To order additional copies, please send a check
payable to Auxiliary-Twigs in the amount of
$19.95 per volume plus $2.50 postage and
handling to:

        Auxiliary-Twigs
        c/o St. Louis Children's Hospital
        Gateways Cookbook
        400 South Kingshighway
        St. Louis, Missouri 63110

Dedicated to St. Louis Children's Hospital

St. Louis Children's Hospital was founded in 1879, making it the oldest pediatric hospital west of the Mississippi River and the seventh-oldest in the U.S. Today, Children's has earned an international reputation for leadership in specialty pediatric medicine and surgery. Children's provides for the health needs of all children, from newborns to adolescents, and excels in cases too complex or serious for others.

Its affiliation with the Washington University School of Medicine reflects two of the hospital's major purposes: education and research. This partnership gives Children's access to research that places the staff of more than 1,000 physicians and nurses on the leading edge of knowledge . . . which translates into up-to-date patient care. Transplant surgery is now performed on hearts, livers, kidneys, lungs, corneas, bone marrow and pancreas. Three-dimensional computer imaging techniques have produced the world's largest data base for reconstructive surgery on deformities of the face and skull. The hospital is also a leading center for the research and treatment of diabetes, epilepsy, cancer and immune deficiencies in children.

But St. Louis Children's Hospital's primary commitment is to give quality patient care . . . by caring for the whole child, not just the illness. Children's provides patients and their families with the support and education they need, beginning at admission and continuing after they return home. With the assistance of fund-raising groups like Auxiliary-Twigs, Children's can assume its responsibilities as a resource in pediatric health care for the region's children.

GATEWAYS

Your Entrée to Easy Elegance

Corporate Sponsors
Anheuser-Busch Companies, Inc.
KSDK
Monsanto Company

Sponsors
Neiman Marcus
   Patty Dean
   Linda Schmitz
Wheatstone Bridge
   Kathy Frost
Lammerts
   Pollie Lammert Hughes
   Sharon Carleton
Virtuoso
Santa Fe Gallery
Kawin Chotin Jewelers
Cat's Eye Gallery
Ladue Market
Midwest Ceramic Tile
Hartke Nursery
The Old House In Hog Hollow
The Tack Room
Williams-Sonoma

Menu Consultant
Blayney Catering

Nutritional Consultant
Shannon Jackson R.D.

Wine Consultant
Barbara D. Werley

Marketing Consultant
Adamson Advertising

Gateways thanks those who graciously allowed us
to photograph their gateways.
Mr. and Mrs. J. Arthur Baer, II
Mr. and Mrs. David E. Bouchein
Busch Stadium
Mr. and Mrs. Robert H. Chapman
Ladue School District
Mr. and Mrs. Van C. Parriott
Mrs. Mary E. Stacey

Gateways wishes to acknowledge the support given by Frances Hurd
Stadler, author of *St. Louis Day by Day* in providing and verifying
historical information. James Neil Primm's *Lion of the Valley*,
Barringer Fifield's *Seeing Saint Louis* and Dorothy Daniels Birk's *The
World Came to St. Louis* were invaluable as additional sources.

Design
Bill Suchy

Photo Design and Photography
David Atkinson of The Atkinson Image

Food Styling
Joan Atkinson of The Atkinson Image

Copy
Carol Swartout Klein

Table of Contents

Introduction

Saint Louis has long been known as the Gateway to the West. It was the portal through which millions passed seeking the promise of a new life in the West. Easterners searching for fame and fortune came to Saint Louis expecting to find a wild frontier town.

Instead, they found a city with an already distinguished history, supporting a rich culture with a decidedly French accent. Founded by early French settlers in 1764, the city was named after Louis IX, the patron saint of the ruling King Louis XV of France. The city's location high on the bluffs overlooking the Mississippi offered many natural advantages. Wild game and fresh fruits and vegetables abounded, leading to a gracious way of life with an emphasis on warm hospitality and festive entertaining. Most occasions were celebrated with elaborate feasts. If no holidays were forthcoming, then a reason to celebrate was invented. To this French culinary tradition, layers of Italian, German and Irish influences were added, and these can still be tasted in Saint Louis' finest cuisines to this day.

Today, Saint Louis is known as the Gateway City, as much for its proud history as for the gleaming Gateway Arch towering above the city's skyline. Its simple, yet stunning, architecture serves both as a tribute to our past and as a magnificent modern symbol of our city's future.

Gateways is your entrée to Saint Louis' traditions, customs, and style. Yet in Saint Louis, there is no single style that dominates. If America is the melting pot for the world, then Saint Louis is the melting pot for America. There are some who say the true "Spirit of Saint Louis" is a blend of Eastern sophistication, Southern charm and Western openness, backed by Midwestern values of family, children and friends. We hope you'll find a little of each as you browse through **Gateways.**

Gateways also represents a look at the way our lifestyle, and cooking is changing as we enter a new decade. **Gateways** is an eclectic blend of treasured recipes from the members of St. Louis Children's Hospital Auxiliary-Twigs, ranging from light healthy dishes to traditional hearty stews. And an Entertaining Guide offers sure-to-succeed party suggestions to take you from impromptu family suppers to lavish formal dinners.

Enter **Gateways.** Stay for a moment for a quick recipe idea . . . or come and linger, enjoying the full flavor of the rich and varied culinary backgrounds that makes Saint Louis such a graceful setting for entertaining family and friends.

Entertaining in the Gateway City

An open gate is a symbol of welcome. It is an entrée into the privacy of one's home and an invitation to share the company of friends who are newly discovered or long cherished. An open gate tells you that someone is looking forward to entertaining you.

Entertaining extends beyond food and drink. At its best, entertaining is an art. The gracious hostess creates an atmosphere that puts her guests at ease and ensures their comfort. The ambiance she provides promotes lively discussions. In short, she makes all her guests feel that they belong.

Entertaining has many functions. It is an integral part of business and political relationships. It is a tool with which we teach our children social skills that will increase their self confidence. It is an opportunity to showcase our talents. Most important, it is the best way we know to gather our friends together and enjoy the pleasure of their company.

What follows then is not so much a guide but a direction . . . an opportunity to gain the benefit of our experience in planning your own creative entertaining strategy. A unique feature of this guide, designed to make it more useful, is the grouping of events and menus by lifestyle and type of entertaining. Each of our Gateways opens up a different avenue. And each is filled with ideas designed to fit our lives and lifestyles today.

Use these suggestions as a starting point. Certainly you don't need to have tickets to the Muny to enjoy "The Midnight Supper after the Muny." In fact, you don't even need to own a pool to use the fabulous menu prepared for the "Pool Opening Buffet." What is required is that you add a touch of your own style and let your original ideas take flight. Trust your imagination and creativity. The more creative you are, the more fun you will have entertaining, and the more of yourself you will put into each gathering. That is the magic key that transforms entertaining from a sometimes intimidating task into a true pleasure . . . and an art.

Gateways to Saint Louis

The "Spirit of Saint Louis" is something that is intangible and difficult to define. The name, of course, comes from the plane in which Charles Lindbergh made his historic flight across the Atlantic, thanks to the sponsorship of a group of Saint Louis businessmen.

Yet, the spirit of the city lives on and can still be powerfully felt today. It comes alive at a Cardinals' baseball game, almost always filled to capacity with diehard Redbird fans. It can be heard in the soulful blues notes of some of the city's jazz greats. It can be discovered in the humorous writings of Mark Twain as he described the lore of the riverboat days. It can be seen in the men and women who built the space capsules that carried our astronauts into space. And it can be found in quiet reflection in one of the city's many spots of beauty and tranquility.

Enter this gateway and explore the true "Spirit of Saint Louis" that is alive and well today.

Saint Louis Blues Jazz Brunch

Eggs á la Brennan
Seasoned Rice with Tomatoes
Asparagus Wrapped in Canadian Bacon
Fresh Seasonal Fruit
Beer and Spice Brunch Cake

Saint Louis has a jazz and blues tradition as rich as its neighbors Chicago to the north and New Orleans to the south. Jazz greats like Scott Joplin, Miles Davis, Pat Methany and Clark Terry can all trace their roots to time spent in the Gateway City. And the sounds of this pure American art form can still be heard today, along the cobblestone streets and in the refurbished warehouses of Laclede's Landing.

Enjoy the cool sounds of either yesterday or today, with a hot and spicy jazz brunch. Write your invitations or have them printed on a blank piece of sheet music. Then give your imagination free rein and create the unique atmosphere of a jazz club in your own home. Create a contemporary feel with the use of all black and white dishes, napkins and tablecloths . . . while listening to the hot jazz licks of another Saint Louisan, David Sanborn. Use a trumpet for your centerpiece and either lay it on its side with streamers or set it upright and replace the mouthpiece with flowers arranged in a small florist's cone.

Try if at all possible to have some live music, such as a pianist, or check out the jazz band of your local college. They may be a source of inexpensive yet surprisingly good talent.

Wine Suggestion: A California sparkling wine such as Roederer Estate or Domaine Mumm.

Cold Supper al Fresco

Cold Tomato Lime Soup
Summer Beef and Pasta Salad
French Bread with Cheese Wedges
Platter of Summer Fruit
Amaretto Butter Squares

Plan a delightful evening outdoors while enjoying an elegant supper set in artistic surroundings. For years, Saint Louisans have been prolific collectors and admirers of fine art. Well known artists Ernest Trova, Siegfried Reinhardt, and Max Beckmann have all called Saint Louis home.

Pick a setting to match the sophistication of the meal and share your love of art with your friends by inviting them to share dinner al fresco in a sculpture garden. Laumeier Sculpture Park, set in a 96-acre park in Saint Louis County, features works by more than 60 artists.

Or if you prefer, stay closer to home and show off your own garden in full bloom. Many Saint Louisans are avid gardeners and the city has become known for its many beautiful gardens. In part that is due to the influence of the Missouri Botanical Garden. This 79-acre oasis in the middle of the city is a world leader in tropical and botanical research.

Whether your plan is to dine at home or to take this easy-to-pack supper with you, it will be the perfect complement to a setting of beauty and tranquility.

Wine Suggestion: A blush picnic wine such as Simi Rosé of Cabernet or De Loach white Zinfandel.

Mississippi Nights
Riverboat Party

Red Pepper Bisque with Italian Bread
Riverboat Snapper
New Potatoes and Herb Butter
Vegetables in Poppy Seed Marinade
Peaches and Cream Pie

Piloting a five to six hundred ton riverboat through the snags and treacherous sandbars lying along the muddy Mississippi was no small challenge for the intrepid yet boastful river captains. In the peak of the steamboat days, an average of one hundred or more of the grand flat-bottomed boats would be moored along the Saint Louis levee, three or four deep for a mile or more. Yet due to the hazards on the river, the average life expectancy of a steamboat was less than three years.

In 1870, an historic three day race took place from New Orleans to Saint Louis. The Natchez battled the Robert E. Lee to determine who was the true master of the Mississippi. At each city along the route, crowds lined the banks of the river to cheer the great boats, with the Robert E. Lee claiming final victory. Perhaps the most famous steamboat captain of all, Samuel Clemens, even took his pen name from the river. When steamboats would head into shallows, one of the crew would measure the water depth and then sound the all-clear "Mark Twain" meaning "by the mark two fathoms."

Bring back those glory days on the Mississippi with an authentic riverboat party. Give straw hats to the gentlemen and fans to the ladies. If your crowd enjoys cards, set up several poker tables . . . on the riverboats lots of money changed hands during a game but anyone caught cheating was usually put off on the next convenient sandbar. Today, efforts being made in several states to legalize gambling on the Mississippi may soon bring a return to the glamour, luxury, and exquisite cuisine found on the riverboats of old.

Wine Suggestion: Chardonnay, with a touch of oak; Shafer or Clos du Bois, barrel fermented.

Cardinals World Series Party

Winning Snack Mix
Green Chile Won Tons
Wild Rice Soup
Broiled Parmesan Turkey Sandwich
Vegetable Crudites

Although winning the pennant has become a commonplace occurrence for the red-hot Saint Louis Cardinals, it has in no way made ardent fans blasé about their team. When it's said that Saint Louisans go all out for the Redbirds . . . they mean out to the ballpark, where for each of the last few years more than three million strong have packed Busch Stadium to root for the home team. This makes the Cardinals one of the top three drawing teams in the country, beating out clubs based in much larger cities.

So who would know better how to host a World Series Party than loyal Cardinals' fans who have had plenty of experience? Send Cardinals' baseball cards out with your invitation or glue one to the front of a blank white card and put the party information inside. Decorate with red and white and have score sheets, pom poms and pennants available for your guests. Repeat the baseball card theme in your centerpiece and bring out any and all Cardinals mementos you have.

Put peanuts, Cracker Jacks and snack mix in batting helmets and place them on tables throughout the house. Turn all televisions on the main floor on and put a radio tuned to KMOX in the kitchen and bathroom so guests won't miss a minute of the action. Serve the soup in Cardinals mugs and give them to guests to take home. And don't forget to have plenty of iced Anheuser-Busch beers on hand. Catch the Redbird spirit and be prepared to cheer. As Jack Buck says, "That's A Winner!!"

Gateways to Friendship

True friendships are precious and often too rare. They are to be treasured because they give meaning and importance to our lives. Like most Midwesterners, Saint Louisans recognize that friendships don't just happen, they must be nurtured and encouraged. What is perhaps unique about Saint Louisans is the value they place on friendship at all levels. Friends made in childhood remain friends as adults. Yet despite these old ties, newcomers to the city receive an equally warm welcome and quickly find themselves amongst a circle of new friends. Perhaps that is why anyone who has spent any length of time here understands the expression that Saint Louis is "a large city with small town roots." People actively reach out to one another and soon seem to find they have made connections wherever they go.

The ability to cherish old friends while remaining warm and open to new ones is just one reason why the Gateway City offers true Gateways to Friendship to all who come here.

Couples in the Kitchen Party

Spicy Broccoli Cheese Dip
Tortillitas
Gazpacho Blanco
Fajitas de Mexico
Frijoles de Olla
Fruit with Kahlúa Dip

No matter how you try to avoid it, everyone always gathers in the kitchen. Well, now there's a reason to because that's where all the action is.

Your friends will know that they are a critical "ingredient" to this party's success when they receive their invitations on recipe cards. For your part, the most important element is advance preparation. Have everything ready and in place at job stations set up in the kitchen, including all the necessary utensils and ingredients.

Greet your guests with a margarita and a big tray of Tortillitas and let everyone mingle for half an hour or so. Then invite them into the kitchen . . . not to watch but to help cook! Give each person an apron and wooden utensil tied to a card describing his or her culinary task. Assign work stations, making certain to mix couples. Jobs can include chopping the tomatoes and the green onions and cutting the fruit for dessert. If you have a few friends who can't even boil water, let them choose the music, set the table or even fill a vase with flowers.

For serving dishes, look in your garden for whimsical or decorative clay pots and planters. Line them with lettuce if you put food in them. When all is ready, heap the food onto serving platters in the middle of a big table so your guests can help themselves. Serve your favorite iced Mexican cerveza with dinner. When compliments are offered to the chef, everyone can share in the meal's success.

Pool Opening Buffet

Bahama Mamas

Scrumptious Banana Slush

Island Samosas with Mango Chutney

Southwestern Tortilla Pizza

Broiled Ravioli with Pesto Dip

Belgian Endive with Julienne Vegetables

Marinated Lamb, Shrimp and Chicken Kabobs

Raspberry Mint Sauce

Onion Marmalade

Peanut Sauce

Fresh Fruit Slices with Raspberry Sauce

Nothing signals the beginning of summer in Saint Louis more than opening the swimming pool. Whether the dress code is coat and tie or bermudas and no socks, this colorful party will get things started with a splash. Create an exotic ambiance by floating tropical flowers and candles in the pool. (Be sure the filter is turned off or they may end up in the skimmers.) Repeat the candles' shimmering effect with miniature strings of white lights in trees and bushes. Line the walk leading to the pool gate with luminaries.

Dress the tables in cool colors and place the flowers in glass vases. Let your guests savor the aroma of dinner being grilled over an open fire as they enjoy their appetizers poolside. Then sit back and relax because it's summertime in Saint Louis and the livin' is easy.

Wine Suggestion: With the kabobs, a light fruity red served slightly chilled; Beaujolais Villages or Brouilly.

World's Fare Buffet

International Cheeses with Dutch Bread
Mixed Greens with Chinese Vinaigrette
Tandoori Chicken with Chutney Mayonnaise
Barbecued Beef Strips
Florentine Lasagne Rolls with Shrimp Sauce
Fresh Carrot Puff
Brussels Sprouts with Caraway Seeds
Chocolate Irish Whiskey Cake
Spirit of Saint Louis Waffles with Ice Cream
and Assorted Sauces

In 1904, the world came to Saint Louis to witness the fabulous Louisiana Purchase Exposition. As a part of the World's Fair, the Olympics were held in the United States for the first time.

Everything about the fair was done on a lavish, larger than life scale. The Agricultural Building, the largest at the fair, covered 21 acres of ground, and a huge Ferris wheel could take more than 2,000 spectators at a time to a height of 264 feet. On any given day you could see a full scale farm or mine in operation, then go and watch a complete re-enactment of the Boer War or Ben Hur's Chariot Race. Trains left Union Station every minute to bring the 100,000 people a day to see the new marvels of electricity, the automobile and the telephone. The best the world had to offer was displayed in thousands of exhibits along 142 miles of aisle space in the eight major Palaces alone. Fair goers refreshed themselves by discovering the novel new treats popularized at the fair . . . iced tea, the hot dog and the ice cream cone.

Why not offer your worldly friends international culinary delights with your own "World's Fare?" The scale can be as extravagant or as simple as you like. Invite guests with a mock passport, saying, "We're importing you for our World's Fare!" Decorate with international items, or bring out any World's Fair memorabilia you might have. Play foreign music or hire international dancers or singers. Then toast your guest with a hearty "Salut! . . . and Bon Appetit!"

Wine Suggestion: With cheeses, an easy drinking red Zinfandel, Fetzer. With entrées, a California Chenin Blanc or a Washington State Riesling such as Chateau Ste. Michelle.

Gateways to Romance

When Saint Louisans' thoughts turn to love . . . Saint Louisans turn to the city's many romantic places. The Central West End exudes European ambiance with its open air cafés and specialty shops. Tables for two abound in the pubs and jazz clubs of historic Laclede's Landing. Horse-drawn carriages clip-clop along the curving streets and through the lush greenery of Forest Park. Charming bed and breakfast inns offer a longer romantic interlude as the perfect weekend getaway.

Whatever your style, Saint Louis offers a little bit of everything for the incurable romantic in all of us.

Midnight Supper after the Muny

Artichoke Hazelnut Cream Soup
Grilled Tenderloin with Horseradish Mold
Red Potato Salad with Caraway Seeds
Chilled Asparagus
Rolls Extraordinaire
Strawberry Grand Marnier Sherbet

Every summer Saint Louisans return once more to enjoy Broadway hits while seated under the stars at their beloved Saint Louis Muny. This 12,000 seat amphitheater, set in Forest Park, pioneered the concept of open air theatre and still stands "Alone In Its Greatness" today. Built by Saint Louisans, for Saint Louisans, every show is required to offer a certain number of free seats so that the theatre is truly available to all.

On this particular evening, the show is over and the final bows have been taken. The glamour and glitter of the Great White Way continue into the night with an invitation to dine "After Ten." Following a hot summer's evening spent outdoors, iced coffee and cold drinks will be a sure hit. As everyone revives inside, play the show's music and relive its highlights. Since the food has been prepared in advance and served cold, relax and enjoy a cool, refreshing repast as a perfect Grand Finale.

Wine Suggestion: A mature California Cabernet or a Merlot from Franciscan or Sterling.

Intimate Dinner for Two

Escarole and Red Leaf Salad with
Tomato Vinaigrette
Creole Shrimp Fettuccine
French Hard Rolls
White Chocolate Mousse with Raspberry Sauce

This gateway beckons you to a private place, a respite where the two of you can escape the demanding and hectic times that constantly swirl about us. Something as simple as a quiet evening's supper, after the children are asleep is a time to share warm memories and exciting future plans.

Set a simple table for two on the terrace or by the fireplace. Gather favorite mementos of your life together to use as a centerpiece. As you both relax from a busy day, light the candles and open the wine. Then quickly assemble these uncomplicated delectable dishes and enjoy an elegant presentation with a minimum amount of effort.

Wine Suggestion: A medium-bodied, fruity Italian red; a Valpolicella or a Chianti.

Gala Anniversary Celebration

Cheddar Dill Tartlets
Toasted Tomato Rounds
Terrine of Veal with Chive Mayonnaise
Chicken Bristol
Rice with Tarragon and Hazelnuts
Steamed Broccoli Florets
Sherried Pears with Crème Anglaise
Norwegian Butter Cookies

Whether it's the 10th, 20th or 40th year, an anniversary of a happy, successful marriage is truly something to celebrate. To make this celebration unique and special, tailor the party to fit the background and shared interests of the couple you are honoring.

We have chosen a love of dance. When the music starts, who can resist an invitation to float across the floor cheek to cheek? The evening begins with an elaborate dinner, served with your best china, crystal and table linens. Have special reminders and photographs from the couple's wedding day on display.

After dinner, move to the patio if the weather is nice or roll up the rugs and turn the living room into a mini-ballroom. Live music would be wonderful but not at all a must. You would be just as clever to hire an instructor from a local dance studio to teach the latest dances from Latin America or the Caribbean. Once the music starts you can be sure that the party will really begin to swing.

Wine Suggestion: With appetizers, a dry sherry, Tio Pepe, or white Taylor Chip Dry Port. Serve either chilled. With entrée, a light fruity Pinot Noir from Oregon or California.

Gateways to Family Fun

Newcomers to the area often remark on what an easy place Saint Louis is to raise a family. The area offers many excellent public and private preparatory schools, as well as the fine educational opportunities available at Washington University, Saint Louis University, and the University of Missouri-Saint Louis.

After some serious learning there is time for some serious fun. There are many attractions that are geared toward the younger set and their parents . . . from the landmark Gateway Arch where a brief train ride takes its passengers soaring 630 feet above the city's skyline . . . to the Six Flags family amusement park . . . to the St. Louis Science Center in Forest Park where science (and occasionally even a dinosaur) comes alive . . . to the "real" live animals found at the world famous zoo where more than 2800 species live in natural settings in an 83-acre park.

Saint Louis corporations show their commitment to families by sponsoring their own unique attractions. Anheuser-Busch owns and operates Grant's Farm which features a wildlife preserve and stables for the famous Clydesdales. Purina Farms, operated by Ralston Purina, allows the visitor to explore the centuries old relationship between man and animal with educational activities and live demonstrations. And McDonnell Douglas sponsors an on-site museum which showcases man's achievements in space.

Camp Chaos Cookout

Skillet Barbecued Shrimp
Cabbage Slaw
Show Me State Ribs
Grilled Corn on the Cob
Fresh Fruit Salad
Vegetable Cheese French Bread
Devastating Brownies

Remember summer camp? Well, now it's as close as your own back yard. The fun starts with the invitations to a Camp Chaos Cookout for both junior and senior "campers." Be sure to note that khaki pants and white shirts are encouraged but not required.

Dress in full camp regalia including Camp Chaos staff T-shirts, whistles and clipboards to greet the new "campers." Set up a tent in the backyard for the kids and give each child a canteen filled with punch.

Put bunches of wild flowers in tin cans or aluminum teapots on the tables and set out coolers full of ice and soft drinks. While the adults devour the shrimp, keep the kids busy with age-appropriate games. Organize a scavenger hunt, with the younger children scouring the yard for inexpensive toys hidden under bushes and rocks. The older "campers" can look for coded clues that lead from place to place, and eventually to a grand prize . . . maybe movie tickets, ice cream cone coupons, a hot new cassette tape or a CD. Or the older kids can prepare a skit about the senior "campers" to be presented after supper.

After dark, toast marshmallows while everyone shares a favorite camp story. For long lasting memories of the "Day at Camp Chaos" give every guest a polaroid Camp Photo and tuck an extra brownie in a small brown bag as a special "care" package from you.

Wine Suggestion: BBQ ribs have to have a red Zinfandel; Frog's Leap or Lytton Springs.

Fireside Family Supper

Guacamole Quesadillas
Jalapeño Corn Chowder
Mixed Greens with Chive and Garlic Croutons
Flan with Orange, Kiwi, and Strawberry Slices*

Here's a chance to make your family feel extra special without a lot of extra fuss. This supper is perfect as a regular Sunday evening event or as an annual family tradition to celebrate the first snowfall, first fire in the fireplace, or the first fall football game. Choose a night when everyone is home, turn off the television and enjoy a cozy evening. To add to the casual feeling, throw an old quilt over a coffee table by the fireplace and serve the quesadillas there.

Back in the kitchen, arrange inexpensive wicker trays with silverware rolled in brightly colored paper napkins. Children love to use unusual dishes and glasses . . . drinks in mason jars and food on terra cotta saucers would be a big hit. Serve the chowder in ceramic or pottery mugs to add a rustic touch. After filling your plate, kick off your shoes, warm your toes in front of the fire and enjoy a delicious supper.

*recipe not included

Mother and Daughter Tea

Smoked Salmon Tea Sandwiches
Tea Sandwiches with Fresh Vegetable Spread
Cucumber Sandwiches with Herb Mayonnaise
Summer Berries and Cream Bread
Orange Blossoms
English Scones*
Strawberry Butter
Lime Tartlets with Fresh Fruit Garnish

The English tradition of afternoon tea is finding new life in modern day America. This civilized notion of an afternoon pause for refreshment makes more and more sense as a way to slow down our hectic, over-committed lives.

Picture this party in the spring around Mother's Day or on a Saturday during the holidays. Mothers and daughters, or grandmothers and granddaughters, will treasure this gracious afternoon. A proper tea table will offer a variety of teas in porcelain and brightly polished teapots.

Invite the little girls to wear their fanciest dresses and frilliest bows. You may wish to set up a separate tea table and let them have their own tea party with miniature dishes. Then give each child a small nosegay as a remembrance of this special occasion. If you're feeling extravagant, especially at Christmas, you could splurge on a photographer to take photos and send each guest a copy as your special gift.

Wine Suggestion: Kir Royale with a lively, sparkling wine such as Shadow Creek, and crème de cassis.

*recipe not included

34

Gateways to Success

Saint Louis has shown many of its citizens Gateways to Success in business, medicine, sports and entertainment. With 17 of the Fortune 500 Industry and Service companies choosing to locate their headquarters here, this is a city that gets down to business. With a diverse business core ranging from heavy manufacturing to service based industries, Saint Louisans usually find that a temporary downturn in one sector is balanced by healthy growth in another.

Yet ours is a city that chooses to enjoy its success quietly. This quiet prosperity can be seen along the gracious tree-lined streets where sweeping lawns lead to classic traditional homes. Reflecting this unpretentious attitude, Saint Louisans have a strong tradition of sharing their good fortune with those less fortunate. In this city, business plays a leading role in the community's cultural, charitable and civic well-being.

Business dinners take on an unassuming, genuine quality as well, with many events and dinners set in the home. Following are some ideas you can in "corporate" for your next business function whether it's a working lunch or an informal yet sophisticated dinner for business associates.

Grilled Dinner for a Job Well Done

Bleu Cheese Moulé with Apple Slices and Crackers

Tomato and Marinated Cream Cheese Salad

Grilled Swordfish Steak with Pepper

Grilled Seasoned Vegetables

Wild Rice with Spinach and Pecans

Jalapeño Cornbread

Mousse au Chocolat

Whether it's to celebrate meeting a sales goal or as an annual thank you to the employees in the office, an invitation into one's home is the ultimate compliment. Showing appreciation for successful teamwork is important in any business.

Keep things uncomplicated and easygoing . . . nothing makes a business dinner more awkward than an air of forced formality. Encourage the air of easy elegance by placing your tables outside covered with pretty colored tablecloths. Placecards with guests' names written on both sides are a subtle help to spouses who may not know everyone at the table. This easy grilled menu allows you to spend as much time as possible circulating among your guests, helping everyone to feel comfortable. Whoever said it's not possible to mix business with pleasure?

Wine Suggestion: For a really big job well done, a 1983 red Burgundy. A Pinot Noir from Acacia or Edna Valley will also work.

Dinner for the New Associate

Grilled Veal Chops with Mustard Herb Butter
Purée of Acorn Squash
Apricot Jam Muffins
Spinach Salad with Pears and Onions
Chocolate Almond Cheesecake

As Saint Louis based companies continue to grow and thrive, welcoming a new business associate from out of town is a common occurrence. And what's fun about welcoming someone to the Gateway City is that it's like revealing a well kept secret. Most people don't realize the cultural and recreational diversity that Saint Louis offers. To make this evening truly special, plan a surprise introduction to one of our city's cultural jewels.

Serve dinner early, perhaps six o'clock, and when the dishes are cleared announce to your guests that the evening has just begun! To really showcase Saint Louis culture, consider one of the following: an evening at the symphony in elegant Powell Hall, (be sure to mention that the Saint Louis Symphony is the second oldest in the nation and considered one of the finest); a presentation by Dance St. Louis of either classical ballet or spectacular modern dance; an inspiring performance of modern day drama at The Repertory Theatre of St. Louis; an exhilarating evening with the Opera Theatre of Saint Louis, one of the region's leading professional companies; or a night enjoying a Broadway show or Las Vegas revue in the one and only Fabulous Fox, now restored to its original Byzantine splendor.

After the performance, return home for a special dessert. In one evening, your guests will have enjoyed both a taste of Saint Louis culture and Saint Louis hospitality as well.

Wine Suggestion: A robust Côte du Rhône or a Chateauneuf-du-Pape.

Quick and Fit
Business Lunch

Flavored Sparkling Waters
Summer Tomato Soup
Aspen Sandwich
Faux Crème and Berries

Here's a light healthy menu that's perfect for an informal working session away from ringing phones and constant interruptions. A business lunch is a working function so keep things simple and straightforward.

Prepare the meal the day before and keep it chilled until you arrive for lunch. Set the table in advance and use a flowering plant as your centerpiece. Expand your table to allow for two more people than you will actually be serving, so there will be extra room for papers and notebooks.

Serve flavored sparkling waters in oversized wine glasses as soon as everyone arrives. For an elegant touch, freeze raspberries or edible flowers in the ice cubes. Attractive presentation and ease of service are essential. Our menu is refreshing yet filling, designed to energize and to inspire productive thinking during the rest of the day.

Gateways to Festive Holidays

All through the year, we find ourselves looking forward to holidays; to be able to break out of our routines and do something different. Retailers know this well. Holiday decorations appear in stores earlier and earlier every year.

Holidays are special . . . the romance of Valentine's Day, the bursting forth of spring at Eastertime, the excitement of parades and brass bands for Independence Day, the pranks and pretending for Halloween, the abundance of Thanksgiving, and of course, the magic of Christmas and Hanukkah.

The sounds and smells, textures and colors of all these holidays hold an extraordinary fascination to children. Our lives are sometimes so frenetic and overloaded that we forget how much little things mean to a child . . . how good it feels to help mom make cookies or dye Easter eggs or decorate the house. The special pleasures of these times of the year lie in teaching our children what our parents taught us.

No matter which holidays you celebrate, good things to eat always add to the festivities. Especially as the days grow shorter and the weather turns cool, our thoughts turn to preparations for the holiday season. Whether you're icing Christmas cookies or making Hanukkah potato pancakes, stop a minute to savor the richness of this time. And perhaps, too, to lend a hand to those whose plate might not be quite so full. For the true joy of all celebrations is in sharing.

Christmas Eve Dinner Buffet

Brie Quiche
Strawberry Sesame Spinach Salad
Beef Tenderloin Stuffed with Mushrooms
Green Beans with Chardonnay Sauce
Orange Rolls
Snowballs and New Zealand Truffles

We are all children at Christmastime. We all yearn for our family traditions and the chance to share them with relatives and friends. The magic of the season spills over into every part of our lives. Maybe the best part is the permission we give ourselves to splurge . . . on gifts, on decorations, and on food!

As in days past, nothing looks more sumptuous than a glorious Christmas dinner spread on the sideboard. The choices are endless . . . one has to return again and again to fill one's plate.

Throughout the house, this is a time for both sparkle and shine. Who can resist the chance to dress up one's home in its holiday finery? Bring an abundance of nature's decorations into your home with fresh evergreens . . . cedar, spruce, variegated holly. Combine these with fresh and dried flowers, fresh fruit, and ribbons to make garlands and fill baskets. If your colors don't lend themselves to traditional red and green Christmas decorations, use gold trim . . . tassels and braid and big bows with long streamers. Light up every corner with candlelight . . . tall tapers in candlesticks of every size and shape, chunky candles on silver trays, votives lined up along the mantel. All cast a warm glow and graciously welcome those who come to share your holiday.

Wine Suggestion: A mature Bordeaux, 1978 or '79 or a California Cabernet, 1985 or '86.

La Guignolée
Champagne Dinner Party

Queen's Pâté for the King's Friends
Sherried Cream of Fresh Mushroom Soup
Lamb with Chèvre Pesto and Basil Hollandaise
Bouquet de Légumes
Watercress Salad with Rice Vinaigrette
Black Sin Gâteau

From the beginning, Saint Louisans greeted the arrival of the New Year with style and gaiety. The early French settlers celebrated with a custom called La Guignolée where the young men of the village would dress in outlandish costumes and serenade their neighbors house by house, asking for food and contributions to be used for their gala Twelfth Night celebration. Later New Year's celebrations were even more lavish, featuring exotic delicacies like oysters and pâté de foie gras.

This year add a French flair to your "Nouvel An" celebration with this sumptuous dinner très élégant. Of course balloons are de rigueur, but give them additional impact by using only one color or the metallic shades of gold and silver in mylar with coordinating strings. For a change of pace consider having live music and dancing and be sure to pass out noisemakers and streamers well before midnight. Finally, be a considerate hostess and don't let guests who have exceeded their limit drive home. That way you can help ensure a happy and safe New Year for everyone.

Wine Suggestion: A Napa Cabernet, 1985 or '86 or a red Zinfandel.

Valentine's Day Dessert Fantasy

Chocolate Hazelnut Torte
Austrian Raspberry Bars
Brandied Truffles
Apricot Macadamia Cookies
Quick and Easy Chocolate Mousse
Fresh Raspberries with Crème Coconut
Café Bar
Champagne

This party is for true romantics and lovers of the sweet things in life. It would be a perfect gathering after an early evening cocktail benefit or after an hour's walk in the winter snow. When you return, an overwhelmingly delicious scent will envelope your friends as they enter your home.

The fantasy begins at a café bar where everyone can choose from a selection of fine dessert coffees topped with whipped cream. Even more delights await in the dining room where every horizontal surface is laden with one sweet after another. Serve small portions and encourage everyone to sample several selections. Continue the fantasy by surprising your guests with champagne and strawberries tucked away in a hidden corner of your home. Everyone will relish this romantic pause, because like love, fine desserts are most appreciated when carefully selected and slowly savored.

Wine Suggestion: An older vintage French champagne, 1975 Bollinger RD.

Gateways to Caring

On a nationwide scale, Saint Louis benefits from a very high level of volunteer activity. Perhaps it's our native friendliness or our solid Midwestern values . . . whatever the reason, people here seem more likely to care about one another and to want to do something to help. Programs geared toward youth, children and the homeless garner tremendous support from Saint Louis volunteers.

Yet Saint Louisans show their caring spirit in small, personal ways too, such as the giving of baskets or special meals to a dedicated teacher, a new mom, or an enthusiastic coach. Give those you love a taste of your caring spirit by sharing some of the ideas that follow and creating your own unique Gateways to Caring.

Benefit Committee Kickoff Luncheon

Chilled Beet Soup
Fruits de Mer with Watercress Dressing
Miniature Blueberry and Lemon Muffins*
Cappucino Cream

With the unending demands placed on women today, the work of the volunteer has become indispensable. As the ranks of volunteers continue to shrink, the demand for the support and service they provide continues to increase. Words of appreciation expressed to volunteers for their efforts are no longer token expressions of gratitude, but true heartfelt thanks for work that could not have been accomplished any other way.

Here's an opportunity to let your volunteer group know how important they truly are. Once your steering committee is in place, it's time to spark everyone's enthusiasm and move into high gear. This luncheon is designed to do just that.

After everyone has arrived, bring out a large silver platter with a crystal pitcher of the Chilled Beet Soup. Pour each guest's serving into a glass mug or punch cup. Serve the colorful salad on plates with white centers to showcase its beauty.

Keep the centerpiece simple, perhaps a pretty soup tureen filled with ivy, or a basket of ferns mixed with caladiums. Or create your own still life with an Oriental bowl piled high with fresh seasonal fruit. With such a gracious beginning how can your gala event be anything but a smashing success!

Wine Suggestion: A crisp Fumé Blanc; Mondavi or Chateau St. Jean.

*recipe not included

Basket Gifts That Show You Care

Basket gifts are a lovely way to express your thoughts of caring and appreciation. They are an attractive, easy and inexpensive way to "dress up" a homemade specialty. The more creative you can be, the more unique the gift itself becomes . . . and the more it reflects your thoughtfulness.

Basket of Special Sauces

Anyone can use an assortment of sauces in the pantry. This gift would be appreciated by any busy person . . . such as a working mom or a new neighbor still unpacking boxes. To round out the selection you might add a marinade to your collection.

> *Chocolate Royale Sauce*
> *Peanut Sauce*
> *Crème Coconut Sauce for Fruit*

Basket of Holiday Sweets

Holiday time is the perfect opportunity to present a special friend with a basket of sweets. And nothing says you care more than a handmade gift. An inexpensive basket can be sprayed red or green and garnished with a festive bow. When the sweets are gone, it still is a perfect container for a basket of holiday greens. Line the basket with tinsel that can be used later on the tree.

> *Brandied Truffles*
> *Apricot Macadamia Cookies*
> *Chocolate and Raspberry Brownies*

Coach's Basket

After a tough season of coaching little league or the community soccer team, present your dedicated sports enthusiast with a basket of goodies and a few really useful items. Include a shiny new whistle and a decorated thermos. Line this basket with the *Sporting News* or toss in the latest issue of *Sports Illustrated*. Your food items should lend themselves to be enjoyed at a live game or one on the television. Just rewards for a kindhearted coach.

> *Beer and Honey Sauce for Ribs*
> *Winning Snack Mix*
> *Brown Sugar and Almond Bars*

New Baby Basket

Line this gift basket with a delicate baby blanket. Tuck in a few gaily decorated bottles or a supply of pacifiers and diaper pins. There is probably no one who appreciates someone else's home cooking more than a busy new mom. Be sure to include a little toy or coloring book for the older siblings.

Marinated Vegetables with Lemon Vinaigrette
Carbonnades with Sour Cream and
Horseradish Sauce
Orzo with Feta
Fresh Fruit with Raspberry Sauce

A Basket of Starters

Do you have a friend who is having guests in for the weekend? Help out a bit with this thoughtful, timesaving basket of appetizers. It will give the hostess a chance to relax and enjoy her company. Why not include a few sightseeing brochures, a local map and even the name of a great new place you've discovered?

Cranberry Refreshers
Gorgonzola Pastries
Golden Chicken Nuggets with Microwave
Barbecue Sauce
Tortillitas

Teacher's Basket

Teachers are forever dipping into their own pockets for "little things." Try including brightly colored thumb tacks, colored chalk and paper clips. Clever post-it notes, gold stars and a box of red heart stickers would also be put to good use. Make sure food containers will fit into a small refrigerator space in the teachers' lounge. Line the basket with a colorful napkin and include the remainder of the set as part of your gift.

Strawberry Orange Soup
Japanese Pasta Salad
Zucchini Raisin Muffins
No Clo Brownies

APPETIZERS
&
FIRST
COURSES

Gorgonzola Pastries

36 pastries

1   16-ounce package puff pastry, thawed
4   tablespoons Dijon mustard
3   ounces cream cheese, softened
2   ounces Gorgonzola or bleu cheese, softened
1   egg, beaten

Unfold pastry sheets and cut into thirds along creases. Cut each third into 3 equal pieces. Using a pastry brush, brush mustard on each pastry piece. Combine cheeses. Mix well. Place one heaping teaspoon of cheese over mustard. Brush edges with beaten egg and fold over to form triangles. Brush tops lightly with beaten egg. Place on baking sheet. Bake at 425 degrees for 10 minutes or until browned. Cool 10 minutes. Cut triangles in half with serrated knife. Serve warm.

Offer these pastries as an accompaniment to a crunchy salad, a bowl of fresh fruit or a chilled soup.

Glazed Raspberry Cheese Pie

Serves 10 to 12

2   cups shredded Cheddar cheese
2   cups shredded American, brick or provel cheese
6-10   green onions, chopped
1   cup pecans, chopped
4   tablespoons mayonnaise
1½   cups raspberry preserves

Line a 9-inch pie plate with plastic wrap leaving a large overhang. Mix cheeses, onions, pecans and mayonnaise. Press into pie plate, flatten top and fold plastic wrap over to cover. Chill well. When ready to serve, invert onto a serving plate and remove plastic wrap. Frost top and sides with raspberry preserves. Serve with crackers. Cheese pie can be made several days in advance and frosted with raspberry preserves just before serving.

Tandoori Chicken with Chutney Mayonnaise

Serves 8

Tandoori Chicken:

- 2 cups yogurt
- ½ teaspoon ground cumin
- ½ teaspoon ground coriander
- ½ teaspoon chili powder
- 1 tablespoon garam masala
- 3 tablespoons tomato paste
- 3 cloves garlic, minced
- 1 tablespoon freshly grated ginger
- 1 teaspoon salt
- 1 teaspoon paprika
  freshly ground pepper to taste
- 4 boneless chicken breasts, skinned and cut into 1-inch pieces

Chutney Mayonnaise:

- ¼ cup mayonnaise
- ¼ cup sour cream
- 2 teaspoons curry powder
- 2 tablespoons orange juice
- 3 tablespoons chopped mango chutney

Tandoori Chicken:
Place all tandoori ingredients except chicken in a food processor or blender. Purée until smooth. Place chicken in a shallow glass dish. Pour marinade over chicken. Cover and *chill overnight*. Shake excess sauce from chicken pieces and broil until brown. Spear with toothpicks and serve with Chutney Mayonnaise.

Chutney Mayonnaise:
Combine all mayonnaise ingredients and mix well. Chill to blend flavors.

Garam masala is a spice that can be found in Oriental or Indian supermarkets. Curry powder can be substituted for the garam masala.

51

Mousse Raifort

Serves 12 to 15

16 ounces cream cheese
¼ cup horseradish
¼ cup chopped almonds
3 tablespoons chopped fresh parsley
¼ cup chopped red pepper (optional)
¼ cup chopped green pepper (optional)
1½ cups slivered almonds
fresh parsley

Combine first 6 ingredients. Line a pie plate with plastic wrap. Pack mixture into pie plate, being careful to release air bubbles. Chill 2 hours or overnight. Before serving, invert mousse onto platter. Garnish with slivered almonds and fresh parsley. Serve with English biscuits.

Mushrooms en Croûte

48 appetizers

2 8-ounce packages refrigerated crescent rolls
8 ounces cream cheese, softened
1 4-ounce can mushrooms, stems and pieces, drained and chopped
1 teaspoon seasoned salt
1 egg, beaten
1-2 tablespoons sesame seeds

Separate crescent dough into 8 rectangles. Press perforations to seal. Combine cream cheese, mushrooms and seasoned salt. Mix well. Spread mushroom mixture in equal portions over each rectangle of dough. Starting at long side, roll in jelly roll style. Pinch ends to seal. Slice rolls into 1-inch pieces. Place on an ungreased baking sheet. Brush each piece with beaten egg and sprinkle with sesame seeds. Bake at 375 degrees for 10 to 12 minutes. Can be frozen before adding egg and sesame seeds. Thaw at room temperature.

Guacamole Quesadillas

Serves 12 to 16

8   ounces Cheddar cheese, shredded

8   ounces Monterey Jack cheese, shredded

1   tablespoon margarine

1   package 10-inch flour tortillas

1   cup guacamole

1   cup salsa or picante sauce

1   cup sour cream

Combine cheeses in a bowl and set aside. Melt margarine in a large skillet. Place 1 tortilla in skillet. Spread a thin layer of guacamole on tortilla. Sprinkle 5 tablespoons of cheese mixture over guacamole. Add 2 tablespoons of salsa and cover with another tortilla (like a sandwich). Cook until bottom is lightly golden. Turn over and cook other side. Quesadilla is done when cheese is melted. Repeat procedure with remaining tortillas. Cut into wedges and top with salsa and sour cream.

For guacamole in a hurry, buy frozen and add 1 finely chopped tomato or avocado or both.

Island Samosas with Mango Chutney

48 samosas

1   medium onion, chopped

1   green pepper, seeded and chopped

2   tablespoons olive oil

½   pound ground chuck

1   teaspoon ground cumin

½   teaspoon ground oregano

2   tablespoons tomato paste

1   tablespoon vinegar

1½ teaspoons sugar
     salt and freshly ground
     pepper to taste

½   cup raisins

1   package won ton skins

9   ounces mango chutney, finely chopped

Sauté onion and green pepper in olive oil until tender. Add ground chuck and brown. Add remaining ingredients, except won ton skins and chutney and simmer 20 minutes. Adjust seasonings. Place 1 tablespoon of the meat mixture on each won ton; fold in half to make a half moon. Moisten edges with water and seal well. Fry won tons in hot oil until browned. Serve with finely chopped mango chutney as a dip.

Couple these with our Bahama Mamas for an instant island vacation.

Terrine of Veal with Chive Mayonnaise

Serves 8 to 10

Terrine of Veal:

- 2 pounds veal, ground 3 to 4 times
- 6 slices bacon, cooked and diced
- 2 teaspoons salt
- ¼ cup chopped chives
- 2 eggs
- 1 cup heavy cream
- 1 tablespoon chopped fresh thyme
- 1 tablespoon chopped fresh sage
- 1 tablespoon chopped fresh rosemary
- ½ cup shelled, blanched pistachio nuts

Chive Mayonnaise:

- 1 cup mayonnaise
- ½ cup sour cream
- 2 scallions, chopped
- 2 tablespoons chopped chives
- ¼ cup sliced leeks
- 6 spinach leaves

A premier first course.

Terrine of Veal:
Combine all ingredients and mix well. Pack into a 1½-quart buttered terrine or baking dish. Bake at 350 degrees for 1 hour. Cool in terrine. Slice thinly. Serve with Chive Mayonnaise.

Chive Mayonnaise:
Combine mayonnaise ingredients in a food processor or blender and purée. Chill.

In the mid 1800's before there were bridges on the Mississippi, people used to cross the river on foot or horseback when it froze over. Enterprising Saint Louisans set up grog shops in tents, complete with tenpin alleys, as a brief respite on the long walk.

Grilled Quail

Serves 4

- **4 quail**
- **4 slices jalapeño pepper**
- **4 slices cream cheese**
- **4 slices bacon**
- **soy sauce (optional)**

Debone the breasts from each quail. Place a slice of jalapeño and a slice of cream cheese on each quail breast. Fold the breast and wrap with a slice of bacon. Secure with 1 or 2 toothpicks. Bundles may be marinated in soy sauce or grilled immediately. Grill over medium heat until bacon is crisp. Serve 2 breasts (1 quail) per person or slice and pass as an appetizer.

Chicken breasts make a wonderful substitute for the quail.

Queen's Pâté for the King's Friends

Serves 12 to 15

- **½ pound medium hot sausage**
- **¾ pound chicken livers**
- **1 cup finely chopped onion**
- **2 cups mushrooms, chopped**
- **½ cup butter**
- **1½ teaspoons dry mustard**
- **½ teaspoon ground nutmeg**
- **¼ teaspoon ground cloves**
- **½ teaspoon garlic salt**
- **½ teaspoon seasoned salt**
- **coarsely ground pepper**
- **dash of cayenne pepper**
- **3 eggs, hard cooked and chopped**
- **½ pound bleu cheese**
- **⅓ cup cognac**

Absolutely delicious. An excellent, very distinctive taste and texture.

Sauté sausage, chicken livers, onion and mushrooms until tender. Cook until juices are reduced by half. Add remaining ingredients and stir to mix well. Blend mixture in a food processor. Chill in a large bowl or oblong container for flavors to blend. Can be frozen at this point in separate serving portions. Serve with party rye or unsalted rice wafers.

Steak Tartare

Serves 6

2   pounds ground beef
    tenderloin
½   cup chopped red onion
2   tablespoons finely chopped
    capers
3   anchovies, finely chopped
2   egg yolks
2   teaspoons Worcestershire
    sauce
    salt and freshly ground
    pepper to taste

**The ultimate steak tartare created by Tony
Bommarito of the famed Anthony's restaurant.**

Mix all ingredients gently with a fork. Do not over
mix. Serve cold accompanied by toast points or
small slices of pumpernickel bread.

Seafood Mold Picante

Serves 8

1   envelope unflavored gelatin
¼   cup water
1   cup picante salsa
8   ounces cream cheese
¼   cup chopped onion
½   cup chopped celery
2   tablespoons chopped green
    pepper
2   dashes of hot pepper sauce
1   6-ounce can crab
1   pound shrimp, steamed,
    deveined and chopped
1   cup mayonnaise

Dissolve gelatin in water. Heat salsa to a boil. Add
gelatin and stir well. Add cream cheese and whisk
until smooth. Cool. Add onion, celery, pepper, hot
pepper sauce, crab and shrimp. Fold in mayonnaise.
Pour into a lightly oiled mold and chill until firm.
Serve with water crackers or tortilla chips.

Broiled Ravioli with Pesto Dip

48 ravioli

Ravioli:

1   **package frozen cheese ravioli**
    nonstick vegetable spray
    Pesto Dip

Pesto Dip:

2   **tablespoons prepared pesto**
8   **ounces cream cheese**
1   **cup mayonnaise**

A must try!

Ravioli:
Cook ravioli according to package directions. Drain and place in a single layer on a baking sheet. Spray ravioli with nonstick vegetable spray and broil until golden. Turn ravioli over and repeat until browned. Serve at room temperature with Pesto Dip.

Pesto Dip:
Blend all ingredients. Chill for several hours.

Freeze your favorite pesto recipe in ice trays. Pop cubes into a zip lock bag for easy access. Ten cubes of pesto will coat 2 pounds of cooked spaghetti.

Spinach Stuffed Mushrooms with Crab Sauce

Serves 6 to 8

1   **pound large mushrooms, stems removed**
1   **12-ounce package frozen spinach soufflé, thawed**
4   **tablespoons butter, melted**
¼   **cup freshly grated Parmesan cheese**
4   **tablespoons butter**
3   **tablespoons flour**
1   **cup half and half**
1   **6-ounce can crab, drained**
2   **tablespoons dry sherry**
1   **cup shredded Cheddar cheese**
    dash of onion powder
    dash of garlic salt
    dash of lemon pepper

The perfect beginning to a magnificent meal.

Place mushroom caps in a buttered baking dish. Fill each cap with spinach soufflé. Brush with melted butter and sprinkle with Parmesan cheese. Bake at 350 degrees for 20 minutes.

Meanwhile, melt butter in a saucepan and blend in flour. Cook until bubbly. Gradually stir in half and half. Add remaining ingredients. Pour sauce over mushrooms.

Best when served fresh from the oven, but mushrooms can be filled early in the day and chilled unbaked.

Brie Quiche

Serves 8 to 10

4 egg yolks
½ cup half and half
1 pound Brie cheese, mashed
⅛ teaspoon salt
4 egg whites
1 8-inch pie crust
  sour cream (optional)
  caviar (optional)

Beat egg yolks and half and half. Add Brie and salt; mix thoroughly. Beat egg whites until stiff. Stir one third of the egg whites into the Brie mixture. Gently fold in remaining egg whites. Place pie crust in an 8-inch tart pan or pie plate. Bake at 350 degrees for 10 minutes. Pie crust will be only partially cooked. Pour mixture into crust. Bake at 350 degrees for 30 minutes or until set. Cut into wedges to serve. Garnish with sour cream and caviar, if desired.

Quiche can be baked in individual tart shells. Cut pie crust into rounds and press into muffin tins or individual tart pans.

Three Cheese Torte

Serves 8 to 10

16 ounces cream cheese, softened
1½ teaspoons dried Italian seasoning
⅛ teaspoon freshly ground pepper
2 ounces Gruyère or Monterey Jack cheese, shredded
⅓ cup chopped pistachio nuts or chopped pecans
¾ cup chopped fresh parsley, divided
3 ounces Roquefort cheese, crumbled

Combine cream cheese, Italian seasoning and pepper in a mixing bowl. Beat at medium speed until smooth. Line a 6 x 4 x 2-inch loaf pan with plastic wrap, leaving a 2-inch overhang on each side. Carefully spread one third of cream cheese mixture in loaf pan. Next, layer Gruyère and chopped nuts. Top with one half of remaining cream cheese mixture. Layer ½ cup parsley and all the Roquefort cheese. Top with remaining cream cheese mixture, pressing mixture firmly. Cover with overhanging plastic wrap and chill for 8 hours.

To unmold, lift cheese torte out of pan using plastic wrap and invert onto serving plate lined with a doily. Remove plastic wrap and sprinkle with remaining parsley. Garnish with fresh edible flowers or vegetable flowers. Serve at room temperature with crackers or melba toast.

The edible variety of nasturtiums makes a beautiful flower garnish. Fan the leaves around the torte and accent with flowers in various shades. The leaves are edible as well. We suggest tomato roses and beet flowers if you wish to use a vegetable garnish.

Spicy Broccoli Cheese Dip

Serves 6 to 8

1   **pound round rye loaf**
½   **cup finely chopped celery**
½   **cup finely chopped onion**
2   **tablespoons margarine**
1   **pound mild Mexican Velveeta cheese, cubed**
1   **10-ounce package frozen chopped broccoli, thawed and drained**

Cut slice from top of round rye loaf and remove center in pieces leaving a firm shell. Sauté celery and onion in margarine until tender. Add cheese and stir over low heat until melted. Stir in broccoli and heat thoroughly until well blended. Spoon into round rye loaf. Serve warm with bread pieces and assorted vegetables.

Bleu Cheese Moulé

Serves 8 to 10

1   **envelope unflavored gelatin**
⅓   **cup white wine**
4-6   **ounces bleu cheese, room temperature**
1   **tablespoon fresh lemon juice**
⅔   **cup light mayonnaise**
2   **tablespoons chopped fresh parsley**
½   **teaspoon paprika**
1-2   **tablespoons finely chopped green onions**
1   **cup whipping cream apple slices**

Stir gelatin into wine and microwave on high 1 minute. Combine cheese with lemon juice. Blend in mayonnaise; add gelatin mixture and stir until smooth. Add parsley, paprika and onions. Whip the cream until stiff. Fold into cheese mixture. Spray a 1-quart mold with nonstick vegetable spray. Place mixture in mold. Chill for several hours. Unmold and serve with crackers and apple slices. Dip apple slices in lemon water to prevent darkening. Can be made a day in advance.

Southwestern Tortilla Pizza

6 pizzas

1 cup prepared pizza sauce
6 corn tortillas
2-4 ounces diced pimiento
1 14-ounce can quartered
   artichoke hearts, drained
   sliced ripe olives
   sliced jalapeño peppers
1 cup shredded Monterey Jack
   cheese

Spread sauce on tortillas. Top with pimiento, artichoke hearts, olives and jalapeños. Top generously with cheese. Bake at 450 degrees for 15 minutes or until bubbly. Cut pizza into fourths.

Fresh Vegetable Spread

Serves 8

2 tomatoes, peeled, seeded and
   finely chopped
1 cup finely chopped celery
1 small onion, finely chopped
1 green pepper, finely chopped
1 cucumber, peeled, seeded
   and finely chopped
1 envelope plain gelatin
¼ cup cold water
¼ cup boiling water
1 teaspoon salt
2 cups mayonnaise

Drain chopped vegetables on paper towels and pat dry. Dissolve gelatin in cold water; add boiling water. Add salt to mayonnaise and fold into gelatin. Add vegetables. Stir gently to combine. Mold and chill. Serve with crackers.

This spread is good on crackers and great as a crunchy sandwich spread. It's a natural for your family, a luncheon or tea.

Green Chile
Won Tons

30 won tons

East meets West with a blaze of taste.

- 8   ounces jalapeño Monterey Jack cheese, shredded
- 1   4-ounce can chopped green chiles
- 30 won ton skins
- 1   egg white, slightly beaten
- 1   tablespoon water
    guacamole

Combine cheese and green chiles. Place 1 teaspoon of the mixture on each won ton skin. Fold won ton like an envelope. Add 1 tablespoon of water to the egg white to make an egg wash. Brush won ton edges with egg wash to seal. Fry in 2 inches of hot oil until brown, turning to brown both sides. Drain. Serve hot with guacamole dip. Can be frozen. Bake at 350 degrees for 5 minutes to reheat.

Cheddar Dill
Tartlets

24 tartlets

Tartlets:

- 3   ounces cream cheese, softened
- ½   cup butter, softened
- 1   cup sifted flour

Cheddar Dill Filling:

- 4   ounces Cheddar cheese, shredded
- 2   eggs
- ½   cup half and half
- 1   teaspoon dried dill weed
- ¼   teaspoon freshly ground pepper

Tartlets:
Combine tartlet ingredients and blend well. Roll pastry into 1-inch balls. Press and mold pastry balls into miniature muffin pans.

Cheddar Dill Filling:
Place equal amounts of cheese into each pastry cup. Combine remaining filling ingredients and mix well. Fill each pastry cup three fourths full with mixture. Bake at 400 degrees for 20 minutes or until golden brown. Gently remove from pan and serve hot. Can be frozen.

A refrigerated pie crust can be substituted for the tartlets for an even quicker assembly.

61

Toasted Tomato Rounds

30 rounds

2½ **tablespoons finely chopped green pepper**

2½ **tablespoons finely chopped green onions**

½ **cup mayonnaise**

½ **cup shredded Cheddar cheese**

30 **bread rounds, cut with a 2-inch cutter**

5 **tablespoons mayonnaise**

10 **cherry tomatoes, sliced into thirds**

3 **slices bacon, partially cooked and diced**

Combine green pepper, green onions, mayonnaise and Cheddar cheese. Mix well. Spread each bread round with ½ teaspoon mayonnaise. Add a slice of cherry tomato. Top tomato with a dollop of cheese mixture. Top cheese mixture with diced bacon. Place on a baking sheet and broil for 5 minutes or until bubbly.

Cheese mixture, bread rounds and tomato slices can be made a day in advance. Appetizers can be assembled several hours before serving.

Steamboat Escargot

Serves 10 to 12

Escargot:

- **2 cans petit gris California escargot, drained well**
- **2 long loaves French baguettes, sliced**

Snail Butter:

- **1 cup butter**
- **4 tablespoons minced shallots**
- **1 clove garlic, minced**
- **4 tablespoons minced fresh parsley**
- **2 tablespoons lemon juice**
  salt and freshly ground pepper to taste
  freshly ground nutmeg to taste

Escargot:
Melt Snail Butter in a large cast iron skillet and sauté for 5 minutes. Add escargot and heat gently for 5 minutes. Tie a bandana around handle of skillet. Serve with a basket of baguettes and lots of napkins.

Snail Butter:
Combine ingredients in a food processor until well blended. Cover and chill for at least 6 hours. Can be frozen.

Serve with a Chardonnay or white Burgundy. Snail Butter goes well with any broiled fish or chicken.

Tortillitas

35 to 40 tortillitas

- **8 ounces cream cheese, softened**
- **1 cup sour cream**
- **5 green onions, chopped**
- **1 4-ounce can chopped green chiles**
- **1-2 teaspoons garlic salt**
- **6-7 12-inch flour tortillas**
  picante sauce

Combine all ingredients except tortillas and picante sauce. Mix until smooth. Cover 1 tortilla with about 3 to 4 tablespoons of the mixture, spreading to the edges. Place another tortilla on top of this and spread with mixture. Continue layering until tortillas and mixture are used, ending with a tortilla on top. Chill thoroughly and cut into squares. Spear with a toothpick and serve with picante sauce. Can be made a day in advance.

Peking Pecans

Serves 8

2 **tablespoons soy sauce**
½-1 **teaspoon salt**
¼-½ **teaspoon freshly ground pepper**
6 **tablespoons butter**
4 **cups pecans**

Combine soy sauce, salt and pepper. Set aside. Melt butter in a 13 x 9 x 2-inch glass baking dish. Add nuts and roast at 300 degrees for 30 minutes, stirring once or twice. Cool 1 to 2 minutes; immediately toss with soy mixture. Cool completely. Can be frozen.

Packaged in a festive tin, these make a nice and easy gift.

Winning Snack Mix

Serves 16

1 **6-ounce package seasoned croutons**
2 **cups sliced almonds**
2 **cups unsalted pecans**
¾ **cup maple syrup**
1 **3-ounce jar real bacon bits**

Combine first 4 ingredients and mix well. Spray a jelly roll pan with nonstick vegetable spray. Spread mixture evenly on pan. Bake at 300 degrees for 10 minutes. Add bacon bits and mix thoroughly. Bake an additional 10 minutes. Store in a tightly covered container.

Brandy Freeze

Serves 36

2 **cups sugar**
7 **cups hot water**
4 **green tea bags**
2 **cups boiling water**
12 **ounces frozen orange juice concentrate**
12 **ounces frozen lemonade concentrate**
2½ **cups brandy**
8 **12-ounce cans lemon lime carbonated beverage**
orange slices

Dissolve sugar in hot water. Steep tea in boiling water for 20 minutes. Combine frozen concentrates, brandy, sugar water and tea. Freeze. To serve, place a scoop of frozen mixture in brandy snifter or cocktail glass. Pour ⅓ cup of lemon lime beverage over frozen mixture. Garnish with orange slices.

Cranberry Slush

Serves 10

1   **quart cranapple or cranberry juice**
1   **6-ounce can frozen lemonade concentrate**
2   **teaspoons lemon juice**
6   **ounces bourbon**
6   **ounces gin**

Combine all ingredients and mix well. Freeze. Serve in chilled glasses.

A good drink to serve at holiday time.

Bahama Mamas

Serves 4

⅓   **cup dark rum**
⅓   **cup coconut rum**
½   **cup grenadine syrup**
½   **cup orange juice**
2½   **cups pineapple juice**
½   **cup frozen lemonade concentrate, thawed**

Sail away to Paradise Island with this refreshing drink.

Combine all ingredients and mix well. Serve in tall frosty glasses over crushed ice. Garnish with fresh pineapple.

Scrumptious Banana Slush

Serves 20

3   **large bananas**
4   **cups water**
2½   **cups sugar**
1   **12-ounce can frozen orange juice concentrate**
1   **6-ounce can frozen lemonade concentrate**
2   **cups pineapple juice**
    lemon lime carbonated beverage
    orange slices and fresh mint for garnish

Peel and mash bananas. Set aside. Bring water and sugar to a boil. Cool. Combine bananas and sugar water with orange juice, lemonade and pineapple juice. Stir to mix. Freeze at least 2 hours.

    To serve, scoop slush into a tall, frosty glass. Fill glass three fourths full with lemon lime carbonated beverage. Garnish with orange slices and fresh mint.

SOUPS

Strawberry Orange Soup

Serves 5 to 6

2 cups fresh or frozen
   strawberries, drained
1½ cups water
½ cup sugar
½ teaspoon finely
   grated orange peel
2 tablespoons orange juice
2 cups buttermilk

The zest and flavor of summer.

Thaw berries, if frozen, and drain. In a 1½-quart saucepan, combine strawberries, water, sugar, orange peel and orange juice. Bring to a boil. Reduce heat, cover and simmer 20 minutes. Cool 30 minutes.

Pour into a blender, cover and blend until smooth. Stir in buttermilk. Cover and chill thoroughly.

For an elegant presentation, serve in wine or champagne glasses. Garnish with a strawberry fan, orange slice or sprig of fresh mint.

Jalapeño Corn Chowder

Serves 10 to 12

½ cup unsalted butter
1 pound bacon, cooked
   and crumbled
2 large onions, diced
2 tablespoons chopped
   jalapeño pepper
1 large red pepper,
   diced
2 pounds potatoes, peeled
   and diced (about 4 cups)
4 teaspoons salt, divided
1½ teaspoons freshly ground
   pepper
4 cups water
6 cups frozen whole kernel
   corn, thawed and
   divided
1 cup finely diced ham
2 cups milk
2 cups heavy cream

In a large soup pot, melt butter over medium heat. Add bacon, onions and jalapeño pepper. Sauté until soft; add red pepper. Sauté about 10 minutes. Add potatoes, 1½ teaspoons salt, pepper and water. Reduce heat to a low simmer. Cook, covered, 20 minutes or until potatoes are tender.

Meanwhile, place 2 cups of corn in a food processor or blender and purée. When potatoes are tender add puréed corn, remaining 4 cups corn, ham, milk, cream and remaining 2½ teaspoons salt. Heat soup to desired temperature. Can be made a day in advance and reheated.

Artichoke Hazelnut Cream Soup

Serves 8

- 1 **cup butter**
- 1½ **medium yellow onions, chopped**
- 3 **ribs celery, chopped**
- ½ **cup flour**
- 1½ **quarts chicken broth, heated**
- 8 **artichoke hearts, fresh or canned**
- 1 **large potato, peeled and cubed**
- 1 **cup broccoli florets**
- ¾ **cup hazelnuts, blanched**
- 1½-2 **cups heavy cream**
  chopped toasted hazelnuts

Melt butter in a heavy saucepan. Add onions and sauté 10 minutes until soft. Add celery. Cook 5 minutes. Add the flour and stir over low heat 5 additional minutes or until the roux is blended and thick. Add the hot broth. Stir mixture until smooth. Add the artichoke hearts, potato, broccoli and nuts. Cover and cook over medium low heat 45 minutes. Stir occasionally. Purée in a food processor in batches. Strain in a food mill or press the purée through a regular strainer with a wooden spoon. Return the strained purée to the pan and add 1½ cups cream. Season to taste. Add additional cream if a richer taste is desired. Cool and then chill. Serve chilled. Garnish with hazelnuts.

The soup base can be frozen without the cream. To serve, thaw, add cream and chill. Base will keep in refrigerator up to 1 week. Add cream 8 hours before serving and chill.

Any fresh herb can be used as a garnish for this pleasant and unusual soup. Try surrounding several hazelnut halves with small outer leaves of artichokes to create a floral garnish.

On a windy May evening in 1849, the steamboat White Cloud caught fire. The wind quickly spread the fire to other boats, and to cargo on the levee, until soon the entire city was ablaze. The fire fighters tried valiantly to control the fire by cutting loose other ships and eventually by dynamiting buildings to stop the spread. Their efforts were to no avail, because in the end the main fifteen block business district had been destroyed. The next year an ordinance was passed requiring buildings in the area to be constructed of brick, stone and cast iron materials only. Many of the resulting buildings featured cast iron facades and a few fine examples can still be seen on Laclede's Landing.

Cold Tomato Lime Soup

Serves 6

- 1 **tablespoon butter**
- 1 **large onion, chopped**
- 2 **tablespoons chopped shallots**
- 6 **large tomatoes (about 3 pounds) peeled, seeded and chopped**
- ¾ **cup chicken broth**
- 1 **tablespoon tomato paste**
- 1 **tablespoon minced fresh thyme**
- ½ **teaspoon sugar**
  salt and freshly ground pepper
- 1 **teaspoon Worcestershire sauce (optional)**
- ¾ **cup whipping cream**
- ⅓ **cup sour cream**
- 3-4 **tablespoons fresh lime juice**
  dash of hot pepper sauce
  cherry tomatoes, lime wedges, Italian parsley

In a saucepan, melt butter. Add onion and shallots. Cover and cook over low heat 15 minutes until soft. Stir in tomatoes, broth, tomato paste, thyme, sugar, salt, pepper and Worcestershire sauce. Increase heat to medium. Cover and simmer 20 minutes. Remove from heat; cool. Transfer mixture to a food processor. Add whipping cream, sour cream, lime juice and pepper sauce. Purée until smooth. Strain if a finer texture is desired. Chill several hours. Adjust seasoning and ladle into chilled bowls. Garnish with cherry tomatoes, lime wedges and parsley.

Perfect with our Gorgonzola Pastries for a delightful lunch.

Curried Pumpkin Soup

Serves 8

  1 **pound mushrooms, sliced**
  1 **large onion, chopped**
  ½ **cup butter**
  3 **tablespoons flour**
  1 **tablespoon curry powder**
  4 **cups chicken broth**
  1 **16-ounce can pumpkin**
  1 **tablespoon honey**
  ⅛ **teaspoon ground nutmeg**
    salt and freshly ground
    pepper
  1 **cup heavy cream**
  ⅛ **cup pumpkin seeds, toasted**

Sauté mushrooms and onion in butter until softened. Add flour and curry powder, stirring constantly for 5 minutes. Remove from heat; add broth in a stream, whisking. Stir in pumpkin, honey, nutmeg and salt and pepper to taste. Simmer, stirring occasionally, for 15 minutes. Purée in a blender and stir in heavy cream. Reheat until hot. Garnish with toasted pumpkin seeds.

Can be made in advance and frozen, omitting heavy cream. Add heavy cream to thawed soup and gently reheat.

A cleaned pumpkin shell can be used as a tureen. Small pumpkins can be used for individual servings.

Gazpacho Blanco

Serves 8 to 10

  3 **cucumbers, peeled and**
    chopped
  1 **clove garlic**
  3 **cups chicken broth**
  3 **cups sour cream**
  3 **tablespoons white vinegar**
  3 **teaspoons salt**
  4 **tomatoes, diced**
  ½ **cup minced fresh parsley**
  ½ **cup sliced green onions**
  ⅔ **cup almonds, sliced and**
    toasted

Place cucumbers and garlic in a blender and process until smooth. Place mixture in a bowl and gradually stir in broth. Place sour cream in a large bowl. Slowly add mixture to the sour cream, stirring well. Season with vinegar and salt. Chill. Just before serving, top with the tomatoes, parsley, green onions and almonds. Serve in chilled bowls. Can be made a day in advance and will keep refrigerated for up to 1 week.

Red Pepper Bisque

Serves 10 to 12

1 cup unsalted butter
2 tablespoons vegetable oil
4 cups chopped leeks
6 large red peppers, sliced
3 cups chicken broth
  salt
6 cups buttermilk
  white pepper to taste
  chives or lemon slices and caviar

One of our favorite starters.

Melt butter and oil in a large saucepan. Add leeks and red peppers. Reduce heat and cook, covered, until vegetables are soft. Add chicken broth and salt to taste. Simmer, partially covered, over low heat for 30 minutes or until vegetables are very soft.

Blend mixture in a food processor until smooth. Strain into a large bowl. Stir in buttermilk and white pepper to taste. Chill. Garnish with chives or a thin slice of lemon with a small scoop of caviar in the middle.

For single servings, dole the soup into green pepper shells.

Seafood Bisque

Serves 16

1¼ cups butter or margarine, divided
1 cup flour
4 7½-ounce cans minced clams, liquid reserved
8 cups milk
2 cups half and half
6-8 green onions, chopped
1 pound small shrimp, steamed, peeled and deveined
2 pounds crab meat (about 4 cups), fresh, frozen or canned
1 cup dry white wine
⅓ cup dry sherry
  parsley sprigs

Melt ¾ cup butter in a 6-quart heavy bottomed soup pot. Blend in flour and cook until bubbly. Over a bowl to catch liquid, drain clams and set aside. Stir clam liquid into flour mixture, blending well. Slowly stir in milk and half and half and cook until sauce is thickened. In a separate pan, sauté onions in remaining ½ cup butter until tender. Add the shrimp, crab and clams and cook until hot. Add to the soup mixture and stir in white wine and sherry. Simmer until thoroughly heated. Garnish with parsley sprigs.

Herbed Cream of Chicken Noodle Soup

Serves 4

2½ pounds chicken pieces or
   2 whole chicken breasts
 2 cloves garlic, crushed
 1 bay leaf
 2 ribs celery
 2 medium carrots
 1 small onion
 1 tablespoon chopped fresh
   parsley
 1 teaspoon dried basil leaves
   salt and freshly ground
   pepper to taste
½ teaspoon dried tarragon
   leaves
 2 cups half and half
 6 ounces kluski noodles,
   cooked until al dente

In a 3-quart saucepan, cover chicken with water. Bring to a boil, then reduce heat to simmer. Add garlic and bay leaf. Simmer about 40 minutes or until chicken is tender. Remove chicken. Strain and skim fat from broth. Discard garlic and bay leaf. Coarsely chop celery, carrots and onion. Return broth to pan and add vegetables. Stir in parsley, basil, salt, pepper and tarragon. Remove chicken from bones, chop and add to broth. Simmer 20 minutes or until vegetables are cooked. Add half and half and noodles and heat thoroughly. Do not boil.

Garnish with toasted buttered bread crumbs and fresh basil leaves. Egg noodles can be substituted for the kluski noodles.

73

Armenian Soup

Serves 4

2 cups water

½ cup pearl barley

2 tablespoons butter

1 medium onion, chopped

½ pound ground lamb or lean beef

1 cup chopped green onions

salt to taste

1 tablespoon dried mint leaves, crushed

1 tablespoon cornstarch

2 cups chicken broth

2 cups plain yogurt

½ cup chopped fresh parsley

An excellent soup for the adventuresome.

Bring 2 cups water to a boil; add barley. Cover and turn heat to low. Cook for 1 hour. Drain and set aside. In a 3-quart saucepan, melt butter over medium heat. Add onion; sauté until tender. Add ground meat and brown. Add green onions and cook 2 to 3 minutes. Mix in salt, mint and cornstarch. Stir until well blended. Gradually add chicken broth and cook until thickened. Reduce heat to very low setting. In a separate bowl, mix yogurt and barley. Add to meat mixture. Stir well. Garnish with parsley and serve hot. Can be reheated.

For an extra rich taste, melt 2 tablespoons of butter. Add 1 teaspoon of dried mint leaves and combine. Place over soup as a garnish.

Summer Tomato Soup

Serves 4 to 6

  4 **cups tomato juice**
  1 **tablespoon finely grated onion**
  1 **cup light cream**
     dash of hot pepper sauce
     salt and freshly ground pepper to taste
     sour cream
     chopped fresh dill

Pretty and delicious with very little effort.

Combine all ingredients except sour cream and dill. Chill at least 2 hours. Top with a teaspoon of sour cream and chopped fresh dill. Can also be served hot.

Tangy Leek and Potato Soup

Serves 10 to 12

  4 **tablespoons unsalted butter**
  4 **large leeks, (about 6 cups), thinly sliced, using white portion and 2 inches green**
  1 **pound potatoes, peeled and cubed**
  ½ **teaspoon salt**
  ⅛ **teaspoon white pepper**
  6 **cups chicken stock or broth**
  1 **cup heavy cream**
  ¼ **cup fresh lemon juice**
  3-4 **tablespoons fresh dill weed**

Melt butter in a large saucepan over medium heat. Add leeks and potatoes. Season with salt and pepper and sauté for 3 minutes. Add chicken stock. Bring to a boil. Lower heat and simmer, covered, 45 minutes or until vegetables are very tender. Strain soup, reserving solids and liquid separately. Place solids in a food processor; blend until smooth. Return to saucepan. Soup can be prepared ahead to this point and frozen.

Combine cream and lemon juice in a small bowl. Whisk to blend well. Stir cream mixture into warm (or thawed and warmed) soup. Add dill. Cook until thoroughly heated. Do not boil. Serve garnished with additional dill.

The lemon and dill lend a nice tang to this vichyssoise-like soup. It can also be served chilled. Thin the chilled soup with a small amount of additional cream.

Carrot and Tarragon Soup

Serves 4 to 6

2 tablespoons butter or margarine

2 medium onions, chopped

2 cloves garlic, minced or pressed

1½ pounds carrots, peeled and thinly sliced

6 cups chicken broth

½ teaspoon dried tarragon leaves

salt and freshly ground pepper to taste

½ cup orange juice

finely chopped fresh parsley or chopped chives

seasoned croutons (optional)

In a 5 to 6-quart soup pot, melt butter over medium high heat. Add onions and garlic. Cook, stirring until onions are limp, about 5 minutes. Add carrots, chicken broth, tarragon, salt and pepper and bring to a boil. Cover soup pot, reduce heat, and simmer until carrots are very tender, about 45 minutes. Uncover the soup pot and simmer 15 minutes.

In a blender or a food processor, blend the soup until smooth and return to the pan. Stir in orange juice. Season with salt and pepper to taste if necessary. Add additional orange juice if desired. To serve, heat soup thoroughly. Ladle into bowls and sprinkle with parsley or chives and croutons. Can be made several days in advance. Can be frozen.

At its peak in the 1940's, Union Station was the largest and busiest rail terminal in the world. Approximately 300 trains arrived and departed daily, carrying more than 100,000 passengers. In the early 1980's, Union Station underwent a dramatic transformation, in one of the largest historic preservation projects in the world. It is now a marketplace featuring more than 100 specialty shops and restaurants. One of the station's many treasures is a carefully restored stained glass window that portrays young women who personify the great rail cities of the country . . . San Francisco to the west . . . Saint Louis in the center . . . and New York to the east. The window is located under the famous Whispering Arch, where a word whispered on one side can be clearly heard on the other.

Chilled Beet Soup

Serves 6

1 16-ounce can sliced beets, drained
16 ounces beef bouillon
1 6-ounce can frozen lemonade concentrate, thawed
1 egg
sour cream or unsweetened whipped cream

A surprisingly delightful blend of flavors — refreshing on a hot summer night.

Combine first 4 ingredients in a blender. Blend until smooth. Chill thoroughly. Garnish each serving with a dollop of sour cream or unsweetened whipped cream.

This soup's bright magenta hue is highlighted when served in large, clear stem glasses.

Wild Rice Soup

Serves 6

6 tablespoons butter
1 tablespoon minced onion
½ cup flour
3 cups chicken broth
2 cups cooked wild rice
½ cup minced ham
½ cup finely grated carrots
3 tablespoons chopped slivered almonds
½ teaspoon salt
1 cup half and half
2 tablespoons dry sherry
chopped chives or fresh parsley

Melt butter in a saucepan and sauté onion until tender. Blend in flour gradually and add broth. Cook, stirring constantly, until mixture comes to a boil. Boil 1 minute. Stir in rice, ham, carrots, almonds and salt. Simmer 5 minutes. Blend in half and half and sherry. Heat to serving temperature. Garnish with chives or parsley.

Crunchy Broccoli and Mushroom Soup

Serves 6 to 8

¾ **cup butter, divided**
1 **bunch broccoli, chopped**
1 **pound mushrooms, chopped**
1 **medium to large onion, finely chopped**
½ **cup flour**
6 **chicken bouillon cubes, crushed**
1 **teaspoon salt**
1 **teaspoon ground nutmeg**
1 **teaspoon freshly ground pepper**
1 **14½-ounce can chicken broth**
½ **cup water**
4 **cups half and half**

A crunchy update of an old favorite.

In a large soup pot, melt ¼ cup butter. Add broccoli, mushrooms and onion. Sauté. In a small saucepan melt remaining butter. Add flour, crushed bouillon cubes, salt, nutmeg and pepper to make a roux. Add roux to broccoli mixture. Add chicken broth and water. Stir. Add half and half gradually to desired consistency. Cook over medium heat about 1 hour.

Creamed Butternut and Apple Soup

Serves 8

2½ pounds butternut squash,
    peeled and cut into chunks
¾ pound tart apples, peeled,
    cored and quartered
4 cups chicken broth
1-1½ inches stick cinnamon
2 cups whole milk
4 tablespoons margarine
2 tablespoons table syrup
¼ teaspoon ground nutmeg
¼ teaspoon ground ginger
    sweetened sour cream

In a large saucepan, combine squash, apples, broth and cinnamon. Bring to a boil, reduce heat to very gentle boil and cook 20 to 30 minutes until tender. Remove cinnamon. Purée in a blender in 2 or 3 batches. Return to saucepan and add remaining ingredients. Serve hot or chill until very cold. Serve with a dollop of sweetened sour cream.

Garnish with a small heart-shaped wreath of fresh thyme.

Minted Pea Soup

Serves 4 to 6

1 tablespoon butter
2 leeks, white part only
2 14½-ounce cans chicken
    broth
20 ounces frozen green peas
2 teaspoons fresh lemon
    juice
⅛ teaspoon freshly ground
    pepper
¾ cup heavy cream
2 tablespoons chopped fresh
    mint

Melt butter and sauté leeks. Add remaining ingredients except cream and mint. Boil 1 to 2 minutes, stirring frequently. Purée in a food processor or blender until smooth. Stir in cream and chill. Garnish with mint.

Country Supper Soup

Serves 8

- 1 **pound ground turkey**
- 1 **medium onion, chopped**
- 1 **16-ounce can whole tomatoes**
- 1 **8-ounce can tomato sauce**
- 1 **15-ounce can small red beans**
- ½ **head cabbage, chopped**
- 3 **carrots, sliced**
- 3 **tablespoons rice, uncooked**
- 3 **ribs celery, sliced**
- 2 **chicken bouillon cubes**
- 2 **teaspoons salt**
- ¼ **teaspoon freshly ground pepper**
- 1 **bay leaf**
- ½ **teaspoon dried thyme**
- 3 **cups water**

Search no further for a perfect wintertime meal.

Spray a Dutch oven or soup pot with nonstick vegetable spray. Sauté turkey and onion until onion is transparent. Add remaining ingredients and stir to mix well. Cook, covered, over low heat for at least 1 hour. Can be frozen.

The Gateway Arch's beauty lies in part with its simplicity. Designed by Eero Saarinen, its shape is based on a catenary curve which is the natural shape a chain makes when held by the ends. On its final day of construction, October 28, 1965, there were some tense moments. The warmth of the sun had caused one of the legs to expand making it impossible to put the keystone in place. The Saint Louis Fire Department came to the rescue and sprayed the leg with cool water, causing it to contract. So, after a slight delay, the final section was installed, while 10,000 Saint Louisans observed the historic event.

New England Baked Soup

Serves 6

1½ pounds medium potatoes
2 tablespoons butter or margarine
⅓ cup sliced scallions
1 clove garlic, minced
2 tablespoons flour
½ teaspoon dry mustard
¼ teaspoon celery seed
⅛ teaspoon ground red pepper
1 cup milk
1 tablespoon white wine Worcestershire sauce
1 cup shredded Swiss cheese, divided
2 tablespoons freshly grated Parmesan cheese
2 6½-ounce cans minced clams, drained, juice reserved
1 cup cottage cheese
¼ cup chopped fresh parsley

In a large saucepan, cook potatoes in salted water about 20 minutes or until tender; drain. Peel and cut into 1-inch cubes (about 4 cups). Set aside.

Butter a 1½-quart baking dish. In a medium saucepan, melt butter. Add scallions and garlic. Sauté 2 to 3 minutes until tender. Stir in flour, mustard, celery seed and ground red pepper until smooth. Cook and stir 1 minute. Remove from heat. Stir in milk. Cook and stir 3 to 5 minutes, until sauce thickens. Reduce heat; stir in white wine Worcestershire sauce, ¾ cup Swiss cheese and Parmesan cheese. Simmer 1 minute until cheese is melted. Remove from heat.

In a blender, combine reserved clam juice and cottage cheese. Process until smooth. Stir into cheese sauce. Fold in potatoes, clams and parsley. Spoon into baking dish. Sprinkle top with remaining ¼ cup Swiss cheese. Bake at 350 degrees for 30 minutes until thoroughly heated and lightly browned.

Serve with green salad, crusty French bread and a hearty wine.

Sherried Cream of Fresh Mushroom Soup

Serves 8

- ½ cup butter
- 2 small onions, chopped
- 2 ribs celery, chopped
- 2 pounds fresh mushrooms, sliced
- 6 tablespoons flour
- 5½ cups milk
- ½ cup dry sherry or dry white wine
- 4 cubes or teaspoons chicken bouillon granules
- salt and freshly ground pepper
- chopped chives

Melt butter and sauté onions, celery and mushrooms until tender; stir in flour. Add milk, sherry and chicken bouillon. Cook until mixture boils and thickens, stirring constantly. Season with salt and pepper. Garnish with chives.

Croutons add interest and crunch to soups. Create whimsical croutons by cutting shapes from sheets of puff pastry, using a cookie cutter, and bake according to package directions.

Seafood Gumbo

Serves 10 to 12

- 4 cups P.D.Q. Roux (page 83)
- 6 cups hot water
- 1 tablespoon salt
- 1 teaspoon cayenne pepper
- 2 pounds raw shrimp, peeled and deveined
- 1 pound crab meat
- 1 pint oysters, with liquid
- filé powder (optional)

Pour Roux into a 5-quart baking dish. Add hot water, salt and cayenne pepper. Cover and microwave on high for 15 minutes, stirring every 5 minutes. Add shrimp and crab. Cover and microwave on medium for 20 minutes, stirring every 5 minutes. Add oysters and liquid. Microwave on medium for 10 minutes, stirring after 5 minutes. Add filé powder to thicken gumbo, if desired.

Duck and Sausage Gumbo

Serves 8

3-4 ducks, cleaned
1 large onion, quartered
½ bunch parsley
2 ribs celery with leaves
½ teaspoon cayenne pepper
½ teaspoon salt
2 cups hot water
4 cups P.D.Q. Roux
6 cups hot water or
  duck stock
1 pound lean smoked sausage
  or Andouille, cut into
  ¼-inch slices
2 teaspoons salt
¼ teaspoon cayenne pepper
4 dashes of hot pepper sauce

Cut ducks into 4 pieces with poultry shears. Stew ducks with next 6 ingredients, covered, until tender. To microwave, place above ingredients in a 3-quart baking dish, cover, and cook on high for 20 minutes, stirring every 5 minutes or until tender. Bone ducks, strain stock and reserve.

Place Roux in a 5-quart baking dish. Stir in 6 cups hot water or duck stock. Add duck, sausage, salt, pepper and hot pepper sauce. Cover and microwave on high for 30 minutes. Serve in bowls over fluffy white rice.

P.D.Q. Roux

4 cups roux

⅔ cup vegetable oil
⅔ cup flour
2 cups chopped onions
1 cup chopped celery
½ cup chopped green pepper
4 cloves garlic, minced
¼ cup chopped fresh parsley
¼ cup chopped green onion
  tops
  hot water

Combine oil and flour in a 4-cup measure. Microwave, uncovered, on high for 6 to 7 minutes. Stir at 6 minutes; roux will be light brown. Continue to cook an additional 30 seconds to 1 minute until roux is dark brown (the color of pecans). Add onions, celery and green pepper. Stir and microwave on high for 3 minutes. Add garlic, parsley and green onion tops. Stir and microwave on high for 2 minutes. Pour off any oil that has risen to the top. There should be about 3¾ cups roux. Slowly add hot tap water to bring roux to the 4-cup mark. Stir to blend. Roux will be smooth and dark. Freezes well.

SALADS
&
SALAD
ENTRÉES

Belgian Endive with Julienne Vegetables

Serves 16

- **1 zucchini**
- **1 carrot**
- **1 yellow squash**
- **2 tablespoons diced pimiento**
- **3 tablespoons Italian salad dressing**
- **1 tablespoon prepared mustard**
- **5 heads Belgian endive, washed and separated**

Grate zucchini, carrot and squash. Blanch 10 seconds. Rinse under cold water. Add remaining ingredients, except Belgian endive, and stir to combine. Chill. Place a rounded teaspoon of mixture onto each endive leaf. Serve chilled.

This salad is a convenient one for the buffet. Arrange in a starburst pattern on a large round platter and garnish with edible violets.

Watercress Salad with Rice Vinaigrette

Serves 4

- **½ cup extra light olive oil**
- **½ cup vegetable oil**
- **4 tablespoons rice vinegar**
- **4 teaspoons fresh lemon juice**
- **2 teaspoons Dijon mustard salt and freshly ground pepper to taste**
- **2 cloves garlic**
- **1 bunch watercress**
- **2 heads Bibb lettuce**
- **½ cup walnuts, broken into pieces**

Pour oil into a medium bowl. Slowly whisk vinegar and lemon juice into oil. Continue whisking while adding mustard. Blend well. Add salt and pepper. Puncture garlic cloves in several places with a toothpick and drop into vinaigrette. Place in a covered container for 2 or more hours to blend flavors. Remove garlic and set aside. Toss ⅓ cup vinaigrette with watercress, Bibb lettuce and walnuts. Store remainder of vinaigrette, garlic added, in refrigerator for 1 to 2 weeks.

Escarole and Red Leaf Lettuce with Tomato Vinaigrette

Serves 6

- ¼ cup safflower oil
- 3 tablespoons tomato juice
- 1 tablespoon fresh lemon juice
- 2 teaspoons grated onion
- ¼ teaspoon salt
- ¼ teaspoon freshly ground pepper
- ¼ teaspoon sugar
- ¼ teaspoon dried basil
  escarole and red leaf lettuce

Spinach Salad with Pears and Onions

Serves 8

- 2 cups confectioners' sugar
- 1 tablespoon dry mustard
- 1 teaspoon salt
- 1 cup cider vinegar
- ⅓ cup grated onion
- 3 cups vegetable oil
- 1½ tablespoons poppy seeds
- ½ pound walnuts
- 1 pound ripe pears
- 2 pounds spinach, washed and stemmed
- 1 red onion, thinly sliced
- ½ pound feta cheese, crumbled

An assertive salad with a taste of sweetness.

In a jar, combine dressing ingredients and shake well. Let stand 1 hour to blend flavors. Toss with escarole and red leaf lettuce.

When preparing a salad, toss greens with a small amount of oil before adding dressing; 1 tablespoon for a head of lettuce is sufficient. This conditions the greens against the wilting effects of vinegar and keeps the salad crisp for a longer period of time.

Combine sugar, mustard, salt and vinegar in the top of a double boiler. Heat over simmering water until sugar is dissolved. Place warm (not hot) mixture in a blender or food processor. Add grated onion. With machine running, add oil in a slow, steady stream. Blend until thickened. Add poppy seeds. Mix well. Chill until ready to mix with salad ingredients.

Place walnuts in a pie plate and bake at 325 degrees for 3 minutes or until lightly toasted. Cut each pear in half and cut each half into 4 wedges. Toss the walnuts, pears, spinach, red onion and feta cheese in a large bowl with dressing.

Serve with Roast Turkey Breast with Apple Onion Stuffing for a tantalizing fall meal.

Confetti Rice Salad

Serves 8 to 10

Salad:

- 8 **cups hot cooked rice**
- 1 **red pepper, cut into julienne strips**
- 1 **green pepper, cut into julienne strips**
- 6 **scallions, sliced**
- ½ **pound fresh asparagus, steamed and cut into 1-inch diagonal slices**
- ½ **cup chopped ripe olives**
- ¼ **cup chopped fresh parsley**
- 2 **carrots, grated**

Vinaigrette:

- 1 **tablespoon Dijon mustard**
- 4 **tablespoons red wine vinegar**
- 1 **teaspoon sugar**
- ½ **teaspoon salt**
- ½ **teaspoon freshly ground pepper**
- ½ **cup olive oil**
  minced fresh parsley or chives to taste

Salad:
Place rice in a large mixing bowl and pour 1½ cups of Vinaigrette over rice. Toss thoroughly. Cool to room temperature. Add remaining ingredients and toss thoroughly. Taste and correct seasonings. Add additional Vinaigrette if desired. Serve immediately, or cover and chill for no more than 4 hours. Return to room temperature before serving.

Vinaigrette:
Combine all ingredients and mix well.

Mixed Greens with Chinese Vinaigrette

Serves 6

1 pound mixed salad greens

1 cup peeled, shredded carrots

½ cup finely chopped green pepper

1 tomato, cut into wedges

2 tablespoons crunchy peanut butter

2 tablespoons soy sauce

4 tablespoons rice vinegar

1 tablespoon hot red pepper oil

1 teaspoon hot red pepper powder

½ teaspoon freshly ground pepper

1 cup vegetable oil

1 tablespoon Oriental sesame oil

1 tablespoon finely minced fresh ginger

1 tablespoon finely minced fresh garlic

1 tablespoon finely minced scallions

1 tablespoon sweet rice wine

1 teaspoon dry mustard

½ teaspoon chicken bouillon granules

Toss salad greens, carrots, green pepper and tomato in a serving bowl. Chill until serving time. Combine remaining ingredients in a blender or food processor. Mix well. Toss with salad and serve immediately.

For the faint of heart, reduce amounts of pepper oil and peppers. Some ingredients may require a stop at the Oriental market.

Strawberry Sesame Spinach Salad

Serves 4

½ tablespoon sugar
1 teaspoon salt
   freshly ground pepper
   to taste
2 tablespoons red wine vinegar
¼ cup vegetable oil
2 tablespoons minced green
   onions
2-3 drops of hot pepper sauce
1 pound spinach
20 strawberries, halved
2 tablespoons toasted sesame
   seeds

Combine sugar, salt and pepper. Whisk in vinegar. Add oil, onions and hot pepper sauce. Whisk until dressing is blended.

Wash spinach well under cold running water and pat dry. Tear spinach into small pieces. Toss spinach with strawberries and sesame seeds. Toss with dressing and serve immediately.

Potato and Green Bean Salad with Walnuts

Serves 4 to 6

1½ pounds new potatoes,
   quartered (about 6 cups)
1 cup fresh green beans,
   cut into 1-inch lengths
¼ cup yogurt
¼ cup mayonnaise
   salt and freshly ground
   pepper to taste
½ teaspoon fresh thyme
1 teaspoon fresh lemon juice
½ cup walnuts, coarsely
   chopped
   romaine leaves

A pleasant change from picnic potato salad.

Cook potatoes in boiling water for 7 minutes. Add green beans and cook an additional 5 minutes. Drain and cool.

Whisk together yogurt, mayonnaise, salt and pepper, thyme and lemon juice. Add potatoes and beans. Toss to coat. Cover and chill. Before serving, stir in walnuts. Serve on a bed of romaine leaves. Can be made a day in advance.

Red Potato Salad with Caraway Seeds

Serves 6

- **3 pounds small red potatoes, unpeeled**
- **¼ cup tarragon vinegar**
- **2 tablespoons sugar**
- **¼ teaspoon paprika**
- **salt and freshly ground pepper to taste**
- **⅓ cup chopped green pepper**
- **¼ cup chopped green onions**
- **1 teaspoon caraway seeds, crushed**
- **¼ teaspoon celery seed**
- **½ cup sour cream**
- **½ cup mayonnaise**
- **large Boston lettuce leaves**
- **chopped fresh chives**

Boil potatoes until tender. Drain and pat dry. Cool slightly. Cut into ½-inch slices.

Combine vinegar, sugar, paprika, salt and pepper in a large bowl. Stir in warm potatoes. Marinate 45 minutes. Gently stir in green pepper, onions, caraway and celery seeds. Combine sour cream and mayonnaise and mix into salad. Cover and *chill overnight*. When ready to serve, line a serving bowl with lettuce leaves. Sprinkle fresh chives over salad if desired. Doubles easily.

This potato salad is lighter than most with a refreshing flavor.

Before prohibition, Missouri was the second largest wine producer in the nation, preceded only by New York. But Missouri's earlier contribution to the world's wine was of much greater significance. In the late nineteenth century, a disease known as phylloxera threatened to destroy much of the world's grapevines. When it was discovered that Missouri's hardy vines were resistant to the disease, Missourians sent carloads of rootings to France. This root stock was grafted onto their centuries-old vines, saving the heritage of French wines for future generations.

Cabbage Slaw

Serves 12

- 1 head cabbage, chopped
- 8 green onions, chopped
- 2 3-ounce packages uncooked Ramen noodles
- 2-3 tablespoons butter or margarine
- ½ cup sesame seeds
- ½ cup slivered almonds
- 4 tablespoons sugar
- 1 cup vegetable oil
- 1 teaspoon freshly ground pepper
- 2 teaspoons salt
- 6 tablespoons rice vinegar

By all means, try this new slant on slaw!

Toss cabbage, onions and noodles together. Do not add seasoning packet to noodles. In a small skillet, melt butter and stir in sesame seeds and almonds. Sauté until lightly browned. Toss with the cabbage mixture.

Combine sugar, oil, pepper, salt and rice vinegar in a blender. Mix well. Pour dressing over cabbage mixture and toss. Chill, stirring frequently. Can be made 2 or 3 days in advance.

Strawberry Cranberry Salad

Serves 12

- 4 cups cranberries, ground
- 1½ cups sugar
- 1 3-ounce can crushed pineapple, drained reserving liquid and adding pineapple juice to equal 1 cup
- 2 3-ounce packages strawberry gelatin
- 3 cups boiling water
- ½ cup sugar
- 1 egg yolk
- 3 tablespoons flour
- 2 tablespoons butter
- 1 cup heavy cream

Combine cranberries, sugar and pineapple. Let stand 2 hours. Dissolve gelatin in boiling water. Add to the cranberry mixture and mix well. Pour into a mold which has been sprayed with nonstick vegetable spray. Chill until set.

In a double boiler, combine pineapple juice, sugar, egg yolk, flour and butter. Cook until thickened. Cool. Whip cream until thickened. Carefully fold into egg mixture. Chill topping at least 2 hours.

When ready to serve, invert mold onto a serving plate and spread with topping. Serve any remaining topping on the side.

Light and fruity with a rich topping, this will be a favorite mold for the Thanksgiving table.

Vegetable Salad with Lemon Vinaigrette

Serves 10

- ⅓ cup fresh lemon juice
- 1 teaspoon salt
- 1 teaspoon sugar
- 1 teaspoon dried oregano
- 1 teaspoon dried basil
- ½ teaspoon dry mustard
- ¼ teaspoon freshly ground pepper
- ¼ cup vegetable oil
- 1 pound broccoli
- 1 small head cauliflower
- 1 14-ounce can artichoke hearts
- 8 ounces frozen crinkle-cut carrots
- 1 large green pepper
- 12 cherry tomatoes
- ¼ cup chopped fresh parsley
- 1 4-ounce can ripe olives, sliced
- 4 ounces crumbled bleu cheese

To make Lemon Vinaigrette, combine first 8 ingredients. Whisk to mix well. Slice all vegetables into bite size pieces. Marinate vegetables and parsley in Lemon Vinaigrette for *24 hours* in the refrigerator. Before serving, add the olives and cheese and toss.

Serve this colorful, texture rich salad as an accompaniment to grilled meats.

93

Tomato and Marinated Cream Cheese Salad

Serves 4 to 6

8 ounces cream cheese, chilled

6 tablespoons vegetable oil

¼ cup red wine vinegar

1 tablespoon finely chopped fresh dill

¾ teaspoon salt

¼ teaspoon freshly ground pepper

1 clove garlic, finely chopped

¼ cup sliced pimiento stuffed green olives

2 teaspoons finely chopped jalapeño pepper (optional)

4 ripe tomatoes

6 green onions, cut into 6-inch lengths and cut lengthwise into julienne strips

lettuce

A showstopper for summer's fresh tomatoes!

Cut cream cheese into ½-inch cubes. Chill while preparing dressing. Whisk oil, vinegar, dill, salt, pepper and garlic in a large bowl. Stir in olives and, if desired, jalapeño pepper. Add the cream cheese and toss to coat evenly. Cover and chill at least 1 hour before serving. Core tomatoes and cut into ½-inch wedges. Sprinkle half the green onions on a bed of lettuce arranged on individual serving plates. Arrange tomatoes on top. Sprinkle remaining green onions over tomatoes. Spoon cream cheese over top. Drizzle dressing over the salad.

Place salad plates in freezer a half hour before serving to make salads seem even cooler and crisper.

Fire and Ice Tomatoes

Serves 10

6 large ripe tomatoes
1 large green pepper
1 red onion
¾ cup vinegar
¼ cup cold water
1½ teaspoons mustard seed
4 teaspoons sugar
⅛ teaspoon freshly ground pepper

Peel tomatoes and cut into quarters. Slice pepper into strips. Slice onion into thin rings. Place vegetables in a large bowl and set aside.

In a small saucepan, combine remaining ingredients. Bring to a boil and cook 1 minute. Pour mixture over vegetables and cool. *Chill 24 hours.*

For ease in peeling tomatoes, dip tomatoes in boiling water for a few seconds and rinse in cool water. Skins will pull off easily.

Feta and Spinach Salad with Basil Dressing

Serves 6

½ cup olive oil
¼ cup red wine vinegar
1 tablespoon dried basil leaves, crushed
2 teaspoons sugar
1 clove garlic, minced
   salt and freshly ground pepper to taste
1 pound fresh spinach, washed and torn
1 avocado, peeled and thinly sliced
½ red onion, thinly sliced
½ cup crumbled feta cheese
½ cup coarsely chopped walnuts, toasted
   Greek olives

To make dressing, combine the first 7 ingredients in a blender. Mix well. Chill. Shake well before using.

Combine remaining ingredients, except olives, in a large bowl. Pour dressing over salad. Toss. Garnish with olives.

Use good quality feta cheese. Fresh in brine is the tastiest, if available.

Summer Beef and Pasta Salad

Serves 4

⅓ cup olive oil
3 tablespoons red wine vinegar
2 teaspoons Dijon mustard
1 large clove garlic, crushed
2 teaspoons crushed dried basil
   salt and freshly ground
   pepper to taste
2½ cups skroodle pasta, cooked
1 green pepper, chopped
½ cup minced scallions
½ cup minced pimiento
1 cup frozen peas, thawed
2 tablespoons capers (optional)
2 tablespoons finely chopped
   fresh parsley
3-4 pounds sirloin steak,
   1½-inches thick
   romaine
   cherry tomatoes or tomato
   wedges

Combine oil, vinegar, mustard, garlic, basil, salt and pepper. Set aside. In a large bowl, combine cooked pasta, green pepper, scallions, pimiento, peas, capers and parsley. Pour vinaigrette over pasta mixture and marinate while steak is grilling.

Grill steak to medium rare. Slice into thin strips (about 2½ cups). Toss beef strips with pasta mixture. Let stand in a cool place for 2 to 4 hours. Serve salad in a large bowl lined with romaine leaves and garnish with tomatoes.

Cashew Shrimp Salad

Serves 6

1 10-ounce package tiny
   frozen peas
1 pound shrimp, steamed,
   peeled, deveined and
   chopped into bite size pieces
2 cups chopped celery
1 cup mayonnaise
1 tablespoon fresh lemon juice
1 teaspoon curry powder
   garlic salt to taste
1 cup unsalted cashews
1 5-ounce can chow mein
   noodles

Shrimp salad with a touch of the Orient.

Combine the first 7 ingredients in a large bowl and toss well. Cover and chill at least 30 minutes. Add cashews and noodles and toss again. Serve on lettuce leaves.

Chive and Garlic Croutons

4 to 6 cups croutons

  3 **tablespoons olive oil**
  3 **tablespoons butter**
  2 **tablespoons minced fresh garlic**
  2 **tablespoons minced fresh chives or scallions**
  2 **tablespoons finely chopped fresh parsley**
 ½ **teaspoon salt**
  1 **10-ounce loaf sourdough, French or Italian bread cut into ½-inch cubes**

In a large skillet, heat oil with butter. When butter foams and subsides, add garlic, herbs and salt. Cook 1 minute or until garlic turns pale gold. Add bread cubes and toss gently until they have absorbed all the butter. Spread bread cubes in a single layer on a baking sheet. Bake at 350 degrees for 15 minutes until crisp and golden brown. Serve warm or at room temperature. Let croutons cool before storing. Store in an airtight container. Can be frozen.

These crisp and crunchy croutons might disappear before the salad is tossed. A dynamite snack!

Citrus Shrimp Salad

Serves 8

 1¼ **pounds jumbo shrimp**
  1 **green onion, sliced**
  1 **pink grapefruit, peeled and sectioned**
  1 **white grapefruit, peeled and sectioned**
  1 **head Boston lettuce, washed and torn**
  1 **small head radicchio, washed and torn**
 ¼ **cup olive oil**
  3 **tablespoons grapefruit juice**
 1½ **tablespoons cider vinegar**
  1 **teaspoon prepared mustard**
 ½ **teaspoon sugar**

A fun salad with a burst of citrus.

Steam shrimp. Peel, devein and cool. In a large bowl, mix shrimp with the onion, grapefruit and lettuce.

    Combine remaining ingredients and mix well. Gently toss with the shrimp mixture.

Fruits de Mer with Watercress Dressing

Serves 6 to 8

An exceptionally lovely luncheon salad.

Shrimp:
- 2-3 tablespoons white wine vinegar
- 1 teaspoon Dijon mustard
- ¾ cup light vegetable oil
- dash of hot pepper sauce
- 1½ tablespoons minced shallots
- 1½ tablespoons minced fresh parsley
- salt to taste
- 2½ pounds shrimp, steamed, peeled and deveined

Shrimp:
Combine first 7 ingredients. Mix well. Toss with shrimp and chill.

Scallops and Vegetables:
- ½ cup white wine vinegar
- ½ cup dry white wine
- 1 teaspoon chopped shallots
- 1 cup fish stock or clam juice
- 1½ pounds bay scallops
- 1 large bunch broccoli, florets only
- ¾ pound snow peas, blanched
- Bibb lettuce

Scallops and Vegetables:
In a saucepan, combine vinegar, wine and shallots. Reduce over high heat until almost dry. Add fish stock. Cook until reduced by one half. Add scallops and cook 5 minutes. Remove scallops and add to shrimp mixture. Chill.

Toss shrimp and scallop mixture with broccoli and snow peas. Chill. Serve on a bed of Bibb lettuce with Watercress Dressing.

Watercress Dressing:
- ⅓ cup yogurt
- ⅓ cup sour cream
- ⅔ cup light vegetable oil
- 2 tablespoons minced watercress
- salt and freshly ground pepper to taste
- hot pepper sauce to taste
- beau monde seasoning to taste

Watercress Dressing:
Combine yogurt and sour cream. Add oil, stirring to mix well. Whisk in watercress. Season with salt, pepper, hot pepper sauce and beau monde. Garnish with edible nasturtiums.

Duck Salad with Raspberry Vinaigrette

Serves 6

Duck Salad:

½ cup currant jelly

2 fresh pears, puréed

1 cup red wine

2 bay leaves

4 sprigs fresh thyme
 salt and freshly ground pepper to taste

3 whole duck breasts
 combination fresh salad greens
 toasted walnuts
 fresh raspberries

Raspberry Vinaigrette:

1½ cups extra virgin olive oil

1 cup raspberry vinegar

½ cup raspberries, slightly crushed

2 teaspoons salt
 freshly ground pepper to taste

¼ cup honey

½ teaspoon ground cinnamon

1 tablespoon Chambord

Duck Salad:
Combine first 7 ingredients and blend to make a marinade. *Marinate duck breasts for several days.*
  Grill duck over mesquite or fruit wood. Cool and slice diagonally. Toss greens with Raspberry Vinaigrette. Serve duck on greens and sprinkle with toasted walnuts. Garnish with fresh raspberries.

Raspberry Vinaigrette:
Whisk all ingredients until well blended. Chill for at least 2 hours.

Here is an opportunity to blend some of the interesting oils available. Substitute, for the olive oil, a combination of walnut and olive or hazelnut and olive. Both walnut and hazelnut oils are light and delicate in flavor.

Apricot Chicken Salad with Mustard Mayonnaise

Serves 6 to 8

Salad:

3 **pounds boneless, skinless chicken breasts, poached until tender and cooled**

1 **cup dried apricots, cut into ¼-inch strips**

⅓ **cup cream sherry**

3 **ribs celery, coarsely chopped**

4 **scallions, sliced diagonally**

½ **cup slivered almonds, toasted**

1-3 **teaspoons chopped fresh rosemary, or to taste**
     fresh rosemary sprigs

Mustard Mayonnaise:

2 **large egg yolks**

2 **tablespoons fresh lemon juice**

2 **tablespoons Dijon mustard**

¾ **cup vegetable oil**

⅔ **cup olive oil**

¼ **cup honey mustard**
     salt and freshly ground pepper

Salad:
Slice poached chicken breasts in 2 x ¾-inch strips and place in a large mixing bowl. In a small saucepan, bring the apricots and sherry to a boil. Reduce heat and simmer 3 minutes. Add to the chicken. Add celery, scallions, almonds and rosemary and toss. Combine salad with Mustard Mayonnaise. Chill at least 2 hours before serving. Transfer to a serving bowl and garnish with rosemary sprigs. Can be made a day in advance but do not toss salad with mayonnaise until a few hours before serving.

Mustard Mayonnaise:
Place egg yolks, lemon juice and Dijon mustard in a food processor fitted with a steel blade. Process for 10 seconds. With machine running, add vegetable and olive oils in a thin, steady stream through the feed tube to make an emulsion. Add the honey mustard and process until smooth. Season to taste with salt and pepper.

Mandarin Chicken Salad

Serves 8 to 10

- 4 boneless, skinless chicken breasts, poached and cut into bite size pieces
- 1 cup white rice, cooked according to package directions
- 1 cup wild rice, cooked according to package directions
- 1 11-ounce can Mandarin orange segments
- 2 whole scallions, chopped
- 1 bunch watercress, stems removed, cut into bite size pieces
- ¼ pound snow peas, blanched
- ½ cup fresh lemon juice
- ¼ cup peanut oil
- 2 tablespoons Oriental sesame oil
- 2 tablespoons soy sauce
- 1 teaspoon chili paste with garlic
- 1 tablespoon sugar
- 1 teaspoon salt
- 3 green scallions, chopped
- ¼ cup toasted almonds

Combine the first 7 ingredients in a large serving bowl. Whisk the remaining ingredients, except almonds. Toss the salad with the dressing and garnish with toasted almonds. Chill until ready to serve.

Blanch snow peas for only 5 to 15 seconds and immediately immerse in ice cold water. The snow peas will be crisp and have a bright, rich green color.

One of the key features at the Missouri Botanical Garden is the Climatron, which opened in 1960. The Climatron marks the first time a geodesic dome, invented by R. Buckminster Fuller, was used as a greenhouse. Recently, the Climatron underwent a complete renovation with new energy efficient glass replacing the clouded plexiglass skin. Inside, the Garden's collection of 1200 species of tropical and sub-tropical plants are now flourishing in completely re-landscaped displays.

Cajun Chicken Tostada Salad with Avocado Dressing

Serves 6

Cajun zip heats up this South of the Border favorite!

Salad:

¾	**cup dry black beans**
1	**bay leaf**
3	**cloves garlic, minced**
1	**teaspoon salt**
4-6	**chicken breast halves, skinned and boned**
	Cajun seasoning
½	**head romaine, washed and torn in pieces**
½	**head iceberg lettuce, washed and torn in pieces**
1-2	**tomatoes, chopped**
2-4	**tablespoons feta cheese, crumbled**
1	**cup corn chips, slightly crushed**
	additional chips for serving

Salad:

Soak beans in water overnight. Drain. In a saucepan, add enough water to cover beans, bay leaf, garlic and salt. Bring to a boil and simmer 2½ hours or until soft. Drain and remove bay leaf.

Sprinkle chicken breast halves with Cajun seasoning and broil 20 minutes until done. Shred chicken.

In a large chilled bowl, toss lettuce with tomatoes, feta cheese and corn chips. Add beans and chicken. Toss with Avocado Dressing. Serve with additional chips.

Avocado Dressing:

1	**ripe avocado, peeled**
1	**tablespoon fresh lemon juice**
¼	**cup half and half**
¼	**cup sour cream**
1	**clove garlic, minced**
¼	**teaspoon sugar**
¼	**teaspoon salt**
1-2	**tablespoons minced onion**
⅛	**teaspoon ground cumin**
	dash of cayenne pepper

Avocado Dressing:
In a bowl, mash avocado with a fork. Add remaining ingredients. Cover tightly and chill. Make sure wrap is touching surface. Stir before serving.

Crisp Chicken and Shredded Lettuce Salad

Serves 6 to 8

Do not be deterred by the length of this recipe. It is quite easy and can be prepared in advance.

Salad:

3	chicken breasts, skinned and boned
¼	cup soy sauce
1	clove garlic, crushed
4	teaspoons sugar
1	tablespoon dry sherry
2	teaspoons Hoisin sauce
1	egg yolk, beaten with 1 teaspoon soy sauce
¾	cup sesame seeds
1	cup rice flour
1	cup peanut oil
4	ounces rice sticks (rice vermicelli)
1	large head iceberg lettuce, shredded into long strips
2	bunches green onions, slivered or chopped
1	bunch cilantro, leaves only, chopped
1	tablespoon toasted sesame seeds
¼	cup toasted almonds

Salad:
Marinate chicken breasts at room temperature in soy sauce, garlic, sugar, sherry and Hoisin sauce for 1 to 2 hours. Dip chicken breasts in egg yolk mixture, then in sesame seeds and then in rice flour. In a large skillet, fry chicken breasts in 1 cup hot peanut oil until crisp and brown. Drain on paper towels and cool.

In a large saucepan, heat ½ inch of peanut oil until very hot. Slightly separate rice sticks and drop, one handful at a time, into the oil. Rice sticks will puff up immediately. Remove from oil and drain on paper towels. Repeat with remaining rice sticks. Can be made a day in advance.

Slice chicken into thin strips. Combine with rice sticks, lettuce, green onions, cilantro, sesame seeds and almonds. Toss with dressing.

Dressing:

¼	cup white wine vinegar
¼	cup vegetable oil
2	tablespoons sesame oil
1	tablespoon soy sauce
2	tablespoons sugar
1	teaspoon crushed red pepper (optional)
1-2	cloves garlic, minced
1	green onion, finely chopped
1	tablespoon Hoisin sauce

Dressing:
Combine all ingredients and mix well.

Lumache Milanese

Serves 10 to 12

1 cup olive oil
½ cup red wine vinegar
1 teaspoon salt
1 teaspoon dry mustard
½ teaspoon paprika
½ teaspoon dried oregano
½ teaspoon dried basil
½ teaspoon cracked pepper
2 cloves garlic, minced
2 firm zucchini, ends trimmed
1 pound lumache (snail pasta)
½ cup ripe olives, sliced
½ cup green olives, sliced
1 pint cherry tomatoes, sliced in half
1 red pepper, chopped
½ pound mushrooms, sliced
grated peel of 1 lemon
½ cup chopped fresh parsley

In a jar with a tight fitting lid, combine first 9 ingredients to make a vinaigrette. Shake well. Set aside.

Cook zucchini in boiling water to cover for 10 minutes. Drain and rinse with cold water. Cut lengthwise in fourths, then crosswise in ½-inch slices. Drain on paper towels.

Cook the pasta in 4 quarts of boiling water with a little oil added to prevent sticking. Cook 6 to 7 minutes, until al dente. Drain. In a large bowl, combine warm pasta, olives, tomatoes, pepper, mushrooms and zucchini. Drizzle with two thirds of the vinaigrette and toss well. Chill. One half hour before serving, bring to room temperature. Add the grated lemon peel and parsley. Toss with remaining vinaigrette. Can be made a day in advance.

Tri-colored pasta is pretty in this dish. Adding shrimp, pepperoni or summer sausage will make this salad even more substantial.

Saint Louisans have lived under the flags of first the French and then the Spanish. It wasn't until March 10, 1804, as a result of the Louisiana Purchase, that the flag of the United States flew over the city for the first time.

MIDDAY ENTRÉES

Eggs á la Brennan

Serves 8

Eggs:

  2 **tablespoons butter**
  ½ **cup chopped onions**
  ½ **cup chopped ham**
  8 **tomatoes, hollowed into cups**
  8 **eggs**
  1 **cup Hollandaise**

Hollandaise:

  4 **egg yolks**
     juice of 1 lemon
 1½ **cups unsalted butter, cut into quarters**

Eggs with Cheddar and Dill

Serves 6

  1 **cup shredded Cheddar cheese**
  2 **tablespoons butter**
  ½ **cup cream**
  1 **teaspoon dried minced onion freshly ground pepper to taste fresh dill weed, leaves and stems, to taste**
  6 **eggs, slightly beaten**

Eggs with a jazzy flair.

Eggs:
Melt butter in a skillet and sauté onions until golden. Add chopped ham and sauté 1 minute. Spoon mixture into tomato cups. Place cups in a greased baking dish. Break 1 egg into each tomato. Bake at 350 degrees for 15 minutes or until firm to the touch. Top with Hollandaise and serve immediately.

Hollandaise:
Mix egg yolks and lemon juice in the top of a double boiler. Over boiling water, whisk in butter 1 piece at a time. Continue cooking until sauce is thick.

Sprinkle cheese in a 9 x 9 x 1¾-inch baking dish. Dot with butter. Combine cream and seasonings. Pour one half of cream mixture over cheese. Pour in eggs. Top with remaining cream mixture. Bake at 350 degrees for 30 minutes.

When growing dill, sow seeds every 2 to 3 weeks from May until early August. You will have a continuous supply of refreshing dill all season.

Ripe Olive Quiche

Serves 6

1½ cups whipping cream
½ cup buttermilk
4 eggs, lightly beaten
¼ teaspoon salt
freshly ground pepper to taste
⅓ pound bacon, cooked and crumbled
2 tablespoons sliced green onions with tops
6 ounces large ripe olives, pitted, drained and sliced
2 cups shredded Swiss cheese, divided
1 9-inch deep dish pastry shell chopped fresh parsley (optional)

In a saucepan, heat cream and buttermilk to a simmer. Whisk in eggs and seasonings. Add bacon, onions, three fourths of the olives and 1 cup of the cheese. Remove from heat. Line a deep pie plate with pastry shell. Sprinkle 1 cup cheese evenly over bottom of shell. Sprinkle remaining olives over cheese, reserving four. Pour custard into shell and arrange reserved olives in center. Bake at 375 degrees for 35 minutes until custard is firm and golden. Let stand 5 minutes before serving. Garnish with parsley, if desired. Can be made in advance and frozen.

Scrambled Eggs with Cheddar Sauce

Serves 12

Eggs:

   3 tablespoons butter or
      margarine
   1 cup diced Canadian bacon
      or ham
   ¼ cup chopped green onions
  12 eggs, beaten
   ½ pound mushrooms, sliced
      Cheddar Sauce
   4 tablespoons butter or
      margarine, melted
  2¼ cups soft bread crumbs
      paprika

Cheddar Sauce:

   2 tablespoons butter or
      margarine
  2½ tablespoons flour
   2 cups milk
   ½ teaspoon salt
   ⅛ teaspoon freshly ground
      pepper
   1 cup shredded sharp Cheddar
      cheese

Eggs:
In a large skillet, melt butter and sauté bacon and onions until onions are tender. Add eggs. Cook over medium heat, stirring to form large, soft curds. When eggs are set, stir in mushrooms and Cheddar Sauce. Spoon eggs into a greased 13 x 9 x 2-inch baking dish. Combine melted butter and bread crumbs. Mix well. Spread evenly over egg mixture. Sprinkle with paprika. Cover and *chill overnight*. Bake, uncovered, at 350 degrees for 30 minutes or until thoroughly heated.

Cheddar Sauce:
In a saucepan, melt butter over low heat. Blend in flour and cook 1 minute stirring constantly. Gradually add milk. Cook over medium heat, stirring constantly, until thickened. Add salt, pepper and cheese. Cook, stirring, until cheese melts and mixture is smooth.

Eggs Gruyère

Serves 6

1   6-ounce package Gruyère cheese wedges, divided
10 bacon slices, crisply cooked
6   eggs
½   cup heavy cream
⅛   teaspoon freshly ground pepper

Slice five of the cheese wedges and place slices in a greased 10 x 6 x 2-inch baking dish. Crumble bacon over cheese. Carefully break eggs over bacon. Spoon cream over eggs. Sprinkle with pepper. Shred remaining cheese wedge and sprinkle over eggs. Bake, uncovered, at 325 degrees for 20 minutes or until eggs are set.

Baked Asparagus and Cheese Sandwich

Serves 6

6   slices firm textured bread
6   slices Canadian bacon or lean ham
6   slices Swiss cheese
4   eggs
2   cups milk
1   teaspoon salt
⅛   teaspoon freshly ground pepper
¼   teaspoon ground nutmeg
1   tablespoon finely chopped onion
18 fresh asparagus spears, cooked until tender
½   cup shredded Cheddar cheese

Trim crusts from bread and arrange bread in a lightly buttered 13 x 9 x 2-inch baking dish. Place ham, then Swiss cheese, on bread.

Beat eggs slightly. Add milk, salt, pepper, nutmeg and onion. Pour egg mixture over the cheese. *Chill overnight.*

When ready to serve, bake at 325 degrees for 25 minutes. Remove from oven and place asparagus spears on top. Sprinkle with Cheddar cheese. Bake an additional 10 to 15 minutes until custard is set and golden. Remove from oven and let stand several minutes. Slice into squares and serve immediately.

Broiled Parmesan Turkey Sandwich

Serves 8

- 1 1-pound loaf French bread, cut in half horizontally
- ⅔ cup mayonnaise
- 4 teaspoons Dijon mustard
- 1 pound thinly sliced, cooked turkey breast
- 2 medium tomatoes, cored and cut into ¼-inch cubes
   salt and freshly ground pepper to taste
- ½ cup mayonnaise
- 5 tablespoons finely chopped onion
- 1-3 cloves garlic, crushed
- 1 cup freshly grated Parmesan cheese

A party sandwich for the football crowd.

Remove bread from inside of sliced loaf, leaving a 1-inch shell. Combine ⅔ cup mayonnaise and mustard in a small bowl. Spread mixture over inside bottom and top edges of bread halves. Place bread halves on a baking sheet. Bake at 375 degrees for 5 to 10 minutes or until edges are slightly brown and mayonnaise bubbles. Layer bread halves with turkey and tomatoes. Season to taste. Combine ½ cup mayonnaise, onion, garlic and cheese. Spread mixture over turkey and tomatoes. Return to baking sheet. Broil until heated and top is bubbly and golden. Can be made in advance and reheated in a foil wrap.

Aspen Sandwich

Serves 2

- 4 slices firm textured nut bread
- 3 ounces cream cheese, softened
- 1 ripe avocado, peeled and sliced
- 1 tomato, sliced
   alfalfa sprouts
   salt and freshly ground pepper to taste

Spread bread slices with cream cheese. Arrange avocado slices on bread. Place tomato slices over avocado. Top with alfalfa sprouts; season to taste. Cover with remaining bread slices.

This sandwich is wonderful alone or paired with a chilled summer soup.

Croissants with Turkey, Apples and Walnuts

Serves 4 to 6

2 cups chopped, cooked turkey
1 Granny Smith apple, unpeeled and chopped
1 tablespoon minced celery
½ cup shredded Swiss cheese
½ cup chopped walnuts
  mayonnaise
  salt and freshly ground pepper
  balsamic vinegar
4-6 croissant rolls

In a large bowl, combine turkey, apple, celery, cheese and nuts. Add sufficient mayonnaise to bind. Season to taste with salt, pepper and balsamic vinegar. Spread the mixture on split croissants. Wrap each croissant tightly in foil. Bake at 350 degrees for 20 minutes.

Smoked Salmon Tea Sandwiches

16 sandwiches

8 slices whole wheat or rye bread
8 ounces cream cheese, softened
½ cup chopped fresh dill
4-6 slices smoked salmon

Remove crusts from bread. Spread cream cheese on each of the bread slices. Sprinkle with dill. Top 4 of the bread slices with the smoked salmon. Cover with the remaining 4 bread slices, and cut into triangles.

When making tea sandwiches, slightly freeze bread before slicing for a cleaner, less jagged look.

Avocado Pita Sandwich

Serves 6

6 **pita breads**
8 **ounces cream cheese, softened**
3 **ripe avocados, peeled and sliced**
2 **tomatoes, sliced**
½ **pound fresh mushrooms, sliced**
½ **pound bacon, cooked and crumbled**
  commercial buttermilk salad dressing
  alfalfa sprouts

Cut a 1-inch slice from each pita bread to make a pocket. Spread cream cheese inside each pocket on both sides. Fill with slices of avocado, tomato, mushrooms and crumbled bacon. Drizzle with buttermilk dressing and top with alfalfa sprouts.

Pita breads are easier to open without tearing if they have been slightly warmed.

Cucumber Sandwiches with Herb Mayonnaise

72 tea sandwiches

¾ **cup mayonnaise**
1 **tablespoon finely chopped fresh parsley**
½ **tablespoon finely chopped chives**
½ **teaspoon dried whole tarragon**
⅛ **teaspoon dried dill weed**
  thinly sliced cucumbers
  thinly sliced bread rounds

Combine all ingredients except cucumbers and bread rounds. Chill at least 1 hour to allow flavors to blend.

Spread bread rounds with the Herb Mayonnaise. Top each with a slice of cucumber. Garnish with fresh dill, small shrimp or parsley. Any leftover Herb Mayonnaise can be used on cold meats, chicken or seafood.

Winter Fruit Mélange

Serves 6 to 8

- **1 cup fresh cranberries**
- **3 fresh pears, peeled, cored and thinly sliced**
- **2 tart apples, peeled, cored and thinly sliced**
- **1 orange, peeled and sectioned**
- **3 inches stick cinnamon**
- **6 whole cloves**
- **½ cup light corn syrup**

Arrange all ingredients, except corn syrup, in an attractive pattern in a 2-quart baking dish. Pour corn syrup over fruit and bake, covered, at 350 degrees for 1 hour until pears are tender. Chill before serving. Can be served cold or at room temperature.

The Bevo Mill, an actual working windmill, now turned restaurant, was built for a princely sum of $250,000, by August A. Busch Sr. as a stopping place on his trips from the brewery to Grants Farm. It opened in south Saint Louis in 1917, and is named after Bevo the fictional fox character that was the logo for the brewery's near beer product. Continuing the mill's European feeling are small stone carved gnomes that can be found on every archway.

SEAFOOD

Peppered Fillet of Salmon with Tropical Fruit Salsa

An extraordinary creation from Cardwell's — known for outstanding seasonal cuisine.

Serves 4

Peppered Salmon:
- 2 pounds salmon fillets
- Pepper Blend to taste
- 1 ounce virgin olive oil
- Tropical Fruit Salsa

Pepper Blend:
- 1 tablespoon whole allspice berries
- 1 tablespoon whole black peppercorns
- 1 tablespoon Szechwan peppercorns
- 1 tablespoon whole white peppercorns
- 1 tablespoon pink peppercorns

Tropical Fruit Salsa:
- 1 ripe fresh pineapple, peeled, cored and cut into ½-inch cubes
- 1 ripe fresh papaya, peeled, seeded and cut into ½-inch cubes
- 1-2 teaspoons grated lime peel
- juice of 2-3 limes
- 1 tablespoon minced, fresh ginger
- 1 poblano pepper, split, seeded and finely minced
- 1-2 fresh green jalapeño peppers, split, seeded and finely minced
- 1-2 fresh red jalapeño peppers, split, seeded and finely minced
- ¼ cup honey
- 1 teaspoon kosher salt
- ¼ cup fresh mint leaves, minced

Peppered Salmon:
Slice fillets on the bias into 4-ounce skinless portions. Season with Pepper Blend. Heat oil in a skillet until hot. Quickly sear salmon on both sides. Do not overcook. Place on a warm serving plate. Add Tropical Fruit Salsa to skillet to heat. Serve as garnish with the salmon.

Pepper Blend:
Combine three or more of the peppercorn varieties in a spice mill or a pepper grinder.

Tropical Fruit Salsa:
Combine all ingredients and allow flavors to develop for several hours. Lime peel should be grated before juicing. Green jalapeño peppers can be substituted if red are not available.

Always wear rubber gloves when working with hot peppers. Peppers can cause eye and skin irritation quite easily.

Seafood Strudel

Serves 8

- **2 tablespoons unsalted butter**
- **2 tablespoons flour**
- **½ teaspoon Dijon mustard**
- **pinch of salt**
- **pinch of ground red pepper**
- **¾ cup milk, room temperature**
- **2 tablespoons whipping cream**
- **1 cup bread crumbs**
- **¼ cup freshly grated Parmesan cheese**
- **¼ teaspoon dry mustard**
- **8 sheets phyllo pastry**
- **¾ cup unsalted butter, melted**
- **1 pound crab, shrimp, lobster or halibut or combination, cooked, shelled and cleaned, cut into bite-size pieces**
- **½ cup shredded Swiss cheese**
- **2 hard cooked eggs, chopped**
- **¾ cup sour cream**
- **¼ cup chopped fresh parsley**
- **¼ cup diced shallots**
- **2 tablespoons chopped chives**
- **1 large clove garlic, minced**
- **2 tablespoons chopped fresh parsley**
- **2 tablespoons freshly grated Parmesan cheese**
- **1 tablespoon minced fresh parsley**
- **crab or lobster claws (optional)**

Well worth the effort.

Melt 2 tablespoons butter in a small saucepan over low heat. Stir in flour to make smooth paste and heat gently, stirring constantly, until mixture begins to bubble. Remove from heat and add mustard, pinch of salt and red pepper. Slowly stir in milk. Cook over medium heat, stirring constantly, until mixture bubbles and thickens. Add cream; adjust seasoning. Cover and chill about 2 hours or until very thick and firm.

Combine bread crumbs, Parmesan cheese and dry mustard in a small bowl. Set aside.

Cover a dampened dish towel with a sheet of waxed paper. Unroll phyllo pastry sheets and arrange on top of paper. Fold towel, paper and pastry in half crosswise (like a book). Fold back towel, paper and first leaf of phyllo. Brush phyllo with melted butter and sprinkle with bread crumb mixture. Repeat until you reach center of "book." Fold opposite side over and repeat until all leaves have been brushed with butter and sprinkled with bread crumb mixture. Leaving phyllo "book" open arrange seafood evenly on lower third. Sprinkle with Swiss cheese and chopped egg. Dot with sour cream. Sprinkle with ¼ cup parsley, shallots, chives and garlic and dot with chilled sauce.

Tuck in ends and roll strudel in jelly roll style. Arrange on a buttered baking sheet seam side down. Brush with melted butter. Bake at 375 degrees for 12 minutes. Remove from oven and brush with melted butter. Slice diagonally with serrated knife into 1½-inch pieces. Push slices together to reshape loaf. Add 2 tablespoons parsley to remaining butter and brush again. Bake 35 to 40 additional minutes, brushing with butter three more times during baking, until crisp and golden brown.

Remove strudel from oven and brush with remaining parsley butter. Let cool 10 minutes. Transfer to a warm serving platter using long spatula. Dust with Parmesan cheese and minced parsley. Garnish with crab or lobster claws, if desired.

Do not be concerned if phyllo pastry tears; just pat it back into place and continue. To save time, assemble all ingredients on a large work space. You can purchase cooked shrimp and a cooked crab/fish combination. A food processor greatly speeds any chopping or grating.

Grilled Swordfish Steak with Pepper

Serves 6

3 pounds swordfish steaks
½ cup virgin olive oil
1 clove garlic, chopped
2 tablespoons coarsely ground pepper
juice of 2 lemons

From Tony Bommarito, owner of Anthony's.

Marinate swordfish in olive oil with garlic, pepper and lemon juice for 1 to 2 hours. Grill over a relatively hot fire until fish flakes.

When purchasing fish fillets allow ⅓ to ½ pound per person.

Grilled Lemon Soy Swordfish Steaks

Serves 8

⅓ cup soy sauce
1 teaspoon grated lemon peel
¼ cup fresh lemon juice
1 clove garlic, minced (optional)
2 teaspoons Dijon mustard
½ cup vegetable oil
8 swordfish steaks, 6 to 8 ounces each
lemon wedges
parsley sprigs

Combine soy sauce, lemon peel, lemon juice, garlic and mustard in a small mixing bowl. Add the oil slowly, stirring until well blended. Place the swordfish steaks in a shallow 9 x 13-inch glass baking dish. Pierce each steak with a fork several times before pouring the soy sauce marinade over the fish. Marinate 1 to 3 hours in the refrigerator, turning occasionally. Grill fish over a moderate fire for 5 to 6 minutes per side, or until fish flakes easily. Brush fish with marinade while grilling. (Fish can also be broiled on a preheated broiler pan in the oven. Cooking time is the same.) Garnish with lemon wedges and parsley sprigs.

Orange peel and orange juice can be substituted for the lemon ingredients. Both variations produce a delightful blend of flavors.

Sanibel Snapper

Serves 4

$\frac{1}{2}$ **cup sliced fresh mushrooms**

6 **green onions, chopped**

2 **pounds red snapper**
  salt and freshly ground pepper

1 **tablespoon fresh lemon juice**

2 **tablespoons white wine (optional)**

1 **cup shredded Monterey Jack cheese**

$\frac{1}{2}$ **cup bread crumbs**

$\frac{1}{2}$ **cup butter, melted**

Place mushrooms and onions in a lightly buttered 9 x 13-inch glass baking dish. Cover with the fish. Season with salt and pepper. Add lemon juice and wine. Sprinkle with cheese and bread crumbs. Drizzle melted butter over all.

Crumple and wet a piece of waxed paper and use to cover baking dish. Bake at 400 degrees for 10 minutes. Remove waxed paper and bake for an additional 10 minutes or until fish flakes.

Blue fish and grouper make excellent substitutions for the snapper.

Riverboat Snapper

Serves 6

2 **pounds red snapper**

1 **teaspoon salt**
  dash freshly ground pepper

4 **tablespoons butter, melted**

1 **cup shredded Cheddar cheese**

1 **tablespoon prepared Dijon mustard**

2 **teaspoons prepared horseradish**

2 **tablespoons chili sauce**

Cut fish into serving pieces. Sprinkle with salt and pepper. Brush with about half of the butter. Broil for 5 to 8 minutes, until lightly browned. Turn and brush with remaining butter. Broil until fish flakes. (Cooking time depends on thickness.) Combine cheese, mustard, horseradish and chili sauce and mix well. Place on top of fish and broil until brown. Other fish can be substituted.

To remove the "fishy" odor from any fish, rub with lemon juice and cover with milk. Let sit 30 minutes before preparing.

Crab, Shrimp and Artichoke Gratinée

Serves 6

4 tablespoons butter

½ pound fresh mushrooms

1 clove garlic, minced

2 tablespoons minced shallots

¼ cup flour

½ teaspoon freshly ground pepper

¾ cup milk

8 ounces sharp Cheddar cheese, shredded and divided

⅔ cup dry white wine

2 7½-ounce cans king crab

1 pound shrimp, steamed, peeled and deveined

1 10-ounce package frozen artichoke hearts, cooked and drained

2 tablespoons bread crumbs

1 tablespoon butter, melted

Melt butter in a skillet and add mushrooms, garlic and shallots. Sauté 5 minutes. Remove from heat and stir in flour, pepper and milk. Slowly bring to a boil, stirring constantly. Remove from heat. Add ½ cup of the cheese and stir until melted. Stir in wine. Combine sauce with crab, shrimp, artichokes and remaining cheese. Pour into a 2-quart buttered baking dish. Combine bread crumbs and melted butter. Sprinkle over the mixture. Bake, uncovered, at 375 degrees for 30 minutes or until bubbly and lightly browned.

1 pound of scallops can be substituted for the king crab.

To celebrate the repeal of prohibition, August A. "Gussie" Busch, Jr. presented his father with a special gift . . . the first eight-horse Clydesdale hitch. Now known throughout the world, the strong but gentle giants, weighing about one ton each, can be seen as a part of the Saint Louis Brewery tour, or at Grant's Farm. From its beginnings in 1852, Anheuser-Busch has become the largest brewery in the world and a fitting home for the King of Beers.

Skillet Barbecued Shrimp

Serves 4

- 1½ **pounds large shrimp, raw and unpeeled**
- 6 **tablespoons unsalted butter**
- 3 **tablespoons olive oil**
- 3 **tablespoons chili sauce**
- 1½ **tablespoons fresh lemon juice**
- 1 **tablespoon Worcestershire sauce**
- 2 **cloves garlic, minced**
- 1 **teaspoon minced fresh parsley**
- ¾ **teaspoon liquid smoke**
- ½ **teaspoon dried oregano**
- ½ **teaspoon paprika**
- ½ **teaspoon dried thyme**
- ¼ **teaspoon hot pepper sauce**
  salt and cayenne pepper

A traditional Saint Louis favorite.

Rinse shrimp in cold water, pat dry and set aside. Combine all remaining ingredients in a large saucepan or skillet. Simmer, stirring frequently, about 10 minutes. Add shrimp and cook over high heat, stirring frequently, 5 to 10 minutes or until shrimp turns pink and edges curl. Serve warm.

To fully enjoy this spicy sauce, crusty French bread is de rigueur.

Scallops Parmesan

Serves 4

1 carrot, peeled and cut
    into julienne strips
6 green onions with tops,
    chopped
½ pound mushrooms, sliced
    olive oil
1 cup chicken broth
½ cup white wine
2 tablespoons butter, melted
2 tablespoons flour
    fresh chopped parsley to
    taste
    fresh basil to taste
    white pepper to taste
1 pound scallops
    freshly grated Parmesan
    cheese
    pasta, cooked until al dente
    (optional)

Nice for family or company.

Sauté carrot, onions and mushrooms in small amount of olive oil. Add broth and wine. Cook to reduce liquid by one half. Combine butter and flour. Stir to mix well. Add to vegetable mixture. Bring to a boil, reduce heat and simmer 5 minutes. Add seasonings and mix well. Add scallops and simmer 1 minute. Pour into a baking dish. Cover with Parmesan cheese and broil. Serve over pasta if desired.

Seafood Bouillabaisse

Serves 6

- 5 slices bacon, diced
- 4 tablespoons flour
- 2 large onions, chopped
- 3 cloves garlic, minced
- 1 10½-ounce can beef consommé
- 1 16-ounce can tomatoes, chopped
- 2 10-ounce cans diced tomatoes with green chiles
- 1 6-ounce can tomato paste
- 3½ cups boiling water
- 1 10-ounce package frozen sliced okra, thawed
- 1 4-ounce can mushroom pieces
- 1 bay leaf
- 1 teaspoon salt
- ¼-½ teaspoon cayenne pepper
- ¼ teaspoon plus 3 dashes of hot pepper sauce
- 1½ pounds shrimp, steamed, peeled and deveined
- ¾ pound crab legs, cooked and shelled
- 1 tablespoon filé powder

In a skillet, cook bacon until crisp. Set aside. Reserve drippings. Spoon 2 tablespoons drippings into a Dutch oven. Heat until hot. Stir in flour until well blended and golden brown in color. Stir in onions and garlic. Cook until brown. Pour consommé, tomatoes, tomatoes with green chiles, tomato paste and boiling water into flour mixture. Bring to a boil. Reduce to a simmer. Meanwhile, in skillet, heat remaining bacon drippings. Sauté okra in drippings until light brown. Add okra, mushrooms, bay leaf and spices to tomato mixture. Simmer, covered, 1 hour. Add shrimp, crab meat and bacon. Cook an additional 10 to 15 minutes. Stir in the filé powder. Serve on hot rice. If possible, prepare a day ahead and chill to allow the flavors to blend. Can substitute 1 can crab for the crab legs.

Filé powder is ground sassafras leaves and is used as a thickening agent.

Shrimp and Chicken in Savory Sauce

Serves 4 to 6

  3 tablespoons vegetable oil, divided
½ cup chopped onion
⅓ cup chopped celery
⅓ cup chopped carrots
  4 teaspoons minced shallots
½ teaspoon minced garlic
  1 28-ounce can whole tomatoes
  2 tablespoons tomato paste
½ cup dry white wine
¼ teaspoon dried tarragon
    salt and freshly ground pepper to taste
  1 boneless chicken breast
    salt and freshly ground pepper to taste
  1 pound raw shrimp, peeled and deveined
  2 teaspoons minced shallots
½ teaspoon dried tarragon
  1 teaspoon chopped fresh parsley
  2 tablespoons cognac

Heat 1 tablespoon of oil in a saucepan and sauté the next 5 ingredients until onion is tender. Crush tomatoes. Add tomatoes (including juice), tomato paste, wine and ¼ teaspoon tarragon. Season with salt and pepper. Simmer 15 minutes.

Meanwhile, slice chicken breast in ½-inch strips. Heat 2 tablespoons of oil in a skillet. Add chicken and season with salt and pepper. Sauté 45 seconds. Add shrimp and sauté 1 minute. Add shallots, tarragon and parsley. Sprinkle with cognac. Add to tomato sauce and bring to a boil, stirring frequently. Serve with rice. Can be prepared in advance and reheated. Can be frozen.

For a dinner party, serve on a treasured antique platter.

In the days before everyone worried about cholesterol and saturated fat, Saint Louisans came up with a heavenly but definitely not low-calorie culinary invention. According to legend, Gooey Butter Cake happened when a baker mistakenly put too much sugar, butter and shortening, all at the same time, into an ordinary yellow cake. The flat gooey cake, that can almost be eaten with a spoon, became an instant hit and Saint Louisans still buy the cakes by the thousands.

Shrimp Thermidor

Serves 6

1¼ pounds medium shrimp
2 lemon slices
1¼ teaspoons salt
2½ tablespoons butter, divided
1 tablespoon flour
⅛ teaspoon freshly ground pepper
½ teaspoon dry mustard
½ cup milk
½ cup heavy cream
2 tablespoons brandy
    freshly grated Parmesan cheese

Cook shrimp in 4 cups boiling water with lemon slices and 1 teaspoon salt. Simmer 4 minutes. Drain. Peel and devein shrimp. Melt 1 tablespoon butter in a saucepan; stir in flour, ¼ teaspoon salt, pepper and dry mustard. Cook and stir until bubbly. Slowly add milk and cream, stirring constantly until thickened. Add remaining butter, shrimp and brandy. Pour into a greased 2-quart baking dish. Sprinkle with Parmesan cheese. Bake at 450 degrees for 2 minutes.

Fiesta Fish

A lively fish entrée with a unique blend of flavors.

Serves 4

2 cups coarsely chopped celery
½ cup margarine
2 cups coarsely chopped apples
2 cups coarsely chopped bell peppers, assorted colors
1 cup raisins
1 14-ounce can tomato sauce
    hot pepper sauce
1½ pounds fish fillets (orange roughy, red snapper or grouper)

In a large microwave safe container, microwave celery in margarine for 2 minutes on high. Add apples, peppers, raisins and tomato sauce. Microwave 2 to 3 minutes or until warm. Place fish, skin side down, in a 9 x 13-inch baking dish in a single layer. Pour sauce over fish and season with hot pepper sauce. Bake at 400 degrees for 1 hour or until sauce is bubbly and fish flakes.

Halibut with Mustard Dill Sauce

Serves 4

½ cup dry white wine
½ cup buttermilk
4 halibut steaks, 1-inch thick
   salt and freshly ground
   pepper
1 cup low fat yogurt
½ cup finely chopped red onion
2 tablespoons Dijon mustard
1 teaspoon dried dill weed

Quick to fix.

Combine wine and buttermilk in a shallow glass baking dish. Add halibut; turn to coat evenly. Cover and chill 1 to 2 hours. Drain halibut and discard liquid. Place fish in a lightly buttered flameproof baking dish. Season with salt and pepper. Broil 6 inches from heat 5 minutes. Turn steaks and broil 5 additional minutes.

    Meanwhile, combine yogurt, onion, mustard and dill weed in a small bowl. Remove halibut to a warm serving plate. Spoon a little sauce over each steak and serve. Pass extra sauce.

Salmon and tuna steaks also work well. Brown rice and a spinach salad are the perfect complements for this dish.

Shrimp and Sole Marguery

Serves 5 to 6

1 medium onion, thinly sliced
1 pound sole, poached and
   flaked
¾ pound shrimp, steamed,
   peeled and deveined
1 4-ounce can minced clams,
   drained
1 10¾-ounce can New England
   style clam chowder
½ cup milk, scant
4 ounces mild Cheddar cheese,
   cut into strips
   buttered bread crumbs

Arrange onion in bottom of an 11 x 7-inch buttered baking dish. Cover with layers of sole, shrimp and clams. Combine soup and milk. Pour over layered ingredients. Arrange cheese strips over top and sprinkle with bread crumbs. Bake at 350 degrees for 30 minutes.

Scallops with Angel Hair Pasta and Chives

Serves 4

1½ cups dry white wine
1 teaspoon grated lemon peel
1 pound scallops
3 teaspoons Dijon mustard
½ cup margarine, cut into 8 pieces
salt and freshly ground pepper to taste
8 ounces angel hair pasta
2 tablespoons snipped fresh chives

Bring wine and lemon peel to simmer in a heavy skillet. Add scallops and cook about 1 minute or until almost opaque. Transfer scallops to a bowl with a slotted spoon. Increase heat and boil about 8 minutes, until wine is reduced to ½ cup. Reduce heat to low, whisk in mustard, then margarine, one piece at a time. Add scallops and heat through. Season with salt and pepper.

Meanwhile, cook pasta in rapidly boiling water until al dente. Drain well and divide between plates. Spoon scallops over pasta and sprinkle with chives.

Salmon Soufflé with Rosemary and Basil

Serves 4 to 6

3 tablespoons butter
2 tablespoons flour
1 cup cream
3 egg yolks
1 cup fresh cooked or canned salmon, flaked
1 teaspoon fresh rosemary
1 teaspoon fresh basil
salt to taste
½ teaspoon freshly ground pepper
5 egg whites
1 slice bacon, cooked and diced

In a saucepan, melt butter and add flour to make a white roux. Add cream and whisk until smooth and thick. Cool slightly. Stir in egg yolks, salmon and seasonings. Beat egg whites until stiff. Stir 2 or 3 tablespoons of egg whites into mixture. Fold in remaining egg whites. Pour mixture into a buttered soufflé dish. Bake at 350 degrees for 35 minutes. Sprinkle with diced bacon. Serve immediately.

Sautéed Trout with Almond Sauce

Serves 6

6   trout, rinsed and patted dry
    salt and freshly ground
    pepper to taste
½   cup butter or margarine,
    divided
⅓   cup sliced almonds
9   tablespoons dry vermouth
6   tablespoons fresh lemon
    juice
2   medium to large cloves
    garlic, minced
1   teaspoon salt
    freshly ground pepper to
    taste
    lemon slices and fresh dill

Salt and pepper trout inside and out. Melt 4 tablespoons of butter in a large 12-inch skillet until hot. Place 3 trout in skillet and sauté about 7 minutes on each side (depending on size of the trout). Remove to a platter and place in a warm oven. Continue with remaining trout, using remaining butter. Place on platter in oven. Sauté almonds until golden. Stir in dry vermouth, lemon juice, garlic, salt and pepper. Heat several minutes until mixture starts to bubble. Taste and adjust seasonings if necessary. Cook about 1 minute. Spoon sauce with almonds over fish. Top each fish with a lemon slice and fresh dill sprig. Keep sauce hot. Pass remaining sauce at the table.

To insure freshness, select fish that have clear bulging eyes and bright red or pink gills. Scales should be tight against the body. Fresh fish usually have flesh that is firm to the touch and no odor.

In Saint Louis there is more than one way to serve ravioli. In fact, one variation, Toasted Ravioli, has become a true Saint Louis classic. The story goes that Toasted Ravioli was "discovered" quite by accident when a cook at Angelo's dropped a few in some bread crumbs and decided to see how they would taste deep fried. The result is a unique appetizer that is a required menu item for most of the Italian restaurants in town.

Fillet of Sole Indienne

Serves 4

6 tablespoons butter
1¼ pounds sole fillets
2 large bananas, halved lengthwise
   juice of 1 lemon
   salt to taste
   paprika to taste
2 tablespoons sliced almonds
⅛-¼ teaspoon curry powder
2 cups frozen peas
   cucumber slices
   lemon slices

Flavorful and light.

Melt butter in a jelly roll pan. Place sole and bananas in pan and turn to coat with butter. Drizzle lemon juice over sole and bananas. Season with salt and paprika. Sprinkle sole with almonds and bananas with curry powder. Bake at 450 degrees for 6 to 7 minutes. Cook peas. To serve, place fillet of sole, bananas and peas on each plate. Spoon juice over fish and garnish with cucumber and lemon slices.

Shrimp Avocat

Serves 6

3 ripe avocados, halved
2 tablespoons fresh lime juice
1 pound shrimp, steamed, peeled and deveined
¼ cup sour cream
½ cup French dressing with herbs
¼ cup sliced almonds, toasted
   lime slices

A new presentation for an always popular classic.

Using a melon baller, scoop 2 cups of avocado balls from shells. Toss with lime juice. Carefully remove remaining pulp from shells with a spoon. (Reserve for use in salad or dip.) Arrange avocado balls and shrimp in shells. Blend sour cream and dressing and chill. Just before serving, top shrimp with almonds and drizzle with dressing mixture. Garnish with lime slices.

Two to 2½ pounds of raw, unpeeled shrimp yield 1 pound cooked and peeled, or about 2 cups.

MEATS

Beef Tenderloin Stuffed with Mushrooms

Serves 10 to 12

1 **5-pound beef tenderloin**
1 **pound mushrooms, chopped**
4 **tablespoons butter**
½ **cup chopped celery**
½ **cup chopped onion**
¼ **cup chopped green pepper**
1 **teaspoon salt**
½ **teaspoon freshly ground pepper**
¼ **teaspoon dried sage**
¼ **teaspoon dried thyme**
2 **tablespoons flour**
   fresh parsley

Starting at the widest end of the tenderloin, slice horizontally from end to end and spread apart. Sauté mushrooms in butter until liquid evaporates. Add celery, onion, green pepper and seasonings. Sauté until vegetables are tender. Blend in flour and cook 1 minute. Stuff mixture into pocket of beef. Secure opening with skewers and lace with string. Bake at 325 degrees for 20 minutes per pound for medium rare. Garnish with parsley.

Filet Mignon Cassis

Serves 4

4 **filet mignons, ½-inch thick**
3 **tablespoons unsalted butter, divided**
1 **clove garlic, crushed**
½ **pound mushrooms, sliced**
1 **tablespoon drained capers**
¼ **cup crème de cassis**
2 **tablespoons Maggi seasoning**

In a skillet, sauté filets in 2 tablespoons melted butter over medium high heat 5 minutes per side, or until desired doneness is reached. Remove and keep warm on a heated platter. Add remaining tablespoon of butter to the skillet and sauté garlic and mushrooms until browning begins. Add capers, cassis and Maggi seasoning. Return filets to skillet and heat 1 minute per side. Place on a serving platter and cover with mushrooms and sauce.

The cassis gives this dish a fruity black currant flavor.

Grilled Tenderloin with Horseradish Mold

Serves 4 to 6

Grilled Tenderloin:

  1 **3-pound beef tenderloin, trimmed**
  1 **clove garlic**
      salt and freshly ground pepper
  ¼ **cup melted butter**

Horseradish Mold:

  1 **3-ounce package lemon gelatin**
  1 **cup boiling water**
  ¼ **teaspoon salt**
  2 **tablespoons fresh lemon juice**
  1 **cup heavy cream**
  ¾ **cup drained horseradish**

Grilled Tenderloin:
Rub tenderloin on all sides with fresh garlic. Sprinkle with salt and pepper to taste. On a gas grill, sear all sides of tenderloin on high heat. Reduce heat to medium and cook, uncovered, 25 to 30 minutes for medium rare. Baste occasionally with melted butter. Let stand 10 to 15 minutes before slicing. Serve with Horseradish Mold.

Horseradish Mold:
Several hours before serving beef, combine first 4 ingredients and stir until gelatin is dissolved. Chill until slightly jelled. Whip cream until stiff. Fold cream and horseradish into gelatin mixture. Pour into a mold and chill until firm. Can be made a day in advance.

Oriental Beef Tenderloin with Peppers

Serves 4

- 1 **pound beef tenderloin, trimmed and chilled**
- 1 **clove garlic, minced**
- ¼ **cup soy sauce**
- 1 **tablespoon minced shallots**
- 2 **tablespoons olive oil**
- ⅛ **teaspoon freshly ground pepper**
- 3 **tablespoons unsalted butter, divided**
- 3 **tablespoons olive oil, divided**
- 2 **tablespoons dry sherry**
- 1 **large green pepper**
- 1 **medium onion**
- ½ **pound large mushrooms, thinly sliced**
- 1 **16-ounce can Italian tomatoes**
- ⅓ **cup sherry**
    reserved tomato liquid
- 1 **tablespoon cornstarch**
- 10 **ounces beef broth**

Slice chilled tenderloin against the grain into ½-inch pieces. Gently flatten to a ¼-inch thickness and cut into 1 x 2-inch pieces. Combine the next 5 ingredients and *marinate tenderloin overnight* in a reclosable plastic bag.

Drain tenderloin and reserve marinade. In a saucepan, sauté tenderloin in 1 tablespoon butter and 1 tablespoon oil over medium high heat, one third at a time. Deglaze saucepan with 2 tablespoons sherry. Reserve deglazing liquid. Set tenderloin aside.

Slice the green pepper into ½ x 2-inch strips. Slice onion into quarters. Separate into leaves. Sauté in 1 tablespoon butter and 1 tablespoon oil over medium high heat 5 minutes. Reduce heat to medium and cook, covered, 5 additional minutes. Set aside.

Sauté mushrooms in 1 tablespoon butter and 1 tablespoon oil over medium high heat 4 to 5 minutes. Set aside. Cut tomatoes into halves. Drain tomatoes and reserve one half of the liquid. Set tomatoes and liquid aside in separate bowls.

In a saucepan large enough to accommodate all ingredients, combine ⅓ cup sherry and tomato liquid. Dissolve cornstarch in beef broth and add to saucepan. Cook sauce over medium heat 5 minutes or until thick enough to coat a spoon. Add tenderloin, green pepper, onion, mushrooms, tomatoes and reserved marinade and deglazing liquids. Cook 3 to 4 minutes until thoroughly heated. Do not overcook as a slightly firm texture is desirable. Serve in shallow bowls as you would a stew. Accompany with steamed white rice.

Like most Chinese food, this loses something when reheated.

Carbonnades with Sour Cream and Horseradish Sauce

Serves 6 to 8

Carbonnades:

- 1 2½-pound rump roast
- 2 tablespoons butter or bacon drippings
- 2 tablespoons vinegar
- 1 cup beer
- 1½ cups beef broth
- 1 teaspoon sugar
- 3 onions, chopped
- 2 tablespoons butter
- 2 tablespoons flour
- 2 tablespoons catsup

Sour Cream and Horseradish Sauce:

- 1 cup sour cream
- 1½ tablespoons horseradish
- 1 teaspoon sugar
- ½ teaspoon salt
   juice of ½ lemon

Carbonnades:
Cut beef into ½-inch slices. Brown in butter and set aside on a plate. Drain fat from skillet. Add vinegar, scraping crustiness from skillet. Add beer, broth and sugar. Simmer a few minutes. Set aside. In a separate skillet, sauté onions in butter, stir in flour and add catsup. In a baking dish, layer beef and onion mixture alternately. Pour sauce over beef and onions. Cover loosely and bake at 325 degrees for 2 to 2½ hours. Serve with Sour Cream and Horseradish Sauce.

Sour Cream and Horseradish Sauce:
Combine sauce ingredients and mix well.

This recipe offers the ease of pot roast with the elegance of tenderloin.

On the bluffs overlooking the Mississippi, just north of Saint Louis appears the image of a fearsome dragon-like bird the Piasa. According to Illini Indian legend, the man-eating Piasa lived thousands of years ago and preyed on innocent victims of the tribe. Finally, Chief Ouatoga and his warriors were able to kill the beast. The Indians then painted the Piasa's image on an inaccessible portion of the bluff and every brave who passed the figure in his canoe fired an arrow at the painting of the fierce bird.

Show Me State Ribs

Serves 6

3 slabs baby back loin ribs, bone side skinned
  salt and freshly ground pepper
¼ teaspoon onion powder per slab
3 cups barbecue sauce
2 tablespoons cider vinegar
2 tablespoons brown sugar

Missouri "shows" you ribs!

Season meat side of ribs with salt, pepper and onion powder. Roll each slab, bone side in, into a circle. Tie with butcher twine and place on a rack in a shallow roasting pan. Bake at 325 degrees for 1 hour and 15 minutes.

Combine barbecue sauce, vinegar and brown sugar and simmer 1 hour.

Untie and grill ribs over low heat, meat side down, 6 to 8 minutes. Turn ribs and baste with sauce. Cover grill and cook 15 minutes, basting occasionally. To serve, cut slabs into 2 or 3 rib pieces. Combine in large serving dish and cover with remaining sauce.

Beef Brisket

Serves 4 to 6

1 4-pound flat-cut, deckle-off beef brisket
  paprika to taste
  freshly ground pepper
  Worcestershire sauce
1 envelope dry onion soup mix

Turn brisket fat side up. Remove most of fat layer. Sprinkle this side generously with paprika and a dash of pepper. Sprinkle generously with Worcestershire sauce and rub in well. Place brisket in a roasting pan. Add ½ cup water to pan if desired. Bake, uncovered, at 400 degrees for 25 to 30 minutes, until browned. Remove from oven. Sprinkle brisket with onion soup mix. Cover pan and bake at 325 degrees for 2 additional hours. Add more water to pan as needed. Let brisket stand 5 minutes before slicing. Slice against the grain.

Can be frozen (after baking) in smaller portions with a little juice from the pan.

Easy to prepare and makes wonderful leftovers for sandwiches.

New Orleans Pot Roast

Serves 6 to 8

1 **4-pound roast of beef, round or chuck**

12 **large pimiento stuffed olives, halved**

¾ **pound salt pork or bacon, diced**

2 **large onions, chopped**

½ **cup rum**

4 **tomatoes, peeled, seeded and chopped, or 2 cups canned tomatoes**
bouquet garni (parsley sprigs, fresh thyme and bay leaf)

½ **teaspoon dried basil**

2 **cloves garlic, crushed**
freshly ground black pepper
sprig of mint

Make a double row of slits in beef on each side and insert olive halves. Roll meat and tie with string at 2-inch intervals.

In a large, deep flameproof baking dish or Dutch oven cook salt pork on top of stove, stirring occasionally until brown. Remove. Add beef and brown on all sides. Remove. Drain off excess fat, leaving 1 tablespoon, and brown the onions. Replace beef and pork, add rum and flame it by igniting it in the dish over medium heat. (Use caution as flames may rise quite high.) Extinguish after 1 minute by covering with the lid.

Add tomatoes, bouquet garni, basil, garlic and pepper to taste. Cover and cook over very low heat or in a 300 degree oven for 4 to 5 hours or until beef is tender enough to cut with spoon. If baking dish becomes dry during cooking, add a little stock. Transfer beef to a platter and garnish with mint. After removing bouquet garni, spoon sauce over beef and serve.

Bouquet garni is a bunch of herbs traditionally made of 2 to 3 parsley stalks, a sprig of fresh thyme (or a pinch of dried thyme) and a bay leaf. Tie together with string if used in liquids which are to be strained. Otherwise, tie herbs in a piece of cheesecloth for easy removal before serving.

Beef with 15 Chile Peppers

Serves 4

1 small egg white
1½ tablespoons black soy sauce
    freshly ground pepper
    to taste
1 teaspoon rice wine
2 teaspoons sugar
1-2 tablespoons water
1 tablespoon cornstarch
1 tablespoon hot bean sauce
    (or more)
5 tablespoons plus 1 teaspoon
    peanut oil
1 1-pound flank steak, thinly
    sliced and cut into bite
    size pieces
2 cloves garlic, finely chopped
15 red chile peppers
¾ cup water
1 tablespoon black soy sauce
1 teaspoon sugar
1½ teaspoons sesame oil,
    divided
1 pound fresh spinach

In a glass bowl, combine egg white, soy sauce, pepper, rice wine, sugar and water. Add cornstarch and blend to thicken. Stir in bean sauce and 3 tablespoons peanut oil. Add flank steak and marinate several hours.

Sauté garlic and red chiles in 2 tablespoons peanut oil. Add meat and stir-fry until cooked. Add water, soy sauce, sugar and 1 teaspoon sesame oil, simmering until liquid is hot. If the sauce is too thin, add a small amount of cornstarch mixed with cold water. Stir well to thicken.

In a saucepan, bring salted water to a boil. Add spinach and 1 teaspoon peanut oil and cook over medium high heat 1 minute. Drain and toss spinach with ½ teaspoon sesame oil. Serve beef on a heated platter surrounded by spinach.

In 1842, William Lemp first introduced Saint Louisans to the clear golden taste of lager beer. Demand soared and in a few short years the city supported more than 40 breweries and numerous beer gardens. One of the more interesting sites was Uhrig's Cave, located at Washington and Jefferson. Uhrig's Cave boasted theatre and music in three separate pavilions while customers enjoyed the cool refreshment of beer chilled in a large cave.

Fajitas de Mexico

Serves 3 to 4

1½ teaspoons garlic salt
½ teaspoon pepper
    juice of 3 limes
1 1-pound flank steak
12 flour tortillas
1 onion, sliced
1 green pepper, sliced
1 red pepper, sliced
1½ tablespoons vegetable oil
    chopped tomatoes
    chopped green onions
    sliced ripe olives
    guacamole
    sour cream
    picante sauce

An original recipe translated from Spanish.

Combine garlic salt, pepper and lime juice and marinate steak in refrigerator for 6 to 8 hours. Drain marinade from steak and grill 6 minutes on each side. Wrap tortillas in foil and heat in oven at 325 degrees for 15 minutes. While steak is grilling, stir-fry onion and peppers in oil. Slice grilled steak into strips and add to onion and peppers. Stir-fry 1 minute. To serve, arrange remaining ingredients on a platter. Place a small amount of stir-fry mixture in center of each tortilla, top with choice of ingredients from platter. Roll tortilla and enjoy!

We like to grill steak over a mesquite fire. It gives tremendous flavor to this recipe.

Barbecued Beef Strips

Serves 4

1½ pounds lean boneless beef strips
1 tablespoon toasted sesame seeds
6 tablespoons soy sauce
2 tablespoons sugar
1 green onion, thinly sliced
2 cloves garlic, minced
2 tablespoons sesame oil
1 teaspoon grated fresh ginger

Cut beef into thin slices. Combine remaining ingredients in a glass bowl. Add beef, cover and marinate 1½ to 2 hours. Thread beef on skewers and grill over medium coals, brushing occasionally with marinade.

Serve with Onion Marmalade or Peanut Sauce.

Eggplant with Beef

Serves 8

3-4 **medium eggplants**
　　 vegetable oil
2　 **pounds ground beef**
1½　**cups chopped onion**
1　 **cup chopped celery**
1-2　**cloves garlic, chopped**
1　 **6-ounce can tomato paste**
1　 **8-ounce can tomato sauce**
2　 **tablespoons sugar**
　　 salt and freshly ground
　　 pepper to taste
¼　 **cup chopped green olives**
¼　 **cup chopped ripe olives**
2-3　**tablespoons capers, drained**
　　 (optional)
1　 **cup freshly grated Romano**
　　 or Parmesan cheese, divided
1　 **cup bread crumbs, divided**
　　 sliced mozzarella cheese

Peel and slice eggplants ¼-inch thick; place in cold, salted water and soak for 30 minutes. Rinse in cold water; squeeze to remove water. In a skillet, sauté eggplant in oil until golden brown. Drain on paper towels. Cool.

Brown beef, onion, celery and garlic. Drain well. Add tomato paste, tomato sauce, sugar, salt and pepper. Cook 5 minutes and remove from heat. Add olives, capers, ½ cup Romano cheese and ½ cup bread crumbs. Stir to mix well.

In a 9 x 13-inch glass baking dish layer eggplant, meat mixture, half the remaining cheese and half the remaining bread crumbs. Repeat layers. Bake, covered, at 350 degrees for 1 hour. Cover with mozzarella cheese during last 5 minutes or until melted.

Serve this in place of lasagne at your next party. Eggplant makes it different.

Nearly a year before the United States announced plans to orbit a man around the earth - even before NASA was formed - McDonnell Aircraft engineers in Saint Louis began work on Project Mercury. When Alan Shepard Jr. made his successful maiden voyage in 1961, the space program was officially on its way. All Mercury and Gemini space capsules were built here, starting a partnership between McDonnell Douglas and NASA that continues to this day.

Upside Down Pizza

Serves 6 to 8

- ½ **pound ground beef**
- ½ **pound bulk Italian sausage**
- ½ **cup chopped onion**
- 1¼ **cups spaghetti or pizza sauce**
- ¼ **pound mushrooms, sliced**
- 1 **2¼-ounce can sliced ripe olives**
- 6 **ounces mozzarella cheese, sliced**
- 2 **eggs**
- 1 **cup milk**
- 1 **tablespoon vegetable oil**
- 1 **cup flour**
- ¼ **teaspoon salt**
- ⅓ **cup freshly grated Parmesan cheese**

The answer to "What's for dinner?".

Brown ground beef and sausage in a large skillet over medium heat. Add onion; sauté, stirring frequently, until onion is limp and sausage is well browned. Drain liquid from skillet. Add spaghetti sauce, mushrooms and olives; heat until simmering. Pour into a 9 x 13 x 2-inch baking dish. Arrange mozzarella cheese over sausage mixture.

In a blender, combine eggs, milk, oil, flour and salt. Mix until smooth. Pour evenly over mozzarella cheese. Sprinkle with Parmesan cheese. Bake, uncovered, at 400 degrees for 25 minutes or until crust is puffed and golden. Cut into squares and serve hot.

Grilled Veal Chops with Mustard Herb Butter

Serves 4

- 4 **tablespoons butter, softened**
- 1½ **tablespoons Dijon mustard**
- 1 **shallot, minced**
- 1 **tablespoon chopped fresh parsley**
- 1 **tablespoon fresh tarragon**
- 1 **tablespoon chopped chives**
  freshly ground pepper
- 4 **veal chops**

To make Mustard Herb Butter, combine all ingredients, except veal, in a small bowl. Grill veal chops over medium coals, brushing frequently with Mustard Herb Butter. Reserve ample butter to serve on fresh vegetables as an accompaniment.

Choose your veal according to color — pale creamy pink is best. Avoid dark pink or reddish color.

Veal Mediterranean

Serves 6

2 pounds veal cutlets
1 egg, beaten
1 cup seasoned Italian bread crumbs
½ cup butter
½ pound mushrooms, sautéed
1 14-ounce can artichoke hearts, halved
1 2¼-ounce can sliced ripe olives
¼ teaspoon dried oregano
½-1 cup chicken broth
6 tablespoons dry sherry
salt and freshly ground pepper

Slice veal into serving portions. Flatten pieces to ½-inch thickness. Dip into egg and then into bread crumbs. In a skillet, sauté veal in butter 2 minutes on each side. Add remaining ingredients and simmer, uncovered, 30 minutes.

For variation, substitute chicken breast cutlets.

Veal Scallopini Avocado

Serves 2

10 ounces veal scallops
flour
salt and freshly ground pepper
2 tablespoons butter
6 large mushrooms, sliced
¼ cup Marsala wine or sherry
1 ripe avocado, peeled and sliced
freshly grated Parmesan cheese

Place veal between sheets of waxed paper and flatten until very thin. Dredge in flour, shaking off excess. Sprinkle with salt and pepper on both sides. Melt butter in a skillet large enough to hold scallops. Sauté veal 2 minutes on each side until golden. Remove to a heated platter. Keep warm in a 200 degree oven. Add mushrooms to skillet and sauté 2 minutes. Blend in wine and bring to a boil. Add avocado and simmer 3 minutes. Pour over veal and sprinkle with cheese.

For another flavor, prepared veal can also be placed in an ovenproof dish and topped with Swiss or Monterey Jack cheese and broiled until browned.

Veal Cutlets with Asparagus Sauce

Serves 6

6   **veal cutlets**
1   **pound asparagus**
1½ **cups beef or chicken broth**
½   **cup butter, divided**
1   **cup flour, divided**
    salt and freshly ground
    pepper
¼   **cup olive oil**
15 **sprigs Italian parsley,**
    coarsely chopped
    lemon wedges

Flatten veal cutlets and set aside. Snap off tough ends of asparagus. Steam until tender. Drain and let rest several minutes. Slice each stalk in half. Place bottom halves of asparagus in a food processor or blender and finely chop. Place in a saucepan and add chicken broth. Bring to a boil and continue to boil gently. Melt 4 tablespoons of butter in a separate saucepan. When butter is melted, add 1½ tablespoons of flour, stirring with a wooden spoon until flour turns a light brown. Add the boiling broth mixture and stir well. Simmer 10 minutes. Add salt and pepper to taste.

Meanwhile, slice remaining asparagus into 1-inch pieces. Place oil and remaining butter in a large skillet over medium heat. With remaining flour, lightly dust cutlets. When butter is melted, sauté cutlets 2 minutes on each side, sprinkling with salt and pepper. Transfer to a warmed serving platter and cover to keep warm. Add sauce and asparagus to skillet. Simmer 5 minutes. When sauce is reduced, pour over the cutlets. Sprinkle with parsley, garnish with lemon wedges and serve immediately.

Italian parsley, also known as flat-leafed, is chosen to add fragrance to a recipe. It also blends well with any fresh greens and has a special affinity for garlic.

Veal and Artichokes

Serves 2

- ¾ **pound veal scallops**
- 2 **tablespoons flour**
- ¼ **teaspoon salt**
- ¼ **teaspoon freshly ground pepper**
- ¼ **teaspoon paprika**
- 1 **6-ounce jar marinated artichoke hearts, drained, liquid reserved**
- ¼ **cup chopped onion**
- 1 **tablespoon butter**
- ¼ **cup chicken broth**
- 1 **tablespoon fresh lemon juice**
- ½ **cup sour cream**
- 2 **tablespoons freshly grated Parmesan cheese**

Flatten scallops to ¼-inch thickness. In a large bowl, combine flour, salt, pepper and paprika. Dredge scallops in flour mixture. Sauté veal in liquid from artichoke hearts 2 minutes per side. Remove veal with a slotted spoon and keep warm. In a separate skillet, sauté onion in butter until tender. Stir in chicken broth, lemon juice, sour cream and Parmesan cheese. Add artichoke hearts and simmer until thoroughly heated. Pour over veal and serve with a favorite pasta.

Flattening veal scallops to a ¼-inch thickness breaks down the tissue in veal and renders more tender scallops.

146

Pork Tenderloin with Mustard Sauce

Serves 4

Pork Tenderloin:
- ¼ cup soy sauce
- ¼ cup bourbon
- 2 tablespoons brown sugar
- 1 2½-pound pork tenderloin

Mustard Sauce:
- ⅓ cup sour cream
- ⅓ cup mayonnaise
- 1 tablespoon chopped onion
- 1 tablespoon dry mustard
- 1½ teaspoons vinegar
- ¼ teaspoon salt

A cinch to prepare for company or family.

Pork Tenderloin:
Combine soy sauce, bourbon and brown sugar. Marinate pork in mixture 2 hours. Bake at 325 degrees for 1 hour and 15 minutes, basting often. Serve warm with Mustard Sauce.

Mustard Sauce:
Combine all ingredients and mix until well blended.

Apple Glazed Pork Roast

Serves 6 to 8

- 1 12-ounce jar apple jelly
- 4 teaspoons Dijon mustard
- 3 teaspoons fresh lemon juice, divided
- 1 2½-pound rolled pork loin roast
  freshly ground pepper
- 1 tablespoon brandy
  watercress sprigs
- 1 apple, sliced

In a small saucepan, melt jelly over low heat. Stir in mustard and 1 teaspoon lemon juice. Set aside. Rub roast with pepper. Place on a rack in a foil lined shallow roasting pan. Roast at 350 degrees for 45 minutes. Brush lightly with jelly mixture and bake an additional 20 minutes. Brush once more with jelly mixture and bake 20 to 30 additional minutes or until meat thermometer reaches 170 degrees. Remove roast to a warm platter. Scrape any browned drippings into remaining jelly mixture. Add 2 teaspoons lemon juice and brandy to jelly mixture and cook until thoroughly heated. To serve, sauce plate and fan thinly sliced roast on top. Garnish with watercress and apple slices.

Pork Tenderloin with Potatoes and Apples

Serves 4

4 pork tenderloins, ½-⅓
   pound each
   salt and freshly ground
   pepper to taste
2 tablespoons vegetable oil
1 teaspoon dried rosemary
1 onion, halved
8 red potatoes
2 baking apples, unpeeled
   and quartered
¼ cup chicken broth
2 tablespoons fresh parsley
   (optional)

Hearty fall family fare.

Sprinkle pork with salt and pepper. Add oil to a roasting pan large enough to contain the tenderloins in one layer. Brown meat on all sides. Sprinkle with rosemary. Add onion and potatoes. Bake at 375 degrees for 40 to 45 minutes. Add apples and bake an additional 10 minutes.

Remove meat, vegetables and fruit to a warm platter. Add broth to the pan, stir and boil 5 minutes. Pour over sliced meat, vegetables and fruit. Sprinkle with parsley, if desired.

Pork Chops with Orange Slices

Serves 2 to 4

4 pork rib or loin chops,
   ½-¾-inch thick
1 teaspoon salt
1 small onion, thinly sliced
½ cup rosé wine
   grated peel of 1 large orange
   juice of 1 large orange
2 tablespoons brown sugar
¼ teaspoon ground allspice
1 small orange, thinly sliced

In a skillet, brown chops over medium heat. Drain skillet. Sprinkle chops with salt and place onion slices on top. Combine wine, orange peel, juice, brown sugar and allspice. Pour into skillet and bring to a boil. Reduce heat, cover and simmer 30 minutes. Arrange orange slices on chops, cover and simmer an additional 15 minutes. Serve sauced with orange liquid, if desired.

Lamb with Chèvre Pesto and Basil Hollandaise

Serves 6

½ **pound chèvre cheese, without ash coating**

½ **cup pine nuts or walnuts**

½ **cup minced fresh parsley**

3 **medium cloves garlic**

½ **cup walnut oil or olive oil**

4 **tablespoons fresh lemon juice**

1 **cup fresh bread crumbs**

6 **racks of lamb chops, 4 to a rack, backbones removed Hollandaise Sauce (page 108) fresh basil, chopped**

To make pesto, blend cheese, nuts, parsley and garlic in a food processor using on and off turns. With machine running, add oil and lemon juice through feed tube and mix until thick. Spread pesto over meat. Press bread crumbs into pesto to coat meat completely.

Place lamb, meat side up, in a roasting pan. Bake at 400 degrees for 25 to 30 minutes or until thermometer inserted in thickest portion of meat (not touching bone) registers 130 degrees for rare. Let stand 10 minutes. Cut into each rack, separate loosely, keeping 4 chops together. Combine Hollandaise Sauce and basil. Serve with lamb.

Lamb can be prepared early in the day and chilled. Let stand at room temperature 2 hours before cooking.

Chèvre is goat cheese. We recommend Montrachet chèvre as it lends itself well to this recipe.

The first bridge to cross the Mississippi at Saint Louis was the Eads bridge completed in 1874. James Eads' innovative upright arch design called for spans of 500 feet resting on only two piers grounded in bedrock. Workmen laboring in decompressed air chambers, over a hundred feet below the surface, suffered from the then unknown ailment of "the bends" when they returned to the surface too quickly after work.

Fillets of Lamb in Champagne Sauce

Serves 8

8 **loin lamb chops, boned, cut 1-inch thick**
   salt
1 **egg**
1 **tablespoon water**
¾ **cup dry bread crumbs**
¼ **cup finely minced ham**
½ **teaspoon dried rosemary**
½ **teaspoon dried savory**
½ **teaspoon dried thyme**
⅓ **cup butter**
6 **ounces Brut champagne**

Warm a serving platter in a 175 degree oven 20 minutes before serving. Season fillets lightly with salt. Beat egg with water. In a small bowl, combine bread crumbs, ham, rosemary, savory and thyme. Dip each fillet in egg and then bread crumb mixture. Melt butter in a sauté pan over moderate heat. Add fillets and sauté 5 minutes, turning once carefully. Remove fillets from pan and arrange on a warmed serving platter in oven. Pour champagne into the sauté pan and heat rapidly, stirring to mix with the cooking juices. Cook 2 minutes. Pour over fillets and serve immediately.

For the perfect potato with lamb, carefully toss small cooked new potatoes with butter, salt, pepper and chopped fresh mint.

Butterflied Leg of Lamb

Serves 12

1 **6-7 pound leg of lamb, butterflied**
1 **cup dry red wine**
¾ **cup beef broth or bouillon**
3 **tablespoons orange marmalade**
2 **tablespoons red wine vinegar**
1 **tablespoon minced dried onion**
1 **tablespoon dried marjoram**
1 **tablespoon dried rosemary**
1 **large bay leaf, crumbled**
1 **teaspoon seasoned salt**
¼ **teaspoon ground ginger**
1 **clove garlic, crushed**

Place lamb in a shallow roasting pan, fat side down. Combine remaining ingredients in a saucepan and simmer, uncovered, 20 minutes. Pour hot mixture over lamb and marinate at room temperature 6 to 8 hours. Turn and baste frequently.

Barbecue lamb over medium hot coals 30 to 45 minutes. Turn several times and baste with marinade. Do not pierce.

To prepare in oven, place lamb fat side down, under broiler about 4 inches from heat. Broil 10 minutes per side. Transfer meat to oven and bake at 425 degrees for 15 minutes. Carve into ½-inch thick slices.

Serve herb jellies with roasted meat. Natural combinations are rosemary-sherry and tarragon-wine.

POULTRY

Chicken Monterey

Serves 4 to 6

4 **large whole chicken breasts, skinned, boned and halved**
  salt and freshly ground pepper
  flour
½ **cup butter or margarine, divided**
½ **cup chopped onion**
1 **clove garlic, minced**
½ **pound mushrooms, chopped**
2 **tablespoons flour**
1 **teaspoon celery salt**
½ **teaspoon white pepper**
½ **cup chicken broth**
½ **cup white wine**
1 **avocado, mashed**
1½ **cups shredded Monterey Jack cheese, divided**

Place chicken breasts between sheets of waxed paper and flatten to ¼-inch thickness. Lightly sprinkle with salt and pepper and dust with flour. Melt ¼ cup butter in a skillet and quickly sauté breasts a few at a time until golden. Remove; place in a 3-quart baking dish. Melt remaining ¼ cup butter in the same skillet and sauté onion, garlic and mushrooms slowly until vegetables are tender, but not brown. Stir in flour, celery salt, pepper, chicken broth and wine. Cook over low heat until thickened. Stir in mashed avocado and ½ cup shredded cheese, blending well. Spoon avocado mixture on each breast and top with remaining cheese. Bake at 350 degrees for 20 to 30 minutes until chicken is cooked and cheese is melted. Can be made (unbaked) a day in advance.

You will have enough sauce remaining to serve over pasta as a side dish. Serve a bright vegetable with this to set off the avocado coloring.

154

Chicken Bristol

Serves 6

 3 chicken breasts, halved, boned and skinned
 2 tablespoons cognac or brandy
    salt and freshly ground pepper
 ½ teaspoon dried marjoram
 7 tablespoons salted butter, divided
 ⅓ cup dry sherry
1½ cups half and half
 3 egg yolks
 1 teaspoon flour
 ½ teaspoon ground nutmeg
 6 ounces lump crab meat
 6 large mushroom caps
 ⅓ cup shredded Gruyère cheese

Place chicken between sheets of waxed paper and flatten. Moisten each fillet with cognac. Let stand a few minutes. Mix salt, pepper and marjoram; rub on each fillet. Melt 6 tablespoons butter in a sauté pan; heat until foaming. Sauté fillets on both sides until browned and tender. Remove to a plate and keep hot. Add sherry to the pan and cook until nearly evaporated. Remove from heat. In a separate bowl, mix half and half and egg yolks. Blend this mixture and flour into sherry pan. Season with nutmeg, salt and pepper to taste. Can be set aside at this point.

When ready to finish the entrée, carefully reheat the sauce. Do not boil. Add a small amount of sauce to the crab and heat. Sauté mushroom caps in 1 tablespoon butter. Fill mushroom caps with crab mixture. Arrange chicken in a baking pan. Place a mushroom cap on each fillet. Pour sauce over chicken and sprinkle with cheese. Brown under the broiler. Serve immediately.

Chicken l'Orange

Serves 10 to 12

 ½ cup flour
 2 teaspoons curry powder
 ½ teaspoon salt
 ½ teaspoon freshly ground pepper
 3 tablespoons butter
 6 whole chicken breasts, halved, skinned and boned
 1 18-ounce jar orange marmalade
 ½ cup orange juice
 ½ cup orange curaçao or Grand Marnier
 2 tablespoons fresh lemon juice
    toasted almonds
    cooked rice

Combine flour, curry powder, salt and pepper in a bowl. Melt butter in a large baking dish. Dredge chicken pieces in flour mixture and place in baking dish. Combine the next 4 ingredients and pour over chicken. Bake at 350 degrees for 1 hour, basting frequently. Sprinkle each portion with toasted almonds and serve over rice. Can be made early in the day and reheated.

Sautéed Chicken with Shallots and Artichoke Hearts

Serves 4 to 6

 6 **tablespoons butter or margarine, divided**
 2 **tablespoons vegetable oil**
 3 **chicken breasts, halved**
20 **large whole shallots, peeled or 16 1-inch white onions, peeled**
    salt and freshly ground pepper
 2 **bay leaves**
 1 **teaspoon fresh lemon juice**
 1 **9-ounce package frozen artichoke hearts, thawed and drained**
 ½ **cup chicken broth**

In a heavy skillet, melt 4 tablespoons butter and oil over medium heat. Brown chicken, starting skin side down, turning until golden brown. Set aside. Add shallots to skillet and sauté until lightly colored. Pour all but a thin layer of fat from skillet. Add chicken and season with salt and pepper. Add bay leaves and cover. Cook over high heat until fat splutters. Reduce heat and cook over low heat for 30 minutes basting frequently with pan juices. Set skillet aside.

Meanwhile, melt remaining butter in a small skillet. When foam subsides, stir in lemon juice. Add artichoke hearts and toss until they glisten. Season with salt. Cover and cook over low heat 10 to 15 minutes or until artichoke hearts are tender. Discard bay leaves. Arrange chicken on a warm platter and surround with shallots and artichoke hearts.

Pour chicken broth into remaining juices in the first skillet. Bring to a boil over high heat stirring to blend. Boil 2 to 3 minutes until sauce is reduced to ⅓ cup. Pour over chicken and serve immediately.

Chicken Breasts with Crab

Serves 8

4 **large chicken breasts, halved, boned and skinned**

1 **pound mushrooms, stems removed and reserved**

¼ **cup chopped onion**

4 **tablespoons butter**

½ **cup cracker crumbs**

2 **tablespoons chopped fresh parsley**

1 **7-ounce can crab, drained and flaked**

3 **tablespoons butter**

¼ **cup flour**

¾ **cup milk**

¾ **cup chicken broth**

⅓ **cup dry white wine**
  salt and freshly ground pepper

1 **cup sour cream**

An elegant do-ahead recipe.

Flatten chicken breasts between sheets of waxed paper to ⅛-inch thickness. Chill until ready to use.

Finely chop mushroom stems. Sauté onion and stems in 4 tablespoons butter until tender. Mix in crumbs, parsley and crab. Top each chicken breast with about ¼ cup crab mixture. Fold in sides and roll. Place seam side down in a baking dish and chill until ready to bake.

Melt 3 tablespoons butter and blend in flour. Add milk, broth and wine all at once. Cook and stir until mixture thickens and bubbles. Add salt and pepper to taste. Slice mushroom caps. Stir mushrooms and sour cream into sauce. Pour over chicken breasts. Bake, covered, at 350 degrees for about 1 hour. Serve remaining sauce over rice or pasta.

Ornate stone and brick water towers used to be a common sight in America's cities. Today only seven remain in the country and three are in Saint Louis. The Corinthian Column on Grand Avenue is the oldest dating back to 1871. The Bissell Street Tower built in 1887 and Reservoir Park's Compton Hill Tower, completed in 1889 complete the trio.

Chicken Lombardy

Serves 8

6 chicken breasts, boned, skinned and quartered
½ cup flour
1 cup butter or margarine, divided
  salt and freshly ground pepper
1½ cups sliced mushrooms
¾ cup Marsala wine
½ cup chicken broth
½ teaspoon salt
⅛ teaspoon freshly ground pepper
½ cup shredded Fontina or mozzarella cheese
½ cup freshly grated Parmesan cheese
  fresh parsley

Place chicken pieces between sheets of waxed paper and flatten to ⅛ to ¼-inch thickness. Dredge lightly with flour. In a large skillet over low heat, sauté chicken in 2 tablespoons melted butter. Cook 4 minutes per side or until golden. Repeat until all pieces are cooked, adding 2 tablespoons butter each time. Place chicken with edges overlapping in a greased 13 x 9 x 2-inch baking dish. Sprinkle with salt and pepper. Reserve drippings in skillet.

In a separate skillet, sauté mushrooms in 4 tablespoons butter until tender. Sprinkle over chicken. In the first skillet, stir wine and chicken broth into drippings. Simmer 10 minutes, stirring occasionally. Add ½ teaspoon salt and ⅛ teaspoon pepper. Spoon ⅓ of broth mixture over chicken. Sprinkle combined cheeses over chicken. Bake at 450 degrees for 10 to 12 minutes. Place under broiler to lightly brown. Garnish with fresh parsley; serve with remaining sauce.

Herbed Parmesan Chicken

Serves 6 to 8

3 pounds chicken breasts, skinned and boned
¼ teaspoon garlic powder
¼ teaspoon paprika
⅛ teaspoon dried thyme
¼ cup freshly grated Parmesan cheese
1 tablespoon minced fresh parsley
⅓ cup fine bread crumbs
1 tablespoon vegetable oil
2 tablespoons margarine
⅓ cup Marsala wine

Cut chicken breasts into pieces 1½ to 2-inches wide. Combine next 6 ingredients in a paper bag. Coat chicken with mixture a few pieces at a time by shaking the bag. Place chicken in a baking dish and press any remaining seasonings into chicken. Sprinkle chicken with oil and melted margarine. Bake, uncovered, at 350 degrees for 30 minutes. Pour wine over chicken and cover with foil. Reduce heat to 325 degrees; bake 15 additional minutes. Remove foil, raise heat to 350 degrees and bake 10 minutes.

This is a lowfat recipe that can be prepared ahead, frozen and reheated in the microwave.

Chicken Phyllo

Serves 6 to 8

  3 **chicken breasts, skinned, boned and cut into pieces**
      salt and freshly ground pepper
  4 **tablespoons butter**
½ **cup Dijon mustard**
  2 **cups half and half**
10 **sheets phyllo pastry**
½ **cup unsalted butter, melted**
¼ **cup toasted bread crumbs**

Season chicken pieces with salt and pepper. Melt 4 tablespoons butter and sauté chicken until cooked. Set aside. Pour off butter. Add mustard, scraping any brown bits remaining in pan. Add half and half; stir, bringing to boil. Reduce heat and simmer until reduced to about 1 cup. Add chicken and toss to coat. Remove from heat.

Lay one sheet of phyllo on a buttered jelly roll pan. Brush with melted butter and sprinkle with some of the bread crumbs. Repeat with 8 sheets of pastry. Cover with last sheet of phyllo. Place the chicken on the phyllo about 1 inch from bottom and side edges of the phyllo sheets. Turn up bottom edge and fold in sides. Roll in jelly roll style. Brush melted butter over dough and place seam side down on the pan. Bake at 425 degrees for 20 minutes or until golden. Cut into 2-inch slices and serve immediately. Can be prepared a day in advance, unbaked, and chilled. Bring to room temperature before baking.

159

Chicken with Julienne Peppers

Serves 6

8 tablespoons olive oil, divided
6 chicken breasts
  salt and freshly ground pepper
1 cup finely chopped onions
2 carrots, finely chopped
4 cloves garlic, minced
1 cup chicken broth
½ cup orange juice
1 14½-ounce can Italian tomatoes, chopped
1 tablespoon dried rosemary
1 red pepper, cut into julienne strips
1 green pepper, cut into julienne strips
1 yellow pepper, cut into julienne strips
⅓ cup chopped fresh parsley

Beautiful — as pleasing to the eye as to the palate.

Heat 6 tablespoons olive oil in a large skillet. Sprinkle chicken with salt and pepper and sauté in oil 10 minutes or until golden. Remove chicken from skillet and keep warm in a 300 to 325 degree oven. Add the onions, carrots and garlic to oil remaining in the skillet and cook over low heat, covered, 20 minutes. Uncover pan and add broth, orange juice, tomatoes and rosemary. Season to taste with salt and pepper. Simmer mixture 15 minutes. Return chicken pieces to skillet and simmer an additional 20 minutes or until tender. Baste chicken with liquid several times while cooking. In a separate skillet, heat 2 tablespoons olive oil and sauté red, green and yellow peppers 3 minutes until tender but still firm. Using a slotted spoon, transfer peppers to the chicken mixture and simmer 5 minutes. Sprinkle with parsley and serve immediately.

Plum Ginger Chicken

Serves 8

12 6-ounce boneless chicken breasts
1 16-ounce can plums in syrup
2 teaspoons chopped fresh ginger
½ cup brown sugar
2 teaspoons chili paste
  salt and freshly ground pepper to taste

Compliments of Chef Ny Vongsaly of Patty Long Café — one of our favorite gathering spots.

Flatten chicken breasts to ¼-inch thickness. In a food processor, blend the plums in syrup and add remaining ingredients. Stir to mix. In a saucepan, simmer plum mixture over low heat 20 to 30 minutes. Grill chicken over a medium hot fire. Add grilled chicken to plum mixture and simmer until thoroughly heated. Can be served chilled.

Mixed Grill of Chicken and Salsiccia

Serves 4

8 pieces chicken, skinned
2-3 large yellow onions
2 green peppers
1 red pepper
1 yellow pepper
5 cloves garlic
2-3 tablespoons olive oil
6 salsiccia
2 pounds lean pork, cut into cubes (optional)
dried oregano to taste
freshly ground pepper to taste
½-1 cup dry or medium dry Italian red wine

Place chicken in a baking dish and bake at 325 degrees for 30 minutes. While chicken is cooking, coarsely chop onions and peppers. Chop garlic. Generously cover bottom of a large skillet with olive oil. Sauté onions until golden. Add peppers and garlic. Reduce heat to low and sauté until vegetables are tender. Slice salsiccia diagonally into 5 to 6 pieces per sausage. Stir into skillet and cook until sausage is browned. Add pork if desired. Add chicken and stir. Sprinkle with oregano and pepper to taste. Stir. Raise heat to medium high and add wine. Stir and correct seasonings. Cook 10 additional minutes over medium high heat, stirring frequently.

As a timesaver, purchase skinless, boneless chicken breasts and cut into bite size pieces. Add chicken when adding the salsiccia.

161

Summer Marinated Grilled Cornish Hens

Serves 5 to 6

Cornish Hens:

　2　**teaspoons dried oregano**
　2　**teaspoons dried rosemary**
　2　**teaspoons dried thyme**
　4　**cloves garlic**
　1　**teaspoon salt**
　½　**cup fresh lemon juice**
　¼　**cup olive oil**
　3　**Cornish hens**

Curry Sauce:

　¾　**cup mayonnaise**
　1½　**tablespoons chutney**
　1　**tablespoon minced onion**
　1　**teaspoon fresh lemon juice**
　¼　**teaspoon curry powder**

Cornish Hens:
Combine oregano, rosemary, thyme, garlic, salt, lemon juice and oil. Place in a shallow glass dish. Split hens in half, remove back bone; wash and pat dry. Place hens in marinade and cover. *Marinate in refrigerator overnight,* turning a few times. Grill hens 5 to 6 inches above coals approximately 15 to 20 minutes per side, basting with marinade. Grill until juices of the thigh run clear when pricked. Serve immediately with Curry Sauce. Can also be grilled 2 to 3 hours in advance and served at room temperature. Marinade can be made a day in advance.

Curry Sauce:
Combine all ingredients and mix well. Chill for 3 to 4 hours.

The city's Italian section, now known as "The Hill" was originally settled by German and Irish immigrants. Later called La Montagna by its Italian residents, it is now a thriving Italian-American community. This elevated area in south Saint Louis was home to two celebrated sports heroes, Joe Garagiola and Yogi Berra.

Oriental Chicken and Pasta

Serves 6

10 ounces fresh Chinese egg noodles or angel hair pasta

5 tablespoons peanut oil, divided

1 pound chicken breasts, boned, skinned and cut into ¼-inch strips

½ teaspoon garlic salt or garlic powder

½ teaspoon minced fresh ginger

½ small head cabbage, shredded

1 bunch green onions, sliced

1 medium onion, thinly sliced

1 medium carrot, peeled and cut into julienne strips

¼ cup oyster sauce

2 tablespoons lite soy sauce

1 teaspoon mushroom soy sauce dried red pepper flakes

An Oriental pasta that is beyond compare!

Cook noodles in boiling water until al dente. Drain well. In a wok or heavy skillet, heat 2 tablespoons oil over high heat. Add noodles and stir-fry 3 minutes. Remove noodles. Add 3 tablespoons oil to wok and heat until very hot. Add chicken, garlic and ginger; stir-fry until chicken is opaque. Add next 7 ingredients and stir-fry at least 2 minutes. Add noodles; heat and blend. Serve immediately. Pass red pepper flakes at the table.

Chinese egg noodles, oyster sauce and mushroom soy sauce are available at Oriental markets.

Chinese Chicken and Ribs

Serves 10 to 12

2 cups lite soy sauce

3 cups dry sherry, divided

4 cloves garlic, minced

4 teaspoons fresh minced ginger

5 pounds chicken pieces, skinned if desired

5 pounds baby back ribs, membrane removed

1 cup Hoisin sauce

1 cup catsup

½ cup packed dark brown sugar

2 cloves garlic, minced

Mix soy sauce, 2 cups sherry, garlic and ginger to make a marinade. Marinate chicken and ribs in separate plastic bags. *Chill overnight,* turning occasionally. Discard marinade. Combine 1 cup sherry and remaining ingredients in a large glass jar to make sauce. Shake to blend. Grill chicken and ribs over medium hot coals, basting with the sauce. Heat remaining sauce to serve with entrée. Sauce will keep several weeks in the refrigerator.

Hontakka
Chicken

Serves 4

Hontakka Chicken:

- **2 tablespoons cornstarch**
- **4 tablespoons soy sauce**
- **4 tablespoons sweet rice wine**
- **2 tablespoons rice vinegar**
- **4 chicken breast halves, skinned, boned and cut into bite size pieces**
- **2 teaspoons Hot Pepper Oil**
- **2 tablespoons peanut oil, divided**
- **3 cloves garlic, minced**
- **3 scallions, minced**
- **1 bunch broccoli, cut into florets, plus several stems thinly sliced**
- **3 cups cooked rice**
  sesame seeds

Hot Pepper Oil:

- **1 cup peanut oil**
- **1 cup whole Chinese red chili peppers (Hontakka)**

You can open your own Chinese restaurant with this one.

Hontakka Chicken:
Combine cornstarch, soy sauce, rice wine and vinegar in a bowl. Add chicken and marinate 20 minutes, stirring occasionally. When ready to serve, heat Hot Pepper Oil and 1 teaspoon peanut oil in a wok until smoking. Quickly stir-fry garlic and scallions. Add broccoli and stir-fry 5 minutes, stirring constantly. Remove from wok. Remove chicken from marinade. Stir-fry chicken in remaining peanut oil until well cooked. Return broccoli to wok. Heat and serve over rice. Garnish with sesame seeds.

Hot Pepper Oil:
Heat oil in wok until smoking. Add peppers, cover quickly and carry wok outside. Let set outside until cooled. Strain; store in a covered glass jar in the refrigerator. Keeps very well.

This oil has more flavor and zip than prepared chili oil. It is well worth keeping on hand.

Roast Turkey Breast with Apple Onion Stuffing

Serves 8

Turkey:

1 **5-pound bone-in turkey breast, thawed**

½ **lemon**

½ **teaspoon salt**

¼ **teaspoon freshly ground pepper**
  Apple Onion Stuffing

4 **tablespoons butter or margarine, melted**

Apple Onion Stuffing:

5 **tablespoons butter or margarine, divided**

1 **cup diced onions**

2 **cups unseasoned cube stuffing mix**

2 **Golden Delicious apples, cored and chopped (2-2½ cups)**

½ **cup plus 1 tablespoon apple cider**

¼ **cup Zante currants**

2 **tablespoons lemon juice**

½ **teaspoon salt**

¼ **teaspoon ground nutmeg**

¼ **teaspoon ground allspice**

Turkey:
Rinse turkey and pat dry with paper towels. Rub skin and cavity with lemon and sprinkle with salt and pepper. Turn turkey skin side down. Loosely fill cavity with stuffing. Place sheet of foil firmly over stuffing. Turn turkey over to pinch ends of foil together. Place turkey skin side up in a shallow roasting pan and brush with melted butter. Roast turkey at 325 degrees for 2 to 2½ hours. Baste with butter every half hour until thermometer inserted into thickest part registers 170 to 175 degrees. Let stand 20 minutes at room temperature before carving.

Apple Onion Stuffing:
In a heavy skillet, melt 2 tablespoons butter over medium high heat. Add onions and cook 3 to 4 minutes, stirring once or twice until translucent. Place stuffing mixture in a medium bowl; add onions.

Melt remaining 3 tablespoons butter in skillet. Reduce heat; add apples and 1 tablespoon cider. Cover and cook 5 to 7 minutes, stirring occasionally until apples are tender. Add to stuffing mixture. Bring currants and 1 cup cider to boil. Cover and simmer 3 to 5 minutes over low heat until plump. Add currants and liquid to stuffing mixture. Add remaining ingredients and toss to combine.

Yields 3 cups stuffing. Double recipe for extra servings. Place half in turkey as directed and half in a baking dish. Bake, covered, at 325 degrees for 30 minutes.

Chicken in Pastry with Mushroom Sauce

Serves 4

Chicken:

- **3 tablespoons butter, melted**
- **3 ounces cream cheese, softened**
- **2 tablespoons milk**
- **1-2 tablespoons chopped chives or onions**
- **1 teaspoon chopped pimiento**
- **¼ teaspoon salt**
- **¼ teaspoon freshly ground pepper**
- **2 cups cooked and cubed chicken**
- **1 package crescent rolls**
- **¼ cup stuffing mix**

Mushroom Sauce:

- **4 tablespoons butter, divided**
- **½ pound mushrooms, sliced**
- **3 tablespoons dry sherry**
- **2 tablespoons flour**
- **1 cup milk**

Chicken:
Combine the first 7 ingredients. Add chicken and mix well. Mixture can be chilled overnight. Form 4 rectangles from crescent roll dough. Fill each rectangle with ½ cup of the chicken mixture. Fold in half and press edges firmly together. Brush tops with water and sprinkle with stuffing mix. Bake at 350 degrees for 20 to 25 minutes or until golden brown. Serve immediately with Mushroom Sauce.

Mushroom Sauce:
In a small skillet, melt 2 tablespoons butter. Add mushrooms and sherry. Sauté until tender and set aside. In a saucepan, melt 2 tablespoons butter over low heat. Add flour and cook until bubbly. Slowly add milk. Simmer, stirring constantly until thickened and smooth. Add mushrooms as sauce starts to boil.

Golden Chicken Nuggets

40 nuggets

- **4 whole chicken breasts, boned and skinned**
- **½ cup unseasoned fine dry bread crumbs**
- **½ cup freshly grated Parmesan cheese**
- **2 teaspoons Crazy Jane salt**
- **1 teaspoon dried thyme**
- **1 teaspoon dried basil**
- **½ cup butter or margarine, melted**

Cut each breast into 1 to 1½-inch nuggets. Combine next 5 ingredients in a reclosable storage bag. Dip nuggets in butter, then shake in crumb mixture. Place in single layer on baking sheets. Freeze. When frozen, transfer to a frozen food storage bag.

When ready to serve, bake desired number of nuggets at 400 degrees for 10 minutes. It is not necessary to defrost nuggets.

Without the fat of commercial nuggets, these will delight your children as snacks and please your guests as an appetizer. But, of course, feel free to make these a meal!

Saint Louis was at one time known as the "Mound City" because of the many prehistoric Indian mounds that were found here. These man-made earthen mounds were built by a group called the Mississippians, primarily for ceremonial activities for the living. Their culture was centered near Cahokia, Illinois, where a State Historical Site contains more than 68 mounds, including the largest prehistoric earthen construction in the new world. It is estimated that nearly 50 million cubic feet of earth was moved by hand, in baskets, to create the many mounds.

PASTA
&
RICE

Fettuccine with Fresh Tomatoes and Brie

Serves 4 to 6

- 2 tablespoons olive oil
- 4 large tomatoes, peeled seeded and chopped
- 1 clove garlic, crushed
- 1 bunch fresh basil, trimmed salt and freshly ground pepper to taste
- 6 ounces Brie cheese, trimmed and cubed
- 1 pound fettuccine

A perfect merger.

Heat olive oil and quickly sauté tomatoes, garlic, basil, salt and pepper. Add Brie and cook until mixture is creamy, stirring constantly. Cook fettuccine according to package directions and drain. Pour sauce over fettuccine and toss. Serve immediately. Egg or spinach fettuccine can be used. Fresh is best.

The word basil is derived from the Greek word for king, basileias. It was once used to make royal perfumes and medicines. Today, basil is one of the most popular herbs used with over 50 varieties available.

Creole Shrimp Fettuccine

Serves 16 to 20

- 3 pounds fettuccine
- 1 cup butter
- 2 cloves garlic, minced
- 2 cups milk
- 4 cups cream
- 2 pounds provel rope cheese
- 2-3 tablespoons creole seasoning
- 4 pounds medium shrimp, steamed, peeled and deveined

A crowd pleaser that can easily be reduced to serve as few as two.

Using a large pot, bring water to a boil and cook pasta according to package directions.

Meanwhile, melt butter in a large saucepan. Add garlic and sauté 1 minute. Add milk and cream. Cook over medium heat, stirring constantly, until hot. Do not boil. Add cheese and stir until melted. Sprinkle with 2 tablespoons creole seasoning. Taste and correct seasoning if desired. Stir in shrimp. Serve warm over fettuccine.

Szechwan Lomein with Szechwan Mayonnaise

Serves 4 to 6

Szechwan Lomein:

1	pound Lomein noodles
1	cup Szechwan Mayonnaise
2	bunches scallions, sliced diagonally
12	ounces pickled baby corn
1	large red pepper, cut into julienne strips
	rice vinegar
	soy sauce
12	ounces frozen snow peas, thawed

Szechwan Mayonnaise:

1	egg yolk
1	tablespoon soy sauce
1	tablespoon rice vinegar
1	teaspoon chile oil
1	tablespoon sesame seeds
1	cup sesame oil

David and Nancy Schwartz, owners of Blayney Catering, are known for their innovative recipes and dramatic presentations.

Szechwan Lomein:
Cook noodles until al dente, according to package directions. Rinse completely under cold water. Toss noodles with Szechwan Mayonnaise. Add vegetables, except snow peas. Taste. Correct seasonings by adding rice vinegar or soy sauce. Add snow peas immediately before serving so they will retain their beautiful green color. Cellophane noodles can be substituted for Lomein noodles, if Lomein are not available.

Szechwan Mayonnaise:
In a food processor, blend first 5 ingredients. While machine is still running, pour sesame oil into top in a steady stream until mixture is emulsified (thickened). Check for seasonings.

Missouri's no-nonsense practicality has earned it the nickname of the "Show Me State." The expression was first used by William Vandiver a little-known congressman from the state. While delivering an address to Congress in 1889, he said, "Gentlemen, frothy elegance neither convinces nor satisfies me. I am from Missouri, you have got to show me."

Crab Vermicelli

Serves 12

- 6 **tablespoons olive oil, divided**
- 6 **tablespoons butter or margarine**
- 3-4 **cloves garlic, minced**
- ½ **cup finely chopped fresh parsley**
- 3 **teaspoons salt, divided**
- ¼ **teaspoon cayenne pepper**
- 1½ **cups milk**
- 1½ **cups heavy cream**
- 2 **cups freshly grated Parmesan cheese**
- 1 **pound fresh crab meat**
- 1½ **pounds vermicelli**

In a saucepan, heat oil and butter. Add garlic and sauté 1 to 2 minutes. Add parsley, salt and cayenne pepper. Mix well. Add milk and cream. Heat thoroughly and add cheese. Mix well. Add partially shredded crab. Cook vermicelli with 1 tablespoon olive oil and 1 tablespoon salt. Drain well. Toss with sauce and serve immediately.

Spicy Chicken Vermicelli

Serves 4 to 6

- 4 **tablespoons butter or margarine**
- 1 **yellow onion, chopped**
- 4 **whole chicken breasts, skinned, boned and cut into bite size pieces**
- 2 **14½-ounce cans Mexican stewed tomatoes**
- ½ **teaspoon baking soda**
- 1 **pound mild Mexican Velveeta cheese, cubed**
- 8 **ounces vermicelli, cooked**

Melt butter in a skillet; add onion and sauté until tender. Add chicken and sauté 5 to 8 minutes. Add tomatoes and bring to a boil. Sprinkle baking soda over tomatoes and stir to blend. Add Velveeta cheese, stirring until melted. Combine mixture with vermicelli and pour into a 2-quart baking dish. Bake, uncovered, at 350 degrees for 15 to 20 minutes. Can be frozen or made in advance. Reheats well in the microwave.

Baking soda neutralizes the natural acidity of the tomatoes.

Pasta with Parsley and Walnuts

Serves 4 to 6

- 2 **cups fresh parsley, stems removed**
- 1 **teaspoon dried basil**
- 1 **teaspoon dried oregano**
- 1 **teaspoon dried marjoram**
- 1 **teaspoon salt**
- ½ **teaspoon freshly ground pepper**
- ½ **teaspoon garlic powder**
- ½ **cup olive oil**
- 1 **pound spaghetti**
- 2 **tablespoons butter**
- ½ **cup chopped walnuts**
- ½ **cup freshly grated Parmesan cheese**

Place parsley, herbs, seasonings and oil in a blender or food processor. Blend until well mixed. Cook spaghetti according to package directions; drain well. Transfer to a large serving bowl. Add butter and nuts and toss. Add parsley sauce and toss. Top with Parmesan cheese.

Tortellini Alla Panna

Serves 8

- 1 **teaspoon salt**
- 2 **pounds fresh tortellini**
- 4 **tablespoons butter**
- 8 **ounces prosciutto, cut into julienne strips**
- 8 **ounces sliced fresh mushrooms**
- 2 **ounces dry sherry**
- 4 **ounces cream**
- ¼ **teaspoon freshly ground pepper**
- 4 **ounces freshly grated Parmesan cheese**

Sample fare from Giovanni Gabriele, owner of a Saint Louis favorite, Giovanni's.

Bring 2 quarts of water to a boil in a large saucepan. Add salt and tortellini. Bring to a second boil and cook pasta 7 to 8 minutes or until tender. Drain and set aside. In a skillet, melt butter and sauté prosciutto 2 minutes until browned. Add mushrooms and sauté 1 minute. Add tortellini and sherry. Cook over low heat 2 minutes. Add cream and pepper. Cook 2 minutes or until cream thickens slightly. Stir gently to mix thoroughly. Add cheese and toss gently. Serve on warm plates with additional Parmesan cheese.

Florentine Lasagne Rolls with Shrimp Sauce

Serves 8

Lasagne Rolls:

- 8 lasagne noodles
- 2 10-ounce packages frozen chopped spinach, cooked and well drained
- 2 eggs, lightly beaten
- ½ cup freshly grated Parmesan cheese
- 2 cloves garlic, minced
- ¼ teaspoon ground nutmeg
- ½ teaspoon salt
- ¼ teaspoon freshly ground pepper
- 1 cup ricotta cheese
- 4 teaspoons olive oil

Shrimp Sauce:

- 2 tablespoons butter
- 1 teaspoon minced shallots
- ½ cup half and half
- 1 10¾-ounce can cream of shrimp soup
- ½ cup sour cream
- 3 tablespoons light dry sherry
- 32 shrimp, steamed, peeled and deveined
  freshly grated Parmesan cheese

Lasagne Rolls:
Cook noodles according to package directions. Meanwhile, lightly coat a 9 x 13-inch baking dish with olive oil. Combine spinach, eggs, Parmesan cheese, garlic, nutmeg, salt, pepper and ricotta. Drain noodles, pat dry with paper towel and place on waxed paper. Brush each noodle with ½ teaspoon olive oil. Spread 4 to 5 tablespoons spinach mixture over noodle, carefully roll and place seam side down in baking dish. Bake, covered, at 350 degrees for 35 minutes.

Shrimp Sauce:
Melt butter and sauté shallots until limp. Pour in half and half and cook until bubbly. Add remaining ingredients and stir until hot. Do not boil. Spoon sauce over lasagne rolls, dividing shrimp evenly. Sprinkle with Parmesan cheese.

Spinach Lasagne

Serves 8 to 10

 4 cloves garlic, minced
 1 medium onion, minced
 3 tablespoons olive oil
 1 teaspoon dried oregano
 ½ teaspoon dried basil
 2 28-ounce cans tomatoes, undrained and crushed
 3 10-ounce packages frozen spinach, thawed and drained
 2 15-ounce cartons ricotta cheese
 ½ pound lasagne noodles
 1 pound fresh mushrooms, thinly sliced
 2 tablespoons butter
16 ounces mozzarella cheese, shredded
   salt and freshly ground pepper to taste
 ½ cup freshly grated Parmesan cheese

Lightly brown garlic and onion in olive oil. Add oregano and basil. Stir to combine flavors. Place crushed tomatoes and onion garlic mixture in a saucepan. Simmer, covered, stirring occasionally, 2 to 3 hours or until sauce has thickened and some of the liquid has evaporated.

Combine spinach and ricotta cheese in a bowl. Set aside. Cook the lasagne noodles according to package directions. Drain and run under cold water. Drain again. Sauté mushrooms in butter for several minutes. Set aside.

Spread one fourth of tomato sauce evenly in bottom of a 10 x 12 x 2-inch baking dish. Layer half of the noodles over the sauce; add another layer of sauce. Layer half of the spinach mixture and half of the mushrooms. Top with half of the mozzarella cheese and sprinkle with salt and pepper. Repeat layers with remaining ingredients. Sprinkle with Parmesan cheese. Bake at 325 degrees for 45 minutes. Let stand 10 minutes before serving.

Japanese Pasta

Serves 6

 ½ pound linguini
 1 bunch green onions, thinly sliced
 1 pound shrimp, steamed and peeled (optional)
 ¼ cup sesame oil, divided
 ¼ cup peanut oil, divided
 1 pound snow peas
 ½ pound button mushrooms
 2 tablespoons grated fresh ginger
 2 cloves garlic, minced
 ⅓ cup soy sauce
 ¼ cup sesame seeds, toasted

Cook linguini in boiling salted water until al dente. Drain and rinse under cold water. Transfer noodles to a large bowl. Add onions and shrimp if desired. Toss with ⅛ teaspoon of the sesame oil and ⅛ teaspoon of the peanut oil. Briefly steam snow peas; remove when still very crisp. Add snow peas to linguini. Sauté mushrooms, ginger and garlic in remaining sesame and peanut oils. Add to linguini. Add soy sauce and toasted sesame seeds. Toss to mix well. Cover and chill at least 2 hours.

Pasta with Peppery Beef and Vegetables

Serves 2

4 ounces spaghetti

1 tablespoon cornstarch

¼ cup soy sauce

⅛ teaspoon ground red pepper (optional)

½ teaspoon freshly ground black pepper

½ cup cold water

1 clove garlic, minced

½ cup chopped green pepper

1 cup snow peas

1 cup mushrooms

1 tablespoon vegetable oil

¾ pound flank steak, cut against the grain into bite size pieces

Cook spaghetti according to package directions. Drain and keep warm. Combine cornstarch, soy sauce, red pepper, black pepper and cold water. Set aside. Spray wok or skillet with nonstick vegetable spray. Stir-fry garlic over medium high heat 30 seconds. Add green pepper, snow peas and mushrooms. Stir-fry 1 to 2 minutes. Remove vegetables and set aside. Add oil and stir-fry beef 3 to 4 minutes. Add cornstarch mixture, stirring constantly until thick and bubbly. Return vegetables to mixture and stir 1 minute. Toss with spaghetti.

Oriental soy sauces are made by fermenting soy beans, roasted wheat, salt, yeast or malt and sugar. They are often fermented 12 to 18 months and range in color from light to very dark.

Crab and Fresh Asparagus Linguini with Lemon Cream

Serves 4 to 6

9 ounces fresh linguini

4 tablespoons butter

2 tablespoons finely grated fresh lemon peel

2 tablespoons dry vermouth

1⅔ cup whipping cream
   several dashes of cayenne pepper

4 tablespoons butter, softened

½ cup freshly grated Parmesan cheese
   salt and freshly ground pepper to taste

¾-1 cup crab meat, flaked

6 fresh asparagus spears, trimmed, peeled, cut into 1-inch pieces and blanched 3-5 minutes

Cook linguini according to package directions. Drain. Meanwhile, in a 10-inch skillet melt 4 tablespoons of butter over medium heat. Add grated lemon peel and cook 2 to 3 minutes. Add dry vermouth and cook another 2 to 3 minutes. Mixture will be slightly thickened. Add cream and cayenne and cook, stirring, about 2 minutes.

Add cooked pasta to skillet. Remove from heat and add 4 tablespoons softened butter (cut into pieces), Parmesan cheese, salt and pepper to taste, crab and fresh asparagus. Heat briefly until all ingredients are thoroughly heated. Garnish as desired and serve immediately.

This dish lends itself to several different garnishes. Try sprinkling 1 to 2 tablespoons of fresh chives, snipped, over the pasta with a blanched asparagus tip placed in the center. Or, cross chive stems and top with a brilliant red crab claw for nautical emphasis.

Linguini with Ham

Serves 4 to 6

½ **pound ham, thinly sliced**
2 **tablespoons olive oil**
½ **pound fresh mushrooms, thinly sliced**
1 **tablespoon finely minced garlic**
2 **ripe tomatoes, peeled, seeded and diced**
1½ **cups frozen peas, thawed and drained**
  salt and coarsely ground pepper to taste
½ **cup heavy cream**
  fresh basil to taste
¾ **pound linguini**
1 **egg, well beaten**
  freshly grated Parmesan cheese

Slice ham into julienne strips. Set aside. In a skillet, heat olive oil and sauté mushrooms 2 minutes. Add garlic, tomatoes and ham. Stir to blend. Cook over high heat 2 minutes. Add peas, salt and pepper. Add cream and basil and bring mixture to a boil. Reduce heat. Simmer to blend flavors. Keep warm.

Cook linguini until al dente. Drain. Place egg in a large, warm mixing bowl. Add linguini and toss. Add sauce and toss to combine. Serve immediately.

Orzo with Feta

Serves 6

2 **tablespoons butter**
2 **scallions, sliced**
1½ **cups orzo or rosamarina**
2 **ounces feta cheese, crumbled**
1 **tablespoon chopped fresh parsley**
  salt and freshly ground pepper

Cook orzo according to package directions. In a skillet, melt butter and sauté scallions until tender. Stir in orzo, feta cheese and parsley. Season with salt and pepper and serve immediately.

Capellini Primavera

Serves 4

1 tablespoon olive oil

½ medium onion, coarsely chopped

3 large tomatoes (1½ pounds) peeled, seeded and chopped

1 cup chicken broth

½ cup whipping cream

1 pound broccoli florets, coarsely chopped

1 large carrot, cut into julienne strips

1 pound capellini pasta

2 medium zucchini, peeled and cut into julienne strips

1½ cups freshly grated Parmesan cheese

4 tablespoons unsalted butter, softened

salt and freshly ground pepper to taste

Bring a large pot of salted water to a boil. Meanwhile, in a large skillet, heat olive oil. Add onion and sauté 5 minutes or until lightly colored. Add tomatoes and sauté 1 to 2 minutes while stirring. Stir in broth and cream. Remove sauce from heat and keep warm.

Add broccoli to boiling water. When water returns to boil, stir in carrot strips and capellini. When water again returns to boil, cook 3 minutes. Add zucchini and cook 2 to 3 additional minutes until pasta is al dente. Drain well. Transfer pasta mixture to a large serving bowl. Add Parmesan cheese and butter and toss to blend. Add sauce and toss gently. Season with salt and pepper. Can be made 1 hour in advance and kept warm.

As a first course, this will serve 8 to 10.

Seasoned Rice with Tomatoes

Serves 8

- **4 tablespoons butter or margarine**
- **½ cup minced onion**
- **1 green pepper, diced**
- **1 clove garlic, finely minced**
- **1 15-ounce can tomatoes**
- **¼ teaspoon cayenne pepper**
- **¼ teaspoon dried thyme**
- **1 tablespoon Worcestershire sauce**
- **3 cups cooked rice**
- **2 tablespoons minced fresh parsley**
- **½ cup shredded Cheddar cheese**

In a skillet, melt butter and sauté onion and green pepper until tender. Add garlic, tomatoes, cayenne pepper, thyme and Worcestershire sauce. Simmer gently 5 minutes to blend flavors. Add rice and parsley; mix well. Pour into a greased or sprayed 1½-quart baking dish. Sprinkle with cheese. Bake at 350 degrees for 15 minutes or until cheese has melted and rice is hot.

Rice with Tarragon and Hazelnuts

Serves 6

- **1 6-ounce package long grain and wild rice chicken broth**
- **1 tablespoon fresh lemon juice**
- **½ teaspoon dried tarragon**
- **¼ cup finely chopped mushrooms**
- **4 tablespoons butter**
- **¼ cup dry sherry**
- **2 tablespoons chopped fresh parsley**
- **½ cup toasted, coarsely chopped hazelnuts**

Prepare rice according to package directions, substituting chicken broth for water, omitting the butter and adding lemon juice and tarragon. Stir and bring to a boil. Simmer until liquid is absorbed. Meanwhile, sauté mushrooms in butter. When mushrooms are dark and tender add sherry and parsley. Toss into cooked rice. Top with toasted hazelnuts. Can be made in advance. Doubles easily.

Ask for hazelnuts or filberts; they are one and the same.

Fruit and Vegetable Rice

Serves 6

- ¼ cup raisins
- ½ cup water
- 2 cups chicken broth
- 1 cup uncooked long grain rice
- 1 tablespoon butter or margarine
- ½ teaspoon salt
- ½ teaspoon poultry seasoning
- ⅛ teaspoon freshly ground pepper
- 1 carrot, grated
- 1 apple, chopped
- 1 rib celery, thinly sliced
- ¼ cup slivered almonds, toasted
  apple wedges

Combine raisins and water in a small saucepan. Cover and cook over medium heat 5 minutes until raisins are soft. Drain the raisins and set aside. Combine chicken broth, rice, butter, salt, poultry seasoning and pepper in a saucepan. Cover and bring to a boil. Reduce heat and simmer 15 minutes. Remove from heat and stir in carrot, apple, celery, almonds and raisins. Cover and let stand 5 minutes. Serve with apple wedges as garnish.

Fried Rice

Serves 6

- 1 cup short grain rice, cooked and chilled 6 to 8 hours
- 3 teaspoons peanut oil, divided
- 8 slices bacon, cooked and crumbled
- 1 cup sliced mushrooms
- 4 scallions, sliced
- 1 cup frozen peas, thawed
- 6 water chestnuts, chopped
- 2 eggs, slightly beaten
  soy sauce to taste
- 1 cup fresh bean sprouts, rinsed and drained

Fluff chilled rice with a fork and set aside. Bring 2 teaspoons of the peanut oil to smoking in a wok over highest heat. Add crumbled bacon and mushrooms and stir-fry 1 minute. Add scallions and peas and cook 1 minute. Add rice and stir-fry until grains are separated.

Meanwhile, heat 1 teaspoon peanut oil in a small skillet. Pour eggs in skillet and cook as an omelet. Turn onto a plate and cut into strips. Set aside. Add soy sauce to wok, stirring, and top with water chestnuts, sprouts and egg strips.

California Rice

Serves 8

1 cup chopped onions
4 tablespoons butter or margarine
4 cups cooked rice
2 cups sour cream
1 cup cream style cottage cheese
1 large bay leaf, crumbled
½ teaspoon salt
⅛ teaspoon freshly ground pepper
1 4-ounce can diced green chiles, drained
2 cups shredded sharp Cheddar cheese
chopped fresh parsley

Sauté onions in butter in a large skillet until golden. Remove from heat. Stir in hot rice, sour cream, cottage cheese, bay leaf, salt and pepper. Toss lightly. Layer half the rice mixture in bottom of a lightly greased 2-quart baking dish. Sprinkle with half of the green chiles and then with half of the cheese. Repeat. Bake, uncovered, at 375 degrees for 25 minutes until bubbly. Sprinkle with parsley. Can be frozen.

Rice with Ripe Olives

Serves 8

1 cup chicken broth
1 cup water
1 cup rice
1 cup sliced ripe olives
1 cup yogurt or sour cream
1 teaspoon dried dill weed
3 tablespoons slivered almonds, toasted

Bring chicken broth and water to a boil. Add rice, cover and simmer 15 minutes. Fluff rice with a fork and add olives, yogurt and dill. Mix well and pour into a serving dish. Sprinkle with almonds and serve.

Green Silk Rice

Serves 10

3 cups cooked rice
1 cup chopped fresh parsley
½ cup shredded
  Cheddar cheese
⅓ cup chopped onion
¼ cup chopped green pepper
1 clove garlic, minced
1 14½-ounce can evaporated
  milk
2 eggs, beaten
½ cup vegetable oil
1 tablespoon salt
½ teaspoon seasoned salt
½ teaspoon freshly ground
  pepper
  juice and grated peel of
  1 lemon
  paprika

Combine rice, parsley, cheese, onion, green pepper and garlic in a greased 2-quart baking dish. Combine remaining ingredients and add to rice mixture. Sprinkle with paprika. Bake at 350 degrees for 45 minutes.

Wild Rice with Spinach and Pecans

Serves 8

8 ounces mushrooms, sliced
1 onion, chopped
2 tablespoons butter
1 10-ounce package frozen
  chopped spinach, thawed
  and well drained
1 cup chopped pecans
1 cup wild rice
3 cups chicken broth
  salt and freshly ground
  pepper to taste

Sauté mushrooms and onion in butter 5 minutes. Add spinach and sauté several minutes. Add pecans and cook 2 minutes. Stir in rice, broth and seasonings. Place in a buttered 2-quart baking dish and bake at 350 degrees for 1 hour. Can be assembled in advance and baked just before serving.

VEGETABLES

Grilled Seasoned Vegetables

Serves 6

1 cup olive oil
1 tablespoon fresh basil
1 tablespoon granulated garlic or 1½ teaspoons garlic salt
1 tablespoon fresh dill weed
1 onion, quartered
3 yellow summer squash
3 medium zucchini
6 ripe, firm plum tomatoes

Combine the first 5 ingredients in a small bowl. *Let stand overnight.* Slice yellow squash and zucchini lengthwise into thirds. Brush with seasoned oil mixture. Grill over a medium hot fire 8 to 10 minutes. Brush tomatoes with seasoned oil mixture and add to grill. Continue grilling 5 additional minutes until vegetables are just tender.

Bouquet de Légumes

Serves 8

16 baby carrots, peeled
2 tablespoons butter, divided
1 tablespoon honey
8 baby pattypan squash
16 asparagus tips
8 baby zucchini, trimmed and sliced very thin diagonally
2 tablespoons sesame oil

Bring a large pot of water to boil. Separately blanch each group of vegetables until crisp tender. Drain. In a small saucepan, sauté carrots in 1 tablespoon butter over low heat 30 seconds. Toss with honey. In a second saucepan, sauté squash in 1 tablespoon butter over low heat 30 seconds. In a third saucepan, sauté asparagus tips and zucchini in sesame oil 30 seconds. Arrange vegetables on dinner plates in an attractive manner.

Baby vegetables are becoming widely available throughout the country. If you cannot find them locally, simply substitute the smallest best quality vegetables you can find.

Chilled Asparagus

Serves 6

2 pounds fresh asparagus
½ cup white wine vinegar
½ cup water
½ cup vegetable oil
1 teaspoon brown mustard
2 teaspoons Worcestershire sauce
salt and freshly ground pepper to taste
2 tablespoons chopped pimientos
2 tablespoons capers (optional)

Snap off tough ends of asparagus. Steam 5 minutes until crisp tender. Run asparagus under cold water to retain color. Drain and place in a 9 x 13-inch dish. Combine remaining ingredients except pimientos and capers. Pour mixture over asparagus and sprinkle with pimientos and capers. Cover and *chill overnight.*

Asparagus with Toasted Pine Nuts

Serves 4

1 pound fresh asparagus
3 tablespoons pine nuts
¼ cup olive oil
1 tablespoon fresh lemon juice
1 clove garlic, crushed
½ teaspoon dried oregano, crushed
½ teaspoon dried basil, crushed
½ teaspoon salt
freshly ground pepper

Rinse asparagus well under cold running water and snap off tough ends. Steam, covered, 5 minutes until crisp tender.

Meanwhile, toast pine nuts in a dry small heavy skillet over medium heat 3 minutes until golden brown, tossing frequently. Set aside. Whisk remaining ingredients for vinaigrette in a bowl or shake in a tightly closed jar until blended. Heat in a noncorrosive saucepan over medium heat 3 minutes or until hot.

Toss asparagus with vinaigrette and place on a serving dish. Sprinkle with pine nuts. Let stand at room temperature until serving time. Can be made early in the day and basted occasionally.

Remember to double the amount of herbs in a recipe if you are using fresh as a substitute for dried.

Green Beans with Chardonnay Sauce

Serves 8

¼ teaspoon curry powder
1 cup mayonnaise
1 teaspoon fresh lemon juice
¼ cup Chardonnay
2½ pounds fresh green beans

In a saucepan, stir curry into mayonnaise. Stir in lemon juice and Chardonnay. Heat, stirring constantly; do not boil. Steam green beans until crisp tender. Pour sauce over green beans and serve immediately.

Chardonnay sauce transforms virtually any vegetable into company fare.

Herbed Green Beans

Serves 4 to 6

2 tablespoons chopped fresh parsley
8-10 fresh basil leaves, chopped to yield 2 tablespoons
1 teaspoon dried oregano
5 tablespoons wine vinegar
2-3 tablespoons finely chopped onion
2-3 cloves garlic, peeled and crushed
1 pound fresh green beans
⅓ cup extra virgin olive oil
salt and freshly ground pepper to taste

Place parsley, basil, oregano and vinegar in a bowl large enough to accommodate the green beans. Add onion and garlic. Stir and let steep at least 30 minutes.

Snap off ends of green beans. Rinse in cold water and drop into boiling salted water. Cook 3 to 5 minutes; beans should be very firm. Drain and, while hot, add beans to the bowl and marinate at least 1 hour or up to 6 hours. Stir occasionally.

Before serving, add olive oil and season with salt and pepper. Toss. Serve at room temperature. Can be made a day in advance.

Adding a pinch of baking soda to cooking water will decrease cooking time and give vibrant color to green beans.

Fresh Carrot Puff

Serves 8

½ cup butter, softened
¼ cup sugar
3 eggs
1 cup cream or milk
1 tablespoon flour
1 teaspoon salt
¼ teaspoon ground cinnamon
2 tablespoons minced onion
2 cups cooked and puréed carrots
2 teaspoons fresh lemon juice

With an electric mixer, cream butter and sugar. Add eggs and then milk. Blend in flour, salt and cinnamon. Add onion, puréed carrots and lemon juice. Place in a 2-quart baking or soufflé dish. Mixture will only rise slightly and will appear somewhat grainy. Can be refrigerated at this point. Bring to room temperature before baking. Bake at 350 degrees for 50 to 60 minutes.

Spiced Carrots

Serves 4

6-8 fresh carrots
¾ cup sugar
¾ cup vinegar
¾ cup water
2½ inches stick cinnamon
3-5 whole cloves

Peel and slice carrots into 3-inch strips. Cook in boiling water 5 minutes. Drain and cool slightly. Blend the remaining ingredients in a saucepan and simmer over low heat 10 minutes. Pour over carrots. *Chill overnight.* Drain before serving. Doubles or triples easily.

Light and just a bit tart — these carrots are a bright accent.

Brussels Sprouts with Caraway Seeds

Serves 6

1½ **pounds Brussels sprouts**

2 **10½-ounce cans chicken broth**

3 **tablespoons butter or margarine**
  salt and freshly ground pepper to taste

2 **teaspoons whole caraway seeds**
  crumbled bleu cheese (optional)

Wash the Brussels sprouts and trim outer leaves. Cut a small cross in the bottom of each sprout. Pour chicken broth to a depth of 1 inch in a saucepan. Bring to a boil and add sprouts. Return to a boil and reduce to simmer. Cover and cook 10 to 20 minutes until crisp tender. Drain and add butter, salt, pepper and caraway. Crumble bleu cheese on top of each serving if desired.

Purée of Acorn Squash

Serves 8

4 **medium acorn squash**

1 **egg**

2 **egg whites**

¼ **teaspoon ground allspice**

¼ **teaspoon ground cinnamon**

⅛ **teaspoon ground nutmeg**

2 **tablespoons honey**
  ground white pepper to taste

1 **tablespoon melted butter**

Slice squash in half lengthwise scraping off any seeds. Place on a baking sheet and bake at 350 degrees for 1 hour or until soft. Scoop squash meat into a bowl and mash well. In a separate bowl, combine egg and egg whites. Beat lightly. Add the squash mixture, spices, honey, pepper and butter. Pour into a 1½-quart baking dish. Bake at 350 degrees for 30 minutes. Serve immediately.

Eggplant Mélange

Serves 6

  1 large onion, diced
 ⅔ cup olive oil
  2 cloves garlic, minced
  2 small zucchini, diced
  1 medium eggplant, diced
  2 green peppers, diced
  1 cup white wine
    salt and freshly ground
    pepper to taste
    saffron to taste
  2 tomatoes, peeled and cut
    into wedges
    chopped fresh parsley

A spectacular combination of color, texture and flavor.

Sauté onion in a saucepan in olive oil until transparent. Add garlic, zucchini, eggplant and peppers. Sauté lightly; add wine, salt and pepper, saffron and tomatoes. Cook 5 minutes. Place in a serving dish and garnish with chopped parsley.

Eggplant Pepper Relish

Serves 12

  1 large eggplant
  5 red peppers
  5 green peppers
  5 cloves garlic, crushed
  4 tablespoons cider vinegar
  2 tablespoons salt
 ½ cup olive oil

A sophisticated complement for lamb or red meat.

Place eggplant in a pie plate. Bake at 350 degrees for 1 hour or until very soft. Broil or grill peppers until skin is charred. Place peppers in a paper bag and close to steam a few minutes. Cool and peel outside skin. Place peppers in a large mixing bowl. Add garlic, vinegar, salt and oil. Peel eggplant and add to warm pepper mixture. Mash thoroughly. Chill and serve. Keeps well in refrigerator.

Vegetables in Poppy Seed Marinade

Serves 10 to 12

4 stalks fresh broccoli
12 large mushrooms, sliced
1 green pepper, chopped
4 ribs celery, chopped
1 head cauliflower, broken into florets
1/2 cup sugar
1 teaspoon dry mustard
1 teaspoon vinegar
1 cup vegetable oil
1 small onion, grated
2 tablespoons poppy seeds
cherry tomatoes

Remove florets from broccoli and discard stalks. Cut florets into bite size pieces. Combine with mushrooms, green pepper, celery and cauliflower florets. Toss lightly. Combine remaining ingredients, except tomatoes, and pour over vegetables. Toss well. Chill at least 3 hours. Garnish with cherry tomatoes.

Triple Crown Vegetables

Serves 6

2 10-ounce packages frozen mixed vegetables
1 teaspoon salt, divided
1/4 teaspoon garlic salt
6 tablespoons margarine, divided
1/3 cup flour
2 cups milk
1/4 cup freshly grated Parmesan cheese
1/8 teaspoon garlic salt
2 tablespoons dry vermouth
3 tablespoons butter, melted
2 cups herb stuffing mix

A gem for the buffet table!

Cook vegetables until crisp tender. Drain well. Stir 1/2 teaspoon salt, 1/4 teaspoon garlic salt and 2 tablespoons margarine into the vegetables. Set aside.

In a double boiler, melt 4 tablespoons margarine. Add flour to make a roux. Add milk slowly, stirring constantly. Blend well and cook until thickened, stirring frequently. Add Parmesan cheese, 1/8 teaspoon garlic salt, 1/2 teaspoon salt and vermouth.

Combine melted butter and stuffing mix in a bowl and toss gently. Place vegetables in a buttered 2-quart baking dish. Pour cream sauce over vegetables and spread stuffing mixture on top. Bake, uncovered, at 350 degrees for 20 to 30 minutes or until bubbly. Can be made early in the day.

Vegetable Palette on Rice

Serves 4 to 6

   1 cup uncooked rice
 ⅓ cup vegetable oil
 ¼ cup cider vinegar
   2 tablespoons water
   1 .6-ounce package Italian salad dressing mix
   2 teaspoons dried dill weed
   1 cup broccoli florets
 ¼ pound small fresh mushrooms
   1 small onion, thinly sliced
   1 small green pepper, cut into strips

Cook rice according to package directions. Combine oil, vinegar, water, salad dressing mix and dill weed. Mix well. Stir one half of the dressing mixture into hot cooked rice. Cover and chill. Combine vegetables in a bowl and toss with remaining dressing mixture. Chill 8 hours, stirring occasionally. To serve, mound rice on lettuce leaves. Make an indentation in rice and fill with vegetable mixture.

For a pretty salad entrée, use spring vegetables like asparagus, carrots and snow peas.

Texas Caviar

Serves 8

   2 cups dried black-eyed peas
   5 cups water
   3 teaspoons salt
 ¾ cup red wine vinegar
 ½ teaspoon freshly ground pepper
   2 cups olive oil
   1 medium sweet onion, sliced into rings
   2 cloves garlic, crushed
   1 tablespoon chopped fresh parsley

Cook peas in boiling water 2 minutes. Remove from heat and soak 1 hour. Return to heat and add salt. Bring to a boil and then reduce heat. Simmer partially covered 40 to 50 minutes or until peas are tender, but somewhat firm to the bite. Drain. Combine peas with remaining ingredients. *Marinate chilled 2 to 3 days,* stirring occasionally. Drain marinade and serve in chilled bowl garnished with additional parsley. Keeps refrigerated for 2 weeks.

Frijoles de Olla

Serves 12

- **16 ounces dried pinto beans**
- **¼ cup vegetable oil**
- **1 onion, finely chopped**
- **½ cup chopped green pepper**
- **1 tablespoon chopped jalapeño pepper**
- **2 cloves garlic, chopped**
- **1 28-ounce can tomatoes, chopped**
- **freshly ground pepper to taste**
- **2 cups chicken broth**
- **3 cups water**
- **salt to taste**
- **2¼ cups chopped onion**
- **2-3 tablespoons chopped cilantro leaves**
- **1 tablespoon fresh lime juice**

Beans in a pot!

Place beans in a large bowl. Pour boiling water over beans to cover by about 2 inches. Let stand 45 minutes. Drain beans and set aside.

Place oil in a 6-quart stock pot. Stir in onion and sauté 5 minutes. Stir in green pepper, jalapeño and garlic. Cook 2 additional minutes. Add tomatoes and ground pepper; cook 3 additional minutes. Stir in broth and water and add beans. Beans should swim freely in the liquid. Bring to a simmer over moderately high heat stirring occasionally. Cover and simmer slowly 2 to 2½ hours. Slightly condense cooking juices by placing lid ajar for the last 15 minutes. Season with salt.

To serve, turn beans into a large bowl and sprinkle with chopped onion, cilantro leaves and lime juice.

A variation of this recipe is to purée prepared beans in a food processor until smooth. Place in a serving dish. Top with shredded Colby cheese and lightly sauce with your favorite salsa. Olé!

New Potatoes and Herb Butter

Serves 6 to 8

- **1½ pounds new potatoes**
- **3 tablespoons butter or margarine**
- **¼ teaspoon salt**
- **¼ teaspoon fresh thyme**
- **1 tablespoon chopped fresh parsley**
- **½ teaspoon fresh rosemary, crushed well**
- **2 bay leaves**

Boil potatoes in lightly salted water until tender. Drain. Melt butter in a large saucepan and add remaining ingredients. Stir to blend well. Add potatoes and toss gently. Serve warm.

The Herb Butter adds an extra dimension to fresh vegetables. We especially like it tossed with steamed broccoli.

Basil Potatoes

Serves 8 to 10

4   **pounds potatoes, peeled and
    cut into ½ inch cubes**
¾   **cup olive oil**
¾   **teaspoon salt**
¾   **teaspoon dried basil**
½   **teaspoon freshly ground
    pepper**

A subtle potato for a dominant entrée.

Toss potatoes with olive oil and seasonings in a large bowl. Spread on a 15 x 10-inch greased or parchment lined jelly roll pan. Bake at 350 degrees for 1½ to 2 hours, turning potatoes once halfway through baking time.

Sweet Potatoes and Bananas

Serves 8

6   **sweet potatoes**
6   **medium bananas**
2   **tablespoons butter
    salt and freshly ground
    pepper to taste**
⅔   **cup packed brown sugar**
1-2 **tablespoons fresh lemon
    juice**
½   **cup orange or pineapple
    juice**

A sweet potato recipe the children will love.

Boil the potatoes until tender; cool. Peel and slice potatoes and bananas. Layer in a 2-quart greased baking dish ending with a layer of potatoes on top. Dot with butter and sprinkle with salt and pepper. Sprinkle with brown sugar and drizzle with lemon juice. Slowly pour orange juice over potatoes and bananas. Bake at 325 to 350 degrees for 20 to 30 minutes until bubbly.

The Wainwright building on North 7th Street, designed by Louis Sullivan, is one of the country's earliest and finest examples of a steel framed skyscraper. Fortuitously saved from the wrecking ball, the building is now a designated National Historic Landmark and enjoys new life after a total renovation.

195

BREADS

Jalapeño Corn Bread

Serves 6 to 8

- ⅔ **cup safflower oil**
- 2 **eggs, lightly beaten**
- 3 **cups sour cream**
- 1 **16-ounce can creamed corn**
- 2 **tablespoons minced or grated onion**
- 2 **jalapeño peppers, finely chopped**
- 2 **tablespoons chopped green pepper**
- 1½ **cups yellow cornmeal**
- 2 **teaspoons baking powder**
- 1 **teaspoon salt**
- ¼ **cup sugar**
- 1 **cup shredded sharp Cheddar cheese**

A southwestern favorite to complement your summer barbecues.

Spray or grease a 9-inch skillet or heavy baking pan. (A brownie pan works well.) Mix oil, eggs, sour cream and creamed corn. Stir in onion, jalapeño and green pepper. Combine the cornmeal, baking powder, salt and sugar. Add to the liquid ingredients. Mix quickly, leaving a few lumps. Pour half of the batter into prepared pan. Top with cheese. Cover with the remaining batter. Bake at 350 degrees for 45 minutes. Cool at least 10 minutes before serving. Can be frozen.

In 1878, His Mysterious Majesty the Veiled Prophet of Khorassan, first made his appearance in his beloved city of Saint Louis. Organized similarly to the secret social krewes of New Orleans, the Veiled Prophet Ball and Parade were originally planned to help promote the annual Saint Louis Fair in October. The first parade was held at night and lit only by torchlight and Chinese lanterns. It was a huge success, with 100,000 of the city's 350,000 residents turning out to see the spectacle. The first official Queen of Love and Beauty, Esther Bates Laughlin, was crowned a few years later in 1894.

Vegetable Cheese French Bread

Serves 6 to 8

- 1 **cup shredded mozzarella cheese**
- ½ **cup grated carrot**
- 2-3 **green onions, sliced**
- ½ **teaspoon dried Italian herb seasoning**
- ¼ **cup mayonnaise**
- 8 **slices French bread**

Combine all ingredients except bread in a medium bowl. Cover and chill. When ready to serve, place bread slices on an ungreased baking sheet. Broil 2 to 3 minutes until lightly browned. Turn and spread cheese mixture on untoasted side. Bake at 350 degrees until cheese melts. Serve immediately.

Gruyère Shortbread

Serves 4 to 8

- 6 **tablespoons butter, softened**
- ½ **teaspoon salt**
- 2 **egg yolks**
- ¼ **teaspoon cayenne pepper**
- 1 **cup shredded Gruyère cheese**
- 1 **cup flour**

Combine butter, salt, egg yolks, pepper and cheese in a food processor by buzzing 6 times. Process for 6 seconds. Add flour and process until dough begins to mass. Pat dough into an 8 x 4-inch rectangle on an ungreased baking sheet. Cut rectangle in half. Cut each half into 4 triangles; separate with a knife. Bake at 350 degrees for 25 minutes or until golden. If necessary, separate triangles again while hot. Cool on baking sheet 3 minutes. Transfer to a cooling rack and serve warm.

A versatile bread that adds interest to soups and salads or distinction to a dessert course of fruit.

Strawberry Almond Bread

1 loaf

- 1½ cups sugar
- ¾ cup unsalted butter, softened
- 3 eggs
- ¾ cup (3 ounces) sliced almonds, toasted
- 1½ cups fresh strawberries, sliced
- 1 teaspoon almond extract
- ½ teaspoon ground cinnamon
- 1 teaspoon baking soda
- 1 teaspoon baking powder
- ¼ teaspoon salt
- 3½ cups flour
- 4 tablespoons sour cream

This recipe came to us from the Trellis Restaurant in Williamsburg, Virginia.

Combine sugar and butter in the bowl of an electric mixer. Beat on medium for 4 minutes; scrape down sides of bowl. Beat on high for 3 minutes; scrape down sides of bowl. Beat on high for 3 additional minutes until thoroughly creamed. Scrape down sides of bowl.

Place mixer on high speed and add eggs, one at a time, beating for 20 seconds and scraping down sides of bowl after adding each egg. Add toasted almonds, sliced berries, almond extract and cinnamon. Mix on high for 30 seconds. Add baking soda, baking powder and salt. Mix for 5 to 10 seconds.

Add flour and mix on low for 20 seconds. Add sour cream and mix on low for 20 seconds. Remove bowl from mixer. Using a rubber spatula, continue mixing batter until it is smooth and thoroughly combined.

Pour batter into a lightly greased and floured loaf pan. Bake at 325 degrees for 60 to 70 minutes until a toothpick inserted in center of bread comes out clean. Allow bread to cool in pan for 15 minutes. Remove bread from pan. Cool to room temperature before slicing.

Pineapple Cheese Bread

1 loaf

- 2 cups flour
- ¾ cup sugar
- 3 teaspoons baking powder
- ½ teaspoon baking soda
- 1 teaspoon salt
- 1 cup crushed pineapple, undrained
- 2 tablespoons margarine, melted
- 1 large egg, lightly beaten
- ½ cup shredded sharp Cheddar cheese
- ½ cup chopped walnuts

Sift together flour, sugar, baking powder, baking soda and salt. Stir crushed pineapple and margarine into lightly beaten egg. Add dry mixture to pineapple mixture. Stir quickly until moistened. Lightly stir in cheese and walnuts. Turn into a greased 9 x 5 x 3-inch loaf pan. Bake at 350 degrees for 1 hour or until completely cooked in the center. Cool completely before slicing.

Summer Berries and Cream Bread

1 loaf

- 1¾ cups flour
- ½ teaspoon baking powder
- 1½ teaspoons baking soda
- ¼ teaspoon salt
- ¼ teaspoon ground cinnamon
- ½ cup butter, softened
- ¾ cup sugar
- 2 eggs
- ½ cup sour cream
- 1 teaspoon vanilla
- 1 cup fresh strawberries, sliced, or blueberries or raspberries
- flour

Combine 1¾ cups flour, baking powder, baking soda, salt and cinnamon in a large bowl. In a small bowl, cream butter with an electric mixer. Slowly add sugar and beat until light. Beat in eggs, one at a time. Beat in sour cream and vanilla. Stir gently into flour mixture until dry ingredients are moist. Place berries in a plastic bag with a small amount of flour and gently shake. Fold berries into batter. Pour into a greased 9 x 5-inch loaf pan. Bake at 350 degrees for 55 to 60 minutes until a toothpick tests clean.

Pumpkin Pecan Bread

3 small loaves

- 3 eggs
- 1 16-ounce can pumpkin
- ¾ cup vegetable oil
- ½ cup water
- 2½ cups flour
- 1½ teaspoons baking soda
- 2¼ cups sugar
- 1¼ teaspoons salt
- 2½ teaspoons ground cinnamon
- 1 teaspoon ground cloves
- ¾ teaspoon ground nutmeg
- ½ cup chopped pecans
- 1 cup dark raisins
- 4 ounces cream cheese, softened
- 3 tablespoons butter, softened
- 1 teaspoon vanilla
- 1 cup confectioners' sugar

Combine eggs, pumpkin, oil and water. Set aside. Combine the next 7 ingredients. Add pumpkin mixture to the dry ingredients. Beat well. Slowly add pecans and raisins. Pour mixture evenly into 3 small greased loaf pans. Bake at 350 degrees for 45 to 50 minutes.

Combine cream cheese, butter, vanilla and sugar and blend well. Frost the cooled loaves with cream cheese mixture and serve. Can be frozen.

Lemon Ribbon Bread

1 loaf

½ cup butter, softened
1 cup sugar
1 egg
2 teaspoons grated lemon peel
1½ cups flour
1 teaspoon baking powder
½ teaspoon salt
1 cup chopped pecans or walnuts
½ cup milk
6 ounces cream cheese, softened
⅓ cup sugar
1 tablespoon flour
1 egg
1 teaspoon vanilla
confectioners' sugar

In a large bowl, cream butter, sugar, egg and lemon peel. In a small bowl, mix flour, baking powder, salt and nuts. Add to creamed mixture alternately with milk, beating until smooth after each addition. Set aside.

Combine remaining ingredients, except confectioners' sugar, to make filling. Beat until smooth. Spread one half of the bread batter into a greased 9 x 5 x 3-inch loaf pan. Gently spread filling over batter in pan. Spoon remaining half of bread batter evenly over filling. Bake at 350 degrees for 55 to 60 minutes. Sprinkle with confectioners' sugar while warm.

Spiced Cranberry Muffins with Orange Honey Butter

18 muffins

Muffins:

2 cups flour

1 cup sugar

1½ teaspoons baking powder

½ teaspoon baking soda

1½ teaspoons ground nutmeg

1 teaspoon ground cinnamon

½ teaspoon ground ginger

½ cup vegetable shortening

¾ cup orange juice

1 tablespoon vanilla

2 teaspoons grated orange peel

2 eggs, slightly beaten

1½ cups coarsely chopped cranberries

1½ cups chopped walnuts, divided

Orange Honey Butter:

½ cup butter

2 tablespoons honey

1 tablespoon grated orange peel

Muffins:
In a medium mixing bowl, combine flour, sugar, baking powder, baking soda, nutmeg, cinnamon and ginger. Cut in shortening until mixture is the consistency of coarse meal. Combine juice, vanilla, orange peel and eggs. Stir into flour mixture until ingredients are moistened. Gently stir in cranberries and 1 cup of the nuts. Spoon batter into 18 paper lined or greased and floured muffin pans. Sprinkle with remaining nuts. Bake at 350 degrees for 25 to 30 minutes or until toothpick inserted near center comes out clean. Serve warm with Orange Honey Butter. Muffins can be frozen.

Orange Honey Butter:
In a small bowl, beat butter until fluffy. Gradually beat in honey and orange peel. Yields ½ cup.

Apricot Jam Muffins

12 muffins

1⅔ cups flour
½ cup sugar
2 teaspoons baking powder
½ teaspoon salt
⅛ teaspoon ground nutmeg or
   ground cinnamon
⅓ cup shortening
¾ cup milk
1 egg
1 teaspoon vanilla
   apricot jam
   chopped nuts

Combine flour, sugar, baking powder, salt and nutmeg. Cut in shortening until particles are fine. Add milk, egg and vanilla. Mix only until thoroughly blended. Spoon into greased muffin pans. Place 1 teaspoon jam on top of each muffin, pressing into batter slightly. Sprinkle with a few chopped nuts. Bake at 400 degrees for 20 to 25 minutes until tops spring back. Serve warm. Other jams can be substituted.

Blueberry Muffins

12 muffins

½ cup unsalted margarine,
   softened
¾ cup sugar
1 egg
1 teaspoon vanilla
2 cups unbleached flour
2 teaspoons baking powder
¾ cup milk
1 generous cup frozen or
   fresh blueberries
2 teaspoons sugar
¼ teaspoon ground cinnamon

With an electric mixer on high speed, beat margarine, ¾ cup sugar, egg and vanilla together. At low speed, alternately add dry ingredients and milk, ending with dry ingredients and blending after each addition. Gently fold in blueberries by hand. (If blueberries are frozen, rinse first.) Line a muffin pan with cupcake papers. Fill papers with mixture two thirds full. Bake at 375 degrees for 20 to 25 minutes until toothpick tests clean. Combine 2 teaspoons sugar and cinnamon and sprinkle over warm muffins. Freezes very well.

The ingredients make this muffin healthy without sacrificing flavor.

Zucchini Raisin Muffins

8 large or 18 miniature muffins

- ½ **cup sugar**
- 1 **egg, beaten**
- ¼ **cup vegetable oil**
- ¾ **cup flour**
- ¼ **teaspoon baking soda**
- ¼ **teaspoon baking powder**
- ¼ **teaspoon salt**
- ¼ **teaspoon ground nutmeg**
- 1 **cup grated zucchini**
- ¼ **cup raisins**
- ¼ **cup chopped walnuts (optional)**

Combine sugar, egg and oil in a large bowl. In a separate bowl, sift together flour, baking soda, baking powder, salt and nutmeg. Add to the sugar mixture. Add zucchini, raisins and walnuts. Mix just until combined. Fill greased muffin pans two thirds full. Bake at 350 degrees for 20 to 25 minutes or until golden brown. Miniature size muffins need only to be baked 15 to 20 minutes.

A nutritious snack. Children especially like the miniatures.

One of the unique features of Saint Louis was the development of elaborate residential enclosures known as "Private Places." Here the well-to-do built luxurious mansions along private streets on the city's outskirts, in order to escape the smoke, crime and dirt of the inner city. Despite Saint Louis' continuing westward expansion, these homes have remained some of the most elegant and desirable in the area. After entering through elaborate gates, visitors still marvel at the wealth and opulence displayed in the houses, which stand as proud testimony to a prosperous and golden age of Saint Louis' history.

Parker House Rolls
Orange Rolls

48 Parker House Rolls or
36 Orange Rolls

Parker House Rolls:
- 1 **cup water**
- ½ **cup butter or margarine**
- ½ **cup vegetable shortening**
- ¾ **cup sugar**
- 1½ **teaspoons salt**
- 1 **cup warm (105-115 degrees) water**
- 2 **packages dry yeast**
- 2 **eggs, slightly beaten**
- 6 **cups flour**

Orange Rolls:
- ½ **recipe Parker House Rolls dough**
- ½ **cup butter, softened**
- ½ **cup sugar**
- 1½ **teaspoons grated orange peel**
- 2 **cups confectioners' sugar**
- 3-4 **tablespoons orange juice**

Positively 5 star and no fail for the novice baker.

Parker House Rolls:
Bring 1 cup water to boil in a saucepan. Remove from stove. Add butter and shortening. Stir until melted. Add sugar and salt. Cool to lukewarm.

Pour 1 cup warm water into a large bowl. Be sure the water temperature is between 105 and 115 degrees. Sprinkle yeast over water and stir to dissolve. Add butter mixture and eggs to dissolved yeast. Add 6 cups flour or enough to make a thick dough. Mix thoroughly. *Cover and let rise in refrigerator overnight.*

About 2 to 2½ hours before serving, turn dough out on floured board. Roll to ¼ to ⅓-inch thickness. Cut dough with a biscuit cutter and fold each in half. Place in a greased pan. Let rise 1½ to 2 hours. Bake at 400 degrees for 12 to 15 minutes. Rolls can be frozen.

Orange Rolls:
Divide the half recipe of Parker House Rolls dough in half. On a lightly floured surface, roll each portion in a 12 x 8-inch rectangle.

Combine butter, sugar and orange peel. Spread evenly over each rectangle, using all of the mixture. Roll each rectangle in jelly roll style beginning with the long side. Slice each roll into 18 equal pieces. Place slices in cupcake papers in muffin pans or use 3 greased 8 or 9-inch baking pans. Let rolls rise 1½ hours. Bake at 375 degrees for 15 minutes or until lightly browned.

Combine confectioners' sugar and orange juice. Drizzle over warm rolls to glaze. Freezes very well.

These delightful rolls can be baked in "give away" pans and presented as special gifts.

Italian Bread

1 loaf

- **1 tablespoon dry yeast**
- **1¼ cups warm (105-115 degrees) water**
- **2 teaspoons salt**
- **1 tablespoon sugar**
- **1 tablespoon olive oil**
- **3-4 cups all purpose flour (or 2½-3 cups all purpose and ½-1 cup whole wheat) egg white for glaze (optional)**

Dissolve yeast in water and add remaining ingredients, except egg white. When dough stiffens, pour out onto a floured board. Knead until smooth, adding additional flour as necessary. Place in a greased bowl, turning to grease top of dough. Cover and allow to rise until doubled in size. Punch dough down on floured board and shape into a long loaf. Place loaf on a greased baking sheet. Cover and allow to rise either in a warm place, or *overnight in refrigerator.* Before baking, make three to four 1-inch deep slashes in loaf. Brush with egg white diluted with a little water if desired. Bake at 400 degrees for 35 minutes.

In 1845, in an area just south and west of the young city's thriving business district lay a body of water called Chouteau's Pond. It was described as a beautiful "fairy tale lake" and was more than two miles long and a quarter mile wide in places. It was a recreational spot used by citizens young and old. Suffering from pollution and facing continuing expansion from the city the pond was eventually drained. More than a century later, when Union Station was being rehabbed, the developers put a pond under the old train shed in almost exactly the spot where part of the original Chouteau's Pond had been.

French Hard Rolls

36 rolls

- **1 package dry yeast**
- **2 cups warm water, divided**
- **1 tablespoon vegetable oil**
- **1 tablespoon honey**
- **1 tablespoon salt**
- **2 tablespoons instant malted milk powder**
- **5 cups bread flour, divided cornmeal**

A robust dinner roll for a hearty meal.

Dissolve yeast in 1 cup warm water which is 105 to 115 degrees. Set aside. Combine 1 cup warm water with oil, honey, salt and milk powder. Stir. Add to this, 1 cup flour and yeast mixture. Mix well. Add remaining flour, 1 cup at a time, until blended. Knead dough 8 to 10 minutes until smooth and no longer sticky. Place dough in an ungreased bowl. Cover and let rise until doubled in volume, about 1 hour. Punch down, cover and let rise again until doubled, about 30 minutes. Punch down again. Divide dough into 4 equal parts. Roll each part into a strip about 27 inches long and 1 inch wide. Place strips on flat surface; sprinkle with cornmeal. Cover and let rise 20 minutes. With a sharp knife, cut strips into 3 to 4-inch lengths. Place on a baking sheet dusted with cornmeal. Cover rolls and let rise 20 to 30 minutes. Slash diagonally prior to baking and spray lightly with a mist of water. Bake at 425 degrees for 15 minutes.

Bread flour adds that bakery flavor and texture to home baked breads. Check your local market as it is now widely available.

Crusty Herb Bread with Herb Butter

2 loaves

Bread:

1 **cup warm water (105-115 degrees)**
1 **package dry yeast**
1 **teaspoon sugar**
2 **cups bread flour**
1 **cup flour**
2 **tablespoons vegetable oil**
1½ **teaspoons salt**
  Herb Butter (optional)
  shortening
  cornmeal
1 **egg, beaten with ½ teaspoon salt**

Herb Butter:

4 **tablespoons butter or margarine, softened**
2 **tablespoons chopped fresh parsley**
2 **tablespoons freshly grated Parmesan cheese**
1 **clove garlic, minced**
¼ **teaspoon dried Italian herbs or 1 teaspoon chopped fresh herbs**

A no knead yeast bread with French bread character.

Bread:
In a 2-cup measure, combine warm water, yeast and sugar. Set aside until yeast is bubbly, about 5 minutes. In work bowl of food processor, fitted with metal blade, combine flours, oil and salt. Process 5 seconds. With machine running, add yeast mixture through feed tube; process 40 additional seconds. Transfer dough to a greased bowl; cover with plastic wrap and let dough rise 1 to 1½ hours or until dough has doubled in size. Punch dough down and roll out on lightly floured surface into a 10 x 16-inch rectangle.

If desired, spread with Herb Butter within 1 inch of all edges. Cut dough in half to form two 8 x 10-inch rectangles. Roll up each half, jelly roll style, pinching and sealing ends and seams. Grease 2 French bread pans or a baking sheet with shortening and sprinkle with cornmeal. Place dough seam side down in pans. Slash tops of loaves and let rise, covered with a cloth towel, 1 hour or until doubled in size. Gently brush loaves with egg glaze.

Bake at 425 degrees for 20 to 25 minutes or until golden brown. If bottom crust of bread is pale when top crust is golden, turn bread upside down and bake 5 additional minutes. Serve within 6 hours of baking with additional Herb Butter.

If it is not possible to serve bread within 6 hours of baking, wrap bread in foil and freeze 20 minutes after removing from oven. To reheat, place foil wrapped loaf on a baking sheet and heat at 350 degrees for 10 minutes. Open foil and heat until crust is crisp and bread is hot.

Herb Butter:
In a small bowl, combine all ingredients. Blend until smooth.

Oatmeal Bread

2 loaves

- ½ **cup warm (105-115 degrees) water**
- 2 **packages dry yeast**
- 1¾ **cups warm milk**
- ¼ **cup firmly packed brown sugar**
- 1 **tablespoon salt**
- 3 **tablespoons margarine**
- 5-6 **cups unsifted unbleached flour**
- 1 **cup quick rolled oats vegetable oil**

Measure warm water into a large bowl prewarmed in the microwave 20 seconds. Sprinkle yeast in water and stir until dissolved. Add warm milk, sugar, salt and margarine. Add 2 cups of flour. Beat with rotary beater about 1 minute. Add 1 cup flour and oats. Beat vigorously with wooden spoon until smooth. Add enough additional flour to make a soft dough. Turn onto lightly floured board and knead 8 to 10 minutes until smooth and elastic. Cover with plastic wrap and a towel and let rest about 20 minutes.

Divide dough in half. Roll each half into a 12 x 8-inch rectangle. Shape into loaves and place each loaf in a greased 8½ x 4½ x 2½-inch pan. Brush loaves with oil and cover loosely with plastic wrap. Chill 2 hours (no more than 24). When ready to bake, remove from refrigerator, unwrap and let stand 10 minutes at room temperature. Puncture any bubbles with a toothpick. Bake at 400 degrees for 30 to 40 minutes. Bread will sound hollow when done. Serve warm.

Breads are always good with fruit butter. The butter will keep for several days in the refrigerator and indefinitely in the freezer. For fruit butter, combine ½ cup unsalted butter, ⅓ cup of your favorite jam, and ½ teaspoon confectioners' sugar. Serve at room temperature.

Over the years, Saint Louis has been home to some famous and respected poets. Eugene Field, author of "Wynken Blynken and Nod" and "Little Boy Blue" also worked as a journalist. Today his home has been turned into a children's museum housing antique toys. T.S. Eliot was also born here and evidence of his roots can be found in his work. And the recent Poet Laureate of the United States, Howard Nemerov, lives in University City, a suburb just outside the city.

Rolls Extraordinaire

12 rolls

1 **package brown and serve rolls**
Cheddar cheese, shredded
pecans
walnuts
jam
ginger marmalade
cinnamon sugar
poppy seeds
melted butter

Very easy, very pretty and very tasty!

Fill splits in rolls with any one or a combination of the ingredients. Brush tops with melted butter. Bake according to package directions.

Bread in a Minute

Serves 12 to 15

½ **cup butter, salted or unsalted**
1 **package Italian salad dressing mix**
1 **loaf French or Italian bread, sliced lengthwise**

Your guests can be at the door when you start this!

Melt butter and add dressing mix. Stir well. Brush mixture on bread halves. Wrap in foil and heat at 350 degrees for 10 minutes.

Pancake Popover

Serves 4

6 tablespoons unsalted butter
or margarine
5-6 eggs
1½ cups milk
1½ cups flour
¼ cup sugar
1 tablespoon vanilla
fresh peaches, strawberries
or nectarines
confectioners' sugar

Defines a lazy Sunday morning breakfast.

In a 400 degree oven, melt butter in a 9-inch skillet with at least 4-inch sides or a 9-inch soufflé pan. Combine eggs, milk, flour, sugar and vanilla in a blender until smooth. Pour batter into heated skillet. Bake at 400 degrees for 15 to 20 minutes until puffed and lightly browned on top. Slice into wedges. To serve, sprinkle with fruit and dust with confectioners' sugar.

For a tangy taste, drizzle with fresh lemon juice and sprinkle with confectioners' sugar.

Spirit of Saint Louis Waffles

4 large waffles

2 cups Bisquick
1 egg
3 tablespoons vegetable oil
1⅓ cups club soda

Lighter than air!

Combine all ingredients with a whisk. Pour ½ cup of mixture into a preheated waffle maker. Cook 5 minutes or until golden brown. Waffles freeze very well.

When you are feeling organized, prepare 5 or 6 batches of waffles at a time. Freeze between sheets of waxed paper and store in a reclosable freezer bag. Be sure to substitute club soda in your pancake mix so they, too, will be lighter than air.

Blueberry Buttermilk Biscuits

12 biscuits

2 **cups sifted flour**
½ **cup sugar**
1 **tablespoon baking powder**
1 **teaspoon grated orange peel**
1 **teaspoon salt**
¼ **teaspoon baking soda**
⅓ **cup vegetable shortening**
¾ **cup buttermilk**
1 **egg, slightly beaten**
½ **cup frozen blueberries (do not thaw)**
3 **tablespoons butter, melted**
3 **tablespoons sugar**
¼ **teaspoon ground cinnamon**
⅛ **teaspoon ground nutmeg**

Combine flour, ½ cup sugar, baking powder, orange peel, salt and baking soda. Cut in vegetable shortening until mixture resembles coarse meal. Combine buttermilk and egg. Add to dry ingredients. Stir in blueberries. Gently knead on heavily floured surface until dough just holds together. Pat out ½-inch thick. Cut into squares, 3-inch rounds or shape into mounds.

Arrange 1 inch apart on a lightly greased baking sheet. Bake at 400 degrees for 20 minutes or until light brown. At serving time, combine melted butter with 3 tablespoons sugar and spices. Brush over warm biscuits. Serve immediately.

Saint Louis University, founded in 1832, was the first university west of the Mississippi. Originally run by Diocesan priests, it was later put under the administration of the Jesuit Order. Today, the school boasts outstanding undergraduate programs as well as excellent studies in business, law and medicine.

214

Beer and Spice Brunch Cake

Serves 12

Cake:
- 1 18¼-ounce package yellow cake mix
- 1 4-ounce package vanilla or lemon instant pudding
- 1 cup beer
- ½ cup vegetable oil
- 4 eggs
- 1 teaspoon ground cinnamon
- ½ teaspoon ground cardamon (optional)
- ¼ teaspoon ground allspice
- ½ teaspoon ground cloves
- ½ teaspoon ground ginger

Lemon Sugar:
- 1½ cups confectioners' sugar
- 2 tablespoons butter or margarine, softened
- ¼ teaspoon grated lemon peel
- 1-2 tablespoons lemon juice

Cake:
In a large bowl, blend all ingredients. Beat at medium speed 2 minutes. Pour into a greased and floured 10-inch tube pan. Bake at 350 degrees for 50 to 60 minutes or until cake springs back in center when done. Cool right side up in pan 25 minutes before removing. Frost with Lemon Sugar. Can be frozen.

Lemon Sugar:
Combine sugar, butter, lemon peel and lemon juice and blend well.

Saint Louisans choose Budweiser, The King of Beers.

Sauces
&
Marinades

Raspberry Mint Sauce

1¹/₂ cups sauce

1 **10-ounce package frozen raspberries, puréed**
¹/₂ **cup mint jelly**

In a small saucepan, combine ingredients. Cook over low heat until jelly is melted. Cool and serve with grilled lamb.

Onion Marmalade

3 cups marmalade

2 **cups vinegar**
4 **onions, sliced**
1 **teaspoon salt**
1 **teaspoon freshly ground pepper**
1 **cup whipping cream**

In a small saucepan, combine first 4 ingredients and cook over low heat 30 minutes or until onions are soft. Add cream and cook an additional 10 minutes. Cool. Purée mixture in a food processor. Serve with grilled chicken prepared with Chicken Marinade.

Peanut Sauce

1¹/₂ cups sauce

1 **cup peanut butter**
2 **scallions, chopped**
1 **teaspoon granulated garlic or ¹/₂ teaspoon garlic salt**
¹/₂ **cup chicken broth**
¹/₄ **teaspoon red pepper**

In a medium saucepan, combine all ingredients. Cook over low heat, stirring until smooth. Serve with grilled chicken.

Lamb Marinade

1¹/₂ cups marinade

- **1 cup red wine vinegar**
- **¹/₂ cup olive oil**
- **1 teaspoon minced fresh garlic**
- **1 tablespoon fresh oregano**
- **1 tablespoon fresh rosemary**
- **1 tablespoon fresh basil**

Combine all ingredients. Stir until thoroughly mixed. *Marinate lamb overnight* before grilling.

Chicken Marinade

1¹/₂ cups marinade

- **1 cup vinegar**
- **¹/₂ cup vegetable oil**
- **1 teaspoon granulated garlic or ¹/₂ teaspoon garlic salt**
- **1 teaspoon freshly ground pepper**
- **1 teaspoon sugar**
- **1 teaspoon paprika**
- **¹/₄ teaspoon ground ginger**

Combine all ingredients. Stir until thoroughly mixed. *Marinate chicken overnight* before grilling.

Shrimp Marinade

¹/₂ cup marinade

- **1 teaspoon granulated garlic or ¹/₂ teaspoon garlic salt**
- **1 teaspoon shellfish seasoning**
- **2 tablespoons vegetable oil juice of 3 limes**

Combine all ingredients. Stir until thoroughly mixed. Marinate shrimp 2 hours before grilling.

Dijon Cream Sauce

1 cup sauce

- **1 cup heavy cream**
- **1 tablespoon Dijon mustard**
  freshly ground pepper
  to taste
  fresh lemon juice to taste

Combine all ingredients in a small saucepan. Bring to a boil and simmer over low heat 1 minute. Serve hot over fish or veal scallops.

Quick Béarnaise Sauce

¾ cup sauce

- **2 tablespoons tarragon vinegar**
- **½ teaspoon dried tarragon**
- **½ cup mayonnaise**
- **1 egg yolk**
  salt and freshly ground
  pepper

Combine all ingredients in the top of a double boiler. Place mixture over hot, not boiling, water. Blend with a whisk until warm.

Try serving this quick sauce at room temperature as a condiment for cold meats or chicken.

Beer and Honey Sauce for Ribs

5 cups sauce

- **6 ounces honey**
- **½ cup vinegar**
- **12 ounces chili sauce**
- **6 ounces prepared barbecue**
  sauce
- **7 ounces catsup**
- **3 tablespoons horseradish**
- **1 tablespoon mustard**
- **6 ounces beer**
  brown sugar to taste
  (optional)

In a saucepan, heat honey and vinegar over medium heat until combined. Add remaining ingredients except brown sugar. Simmer up to 1 hour. Add brown sugar if a sweeter taste is desired. Keeps well (several weeks) in the refrigerator.

This sauce was created with ribs in mind, but it also enhances chicken, pork or beef.

Microwave Barbecue Sauce

1 cup sauce

- 2 **tablespoons balsamic vinegar**
- 4 **tablespoons water**
- 1 **tablespoon lemon juice**
- 2 **tablespoons Worcestershire sauce**
- 3 **tablespoons catsup**
- ½ **teaspoon hot pepper sauce**
- 2 **tablespoons butter (omit if sauce is for meats high in fat)**
- 3 **tablespoons brown sugar**
- 1 **teaspoon prepared mustard**
- 1 **teaspoon chili powder**
- 1 **teaspoon paprika**
- 1 **teaspoon salt**

Combine all ingredients; heat in a microwave oven. Baste meat with sauce occasionally during cooking.

Baked Potato Topping

2 cups dressing

- ½ **cup butter or margarine, softened**
- 1 **cup shredded Cheddar cheese**
- ½ **cup sour cream**
- 2 **tablespoons chopped green onions**

Combine all ingredients using an electric mixer. Topping can be made in advance and chilled. Bring to room temperature before serving.

This also makes a delicious topping for other vegetables, especially cauliflower and broccoli.

Honey Mustard Dressing

1½ cups dressing

- ¼ **cup wine vinegar**
- ¾ **cup vegetable oil**
- 3 **tablespoons honey mustard**
- 5 **teaspoons honey**
- 1 **clove garlic, minced**
- 2 **tablespoons chopped onion**
- 2 **tablespoons mayonnaise**

Combine all ingredients in a blender until smooth. *Chill several hours or overnight.* Serve as a dip for vegetable crudités, as a spread for ham or chicken or as a dressing for salad greens.

Rum Lime Sauce and Fruit

Serves 12

⅔ **cup sugar**
⅓ **cup water**
1 **heaping teaspoon grated lime peel**
6 **tablespoons fresh lime juice**
½ **cup light rum**
1 **cantaloupe, diced**
⅛ **watermelon, diced**
1 **honeydew melon, diced**
1 **cup fresh blueberries**

In a small saucepan, combine sugar and water. Bring to a boil and simmer 5 minutes. Add lime peel and let cool to room temperature. Add lime juice and rum and blend well. Pour sauce over fruit. Chill, covered, for several hours or even 24 to 48 hours. Stir occasionally. Can easily be doubled or tripled. Other fresh or frozen fruits can be used. Do not use bananas.

The secret to this recipe is fresh lime peel and juice! Design lime peel flowers for an attractive garnish. Make a continuous "snake" of lime peel with a parer or a zester. Arrange "snake" into a flower shape and place a small melon ball or berry in center. Place in the serving bowl and add mint leaves and stems to complete the flower.

Raspberry Sauce for Fruit

1½ cups sauce

1 **cup sour cream**
⅓ **cup red raspberry preserves**
2 **tablespoons finely chopped pecans**
2 **tablespoons milk**
¼ **cup shredded coconut (optional)**

Combine all ingredients. Chill for several hours. Serve with seasonal fruits.

Crème Coconut

1 cup sauce

8 **ounces cream cheese**
   heavy coconut syrup or coconut liqueur

A real fooler — easy and delicious.

Soften cream cheese. Blend coconut syrup with cream cheese until desired consistency and sweetness are reached. Serve with fresh berries or cakes.

Fudge Sauce

3 cups sauce

½ cup butter
2¼ cups confectioners' sugar
⅔ cup evaporated milk
6 ounces unsweetened chocolate

Melt butter in top of a double boiler and add sugar. Add milk and chocolate, stirring occasionally until chocolate is melted. Without stirring, continue to cook over barely simmering water 30 minutes. Remove from heat and beat with a spoon 2 to 3 minutes. Can be stored chilled and warmed before serving. If sauce needs to be thinned, add a small amount of cream.

Sink summer fruits in this rich dark sauce. Whenever possible, leave stems on fruit for that fresh picked look.

Chocolate Royale Sauce

Serves 6

12 ounces semisweet chocolate chips
½ cup unsalted butter
1 cup sugar
1 cup heavy cream
1 teaspoon vanilla

Melt chocolate and butter in a heavy saucepan. Cook over low heat until melted. Add remaining ingredients and simmer over low heat 5 minutes or until smooth.

A cookbook is not complete without a chocolate sauce. This is our hands down favorite.

Kahlúa Dip

Serves 6

8 ounces cream cheese
1 cup nondairy whipped cream
¾ cup brown sugar
1 cup sour cream
¼ cup Kahlúa
⅓ cup chopped nuts

Combine all ingredients in a blender. *Chill 36 to 48 hours to allow flavors to blend.* Serve as a dip with fresh fruit.

Chocolate and Raspberry Brownies

24 brownies

- **4 ounces unsweetened chocolate**
- **½ cup butter**
- **2⅓ cups sugar, divided**
- **1 teaspoon vanilla**
- **4 large eggs**
- **1 cup flour**
- **¼ teaspoon baking powder**
- **¼ teaspoon salt**
- **8 ounces cream cheese, softened**
- **1 egg**
- **¾ cup raspberry jam**

Melt chocolate and butter in a double boiler. When smooth add 2 cups sugar and vanilla. Beat in 4 eggs. Add flour, baking powder and salt. Pour one half of the batter in an ungreased 9 x 13-inch baking pan. In a small bowl, combine cream cheese, ⅓ cup sugar and 1 egg. Mix well and spread over batter in pan. Cover with raspberry jam. Spoon remainder of batter over raspberry jam. Bake at 350 degrees for 35 to 40 minutes. Cool and cut into squares.

Peaches and Cream Pie

Serves 8

- **¾ cup sugar**
- **¼ cup flour**
- **1 cup heavy cream**
- **¼ teaspoon salt**
- **8 large fresh peaches, peeled and sliced**
- **pinch of salt**
- **¼ teaspoon fresh lemon juice**
- **1 9-inch unbaked pastry shell**
- **2 tablespoons butter**
- **2 teaspoons ground cinnamon**

In a medium bowl, combine sugar, flour, cream and ¼ teaspoon salt. In a separate bowl, stir together peaches, pinch of salt and lemon juice. Place pastry shell in a pie plate. Arrange peaches in pastry shell. Pour cream mixture over peaches. Dot with butter and sprinkle with cinnamon. Bake at 425 degrees for 15 minutes. Reduce heat to 300 degrees and bake an additional 40 to 45 minutes.

Peach Yogurt Cake

Serves 12

- 2 cups sugar
- 1 cup butter or margarine, softened
- 3 eggs
- 1 cup peach yogurt
- 2¼ cups flour
- ½ teaspoon salt
- ½ teaspoon baking soda
- 1 teaspoon vanilla
- 1 cup thinly sliced fresh peaches

Cream sugar with butter or margarine. Beat in eggs. Add yogurt and beat well. Gradually add the dry ingredients and beat well. Stir in vanilla and peaches. Bake at 375 degrees in a greased and floured tube or bundt pan for 50 to 60 minutes.

This cake shows its versatility when you substitute other yogurt flavors and add compatible fruits to the batter. Two of the best are blueberry and fresh blueberries or lemon flavored with ½ teaspoon lemon peel.

Austrian Raspberry Bars

24 bars

- 1 cup butter, softened
- 1 cup sugar
- 2 egg yolks
- 2 cups sifted flour
- 1 teaspoon vanilla
- 1½ cups raspberry jam

In a bowl, cream butter and sugar. Add egg yolks, flour and vanilla. Mix thoroughly. Pat half of the dough in a 9 x 13-inch pan. Spread with raspberry jam. Sprinkle with remaining dough and bake at 350 degrees for 25 minutes. Cool and cut into small bars.

Sherried Pears with Crème Anglaise

Serves 6

Sherried Pears:

  3 **medium pears**
 ⅓ **cup packed brown sugar**
 ¼ **cup cream sherry**
  1 **tablespoon vanilla**
  1 **tablespoon lemon juice**
 ½ **teaspoon ground cinnamon**
     Crème Anglaise
     freshly grated nutmeg

Crème Anglaise:

  2 **cups milk**
  5 **egg yolks, slightly beaten**
 ⅔ **cup sugar**
     pinch of salt
  1 **teaspoon vanilla, rum, dry sherry or flavor of choice**
 ½ **cup slivered almonds (optional)**

Sherried Pears:
Halve pears lengthwise. Core and peel. Place halves on cutting board, flat side down. Make lengthwise cuts in pears from end to end, but do not cut all the way through. In a small saucepan, combine next 5 ingredients. Stir over medium heat until sugar is dissolved. Place pears flat side down in a baking dish. Pour sauce over pears. Bake, covered, at 350 degrees for 35 to 40 minutes. Present warm pears in a pool of Crème Anglaise with a splash of freshly grated nutmeg.

Crème Anglaise:
Heat milk to scalding in the top of a double boiler. (Top should not be in the water.) Combine egg yolks, sugar and salt. Slowly blend into hot milk, stirring constantly until mixture starts to thicken. Remove from heat and cool. Stir in flavoring. Cover and chill thoroughly. Before serving, stir in almonds if desired.

Pear and Apple Pie with Black Walnuts

Serves 8

3 large cooking apples,
   peeled and sliced
¾ cup dark raisins
⅓ cup sugar
1 tablespoon whole wheat flour
¼ teaspoon ground cinnamon
¼ teaspoon ground nutmeg
2 medium pears, peeled and
   sliced
   pastry for double crust
   9-inch pie
1 tablespoon dark rum
1½ tablespoons butter or
   margarine, melted
2 tablespoons finely chopped
   black walnuts

Combine first 6 ingredients in a bowl and toss. Cover and chill 20 minutes. In a saucepan, cook pears in a small amount of water 5 minutes or until tender. Drain and mash; set aside.

Roll half of pastry to ⅛-inch thickness on a lightly floured surface. Place in a 9-inch deep dish pie plate. Spoon half of apple mixture into pastry shell. Spread half of pears over apple mixture. Repeat procedure with remaining apple mixture and pears. Sprinkle with rum, butter and black walnuts.

Roll remaining pastry to ⅛-inch thickness; transfer to top of pie. Trim off excess pastry. Fold edges under and flute. Cut slits in top crust. Bake at 425 degrees for 45 minutes. Cover edges of pastry with aluminum foil to prevent excessive browning if necessary. Cut pear shapes from remaining pastry. Brush one side with water and arrange in a cluster on top of pie, wet sides down.

Black walnut trees grow abundantly in Missouri. The nut is round with a thick shell making it difficult to crack. However, its earthy flavor rewards the effort.

Brian Mullanphy, son of the city's first millionaire, wanted to help those in Saint Louis who were less fortunate, without hurting their pride. He once "hired" a poor family to care for a completely furnished house for him, thus giving them a roof over their heads. He also bought a cow and asked a woman to stable it. In return he paid her a wage and let her use the milk for her hungry children. After his death in 1851, his will specified that one-third of his estate be used to help travelers and pioneers coming through Saint Louis on their way west . . . which was the beginning of the Travelers Aid Society.

Chocolate Hazelnut Torte

Serves 8 to 10

Torte:

  10 tablespoons butter

  ¾ cup sugar

  6 eggs, separated

  1 cup toasted ground hazelnuts

  ¾ cup semisweet chocolate chips, melted

Frosting:

  10 tablespoons butter

  4 tablespoons sugar

  2 eggs

  ¾ cup semisweet chocolate chips, melted

  3 tablespoons seedless raspberry jam

Torte:
In a large bowl, beat butter, sugar and egg yolks until creamy. Add nuts and melted chocolate. Beat egg whites until stiff. Gently fold into chocolate mixture. Butter three 9-inch cake pans and dust with cocoa. Divide batter evenly in pans. Bake at 350 degrees for 20 to 25 minutes or until toothpick tests clean. Do not overbake. Cool and wrap each layer. *Chill overnight.*

Frosting:
Cream butter and sugar. Add eggs and mix well. Add chocolate and mix well. Place 1 torte layer on a serving plate. Spread top with frosting. Place second layer on first and spread with jam and then frosting. Place third layer on top and spread with frosting. Leave sides unfrosted. Chill until ready to serve. Keeps well covered in refrigerator.

Specialty shops usually carry toasted hazelnuts. If not, place hazelnuts on a baking sheet in a single layer. Bake at 400 degrees for 10 to 15 minutes. Remove and wrap in a kitchen towel to steam 1 minute. Rub in the towel to remove skins.

Quick and Easy Chocolate Mousse

Serves 6

1 **12-ounce package semisweet chocolate chips**
1½ **teaspoons vanilla**
     dash of salt
1½ **cups heavy cream**
6 **egg yolks**
2 **egg whites**
     sweetened whipped cream

A 10 minute taste sensation.

Combine chocolate chips, vanilla and salt in a blender or a food processor fitted with a steel knife. Mix 30 seconds. Heat cream to boiling point. Add cream to blender and continue mixing 30 seconds or until chocolate is melted. Add egg yolks. Mix 5 seconds. Beat egg whites until stiff peaks form. Fold into chocolate mixture. Place in a serving bowl or individual chocolate cups. Cover and chill. Serve with whipped cream.

Mousse au Chocolat

Serves 8

5 **eggs, separated**
¼ **teaspoon cream of tartar**
1 **cup sugar, divided**
⅛ **teaspoon salt**
2 **teaspoons brandy**
4 **ounces unsweetened chocolate**
2⅔ **cups heavy cream, divided**
     chocolate curls

Simply the very best.

Beat egg whites and cream of tartar until soft peaks form. Gradually add ¾ cup sugar and beat to soft peaks. In a separate bowl, beat egg yolks with salt until thick. Gradually add remaining sugar and brandy. Melt chocolate; cool. Add chocolate and ⅓ cup cream to egg yolk mixture. Beat 1⅓ cups cream until stiff. Fold in chocolate mixture and egg whites and turn into a 2-quart dish. Beat remaining cream until stiff and serve as a topping. Garnish with chocolate curls.

Brown Sugar and Almond Bars

24 bars

- ½ **cup packed brown sugar**
- ⅔ **cup butter or margarine, softened**
- ½ **cup dark corn syrup**
- 1 **egg**
- 1 **teaspoon vanilla**
- 2 **cups flour**
- ¼ **teaspoon salt**
- ⅓ **cup packed brown sugar**
- ⅓ **cup dark corn syrup**
- 4 **tablespoons butter or margarine**
- ¼ **cup heavy cream**
- 1 **tablespoon vanilla**
- 1 **cup sliced almonds**

Mix ½ cup brown sugar, ⅔ cup butter, ½ cup syrup, egg and 1 teaspoon vanilla. Stir in flour and salt. Spread dough in a greased 9 x 12-inch baking pan. Bake at 350 degrees for 20 minutes or until golden brown.

To prepare topping, combine ⅓ cup sugar and ⅓ cup syrup in a saucepan over low heat, stirring constantly until sugar is dissolved. Add 4 tablespoons butter and ¼ cup cream; heat to boiling. Remove from heat. Add vanilla and nuts. Pour mixture over baked crust. Bake an additional 20 minutes or until set. Do not overbake. Cool and cut into bars.

Tower Grove Park, next door to the better-known Missouri Botanical Garden, was another generous gift to the city from the successful English-born businessman Henry Shaw. Inspired by gardens he had seen abroad, Shaw set out to create a Victorian walking park. First 10,000 trees were planted. Then inspirational statues, gingerbread pavilions, and even romantic ruins made from stones of the destroyed Lindell Hotel, were carefully placed throughout the grounds. Today, the magnificent bandstand is home to free concerts by the 60 piece Compton Heights Band where the music of John Philip Sousa, Gilbert and Sullivan and Broadway show tunes can be heard on warm summer evenings.

New Zealand Truffles

60 truffles

½ cup butter, softened
1 cup confectioners' sugar
⅔ cup flaked coconut
3 tablespoons cocoa
1 teaspoon vanilla
¼ cup flaked coconut
¼ cup finely chopped pistachio nuts

A delectable dose of chocolate.

In a bowl, combine the first 5 ingredients and blend well. Shape into small balls. Roll half the balls in coconut and half in the pistachios. Best when made in advance and chilled until ready to serve.

Truffles, because of their delicate nature, require special attention. They are most elegant when served chilled with expresso or cappuccino. Your guests will be flattered.

Brandied Truffles

60 truffles

1 12-ounce package semisweet chocolate chips
1 cup butter or margarine, cut into pieces
4 egg yolks
1½ cups sifted confectioners' sugar
2 teaspoons instant coffee
4 tablespoons brandy
2 teaspoons vanilla
chopped pecans or cocoa

In a saucepan, melt chocolate chips and butter. Beat egg yolks in a medium to large bowl. Add melted chocolate to egg yolks. Gradually stir in sugar. Dissolve coffee in brandy and add to chocolate mixture. Add vanilla and mix well. Chill until mixture can be shaped into balls. Roll in chopped pecans or cocoa. Chill until ready to serve. Can be frozen.

Chocolate Irish Whiskey Cake

Serves 10 to 12

1 18½-ounce chocolate cake
   mix with pudding
3 eggs
1 cup Irish whiskey, divided
½ cup cold water
⅓ cup vegetable oil
2 cups heavy cream
⅓ cup cocoa
½ cup confectioners' sugar
1 teaspoon vanilla

Chocolate and cream — leaves Irish eyes smiling.

In the bowl of an electric mixer, combine cake mix, eggs, ½ cup whiskey, water and oil. Blend and beat on medium speed 2 minutes. Pour into 2 greased and floured 9-inch round cake pans. Bake at 350 degrees for 30 minutes. Cool in pans 10 minutes. Remove from pans and cool on racks.

    To make frosting, stir together cream, cocoa, sugar and vanilla in a large bowl. Beat until stiff. Stir in remaining ½ cup whiskey. Split completely cooled cake layers in half. Spread frosting over layers, top and sides of cake. Chill well.

No Bake Chocolate Cookies

36 to 40 cookies

2 cups sugar
½ cup milk
½ cup cocoa
½ cup margarine
½ cup coconut
3 cups quick oats
1 teaspoon vanilla
   dash of salt

A hot summer night's dream — no oven.

In a saucepan, bring the first 3 ingredients to a boil and boil 1 minute. Add remaining ingredients; mix well. Drop cookies on waxed paper; let set 3 to 4 hours.

Orange Blossoms

120 cakes

1 18½-ounce yellow cake mix, prepared according to package directions
2 oranges
2 lemons
1 1-pound box confectioners' sugar, sifted

A zesty tea time treasure.

Fill miniature greased and floured muffin pans with 1 teaspoon of cake batter. Bake at 350 degrees for 8 to 10 minutes. Do not overbake. Cool and remove from pans. Grate and juice oranges and lemons. Combine juices, grated peels and sugar. Blend well. Dip cooled cakes in frosting and let harden on racks. Decorate with small sugar flowers.

Arrange on a pedestal cake plate and garnish with a sprig of mock orange or kumquat leaves.

Strawberry Grand Marnier Sherbet

Serves 8

6 cups fresh strawberries
2 cups sugar
1½ cups fresh orange juice
½ cup fresh lemon juice
¼ cup Grand Marnier
8 fresh strawberries with stems or orange and lemon slices

Wash and hull strawberries. Combine strawberries and next 3 ingredients in a blender, mixer or food processor. Blend well. Add Grand Marnier and blend. Freeze mixture. When frozen, remove and beat with an electric beater. Refreeze until ready to serve. Spoon into sherbet dishes and garnish with whole fresh strawberries or orange and lemon slices.

Lime Tartlets

Serves 16

Lime Curd:
- ½ cup unsalted butter, cut into pieces
- ½ cup sugar
- 2 tablespoons grated lime peel
- ⅓ cup fresh lime juice
- 2 eggs, slightly beaten

Tartlets:
- 2½ cups flour
- 1 teaspoon salt
- 1 teaspoon sugar
- 1 cup unsalted butter, cold and cut into pieces
- ¼-½ cup ice water

A delightful combination of citrus and pastry.

Lime Curd:
In a saucepan, combine the butter, sugar, lime peel, lime juice and eggs. Cook mixture over moderately low heat, stirring constantly until curd is thick enough to coat the back of a wooden spoon. Do not boil. Transfer curd to a bowl and cool. Cover the bowl with waxed paper and chill 1 hour.

Tartlets:
Place flour, salt and sugar in a food processor. Add cold pieces of butter and process until mixture resembles coarse meal. Add ice water slowly through feed tube until dough holds together. Turn dough onto plastic wrap. Flatten slightly, wrap and chill at least 1 hour. On a lightly floured surface, roll dough to ⅛-inch thickness. Spray 16 4½-inch oblong tart pans with nonstick vegetable spray. Cut dough to fit and press into tart pans. Prick the shells lightly with a fork and chill 1 hour. Line the shells with foil and place on a baking sheet. Bake at 375 degrees for 15 to 20 minutes. When pastry begins to color, remove foil and bake until done. Remove shells from tart pans and let cool completely on a rack. Fill each shell with 1 tablespoon of Lime Curd. Garnish with fresh fruit or mint leaves and pomegranate seeds.

The international tennis classic, the Davis Cup, was founded by Saint Louisan Dwight F. Davis in 1900. A former national doubles tennis champion and Saint Louis Parks Commissioner, Davis was a true advocate of athletics and outdoor sports. He was responsible for laying out baseball diamonds, tennis courts and golf courses in Forest Park. The Dwight F. Davis Tennis Center in the park is named in his honor.

Apricot Macadamia Cookies

20 to 24 cookies

> 2 **refrigerator pie crusts, unbaked**
> 6 **ounces dried apricots**
> ½ **cup macadamia nuts**
> ½ **cup sugar**
> 2 **tablespoons water**
> **flour**
> **milk**
> **sugar**

Let pie crusts stand at room temperature as directed on package. Finely chop the apricots and nuts in a food processor. In a saucepan, combine apricots, nuts, sugar and water and cook over low heat until thoroughly heated. Set aside and cool. Carefully unfold one pie crust on a lightly floured surface. Press fold lines. With a lightly floured rolling pin, roll crust to ⅛-inch thickness. Cut into 2½-inch rounds. Place rounds 1 inch apart on an ungreased baking sheet. Repeat procedure with second pie crust. Spoon apricot filling on one half of each round. Moisten edge with water. Fold in half and press edges to seal. Bake at 375 degrees for 7 minutes. Remove from oven; brush with milk and sprinkle with sugar. Bake an additional 2 to 4 minutes. Cool 1 minute and remove to a wire rack.

Norwegian Butter Cookies

40 cookies

> ½ **cup butter, softened**
> ¼ **cup sugar**
> 2 **hard cooked egg yolks**
> ½ **teaspoon lemon or vanilla extract**
> 1 **cup flour**
> **assorted nuts or cherries**

In a bowl, cream butter, sugar and egg yolks which have been pressed through a sieve. Add lemon extract. Mix in flour and roll dough into ½-inch balls. If dough is hard to handle, chill well. Place on a cookie sheet and press a cherry or nut in the center of each cookie. Bake at 375 degrees for 10 minutes.

Snowballs

144 snowballs

- **1 angel food cake**
- **1 cup milk**
- **1 tablespoon flour**
- **½ cup butter, softened**
- **½ cup vegetable shortening**
- **1 cup sugar**
- **1 teaspoon vanilla**
- **28 ounces flaked coconut**

Here's one for the cookie exchanges!

Slice cake and remove brown pieces. Cut into 1-inch cubes and set aside. Place milk in a saucepan over low heat. Whisk in flour and cook until thickened. Set aside to cool.

With an electric mixer, cream butter and shortening. Add sugar and beat well. Add flour and milk mixture and beat to blend. Add vanilla and blend well. Place coconut in a shallow bowl. Swirl cake cubes in soft mixture and roll in coconut. Store in a tightly covered container. Keeps up to 3 weeks chilled.

A luscious dessert made irresistible — pile high and top with a flurry of Bittersweet Sauce.

Devastating Brownies

24 brownies

- **4 squares unsweetened chocolate**
- **1 cup butter or margarine**
- **2 cups sugar**
- **4 eggs**
- **2 teaspoons vanilla**
- **1 cup flour**
- **pinch of salt**
- **1 12-ounce package semisweet chocolate chips**
- **2 cups miniature marshmallows**

Melt unsweetened chocolate and butter together. Add sugar. Cool mixture. Add eggs, beating well, one at a time. Add vanilla, flour and salt; mix until well blended. Fold in chocolate chips and marshmallows. Pour into a greased 9 x 13-inch baking pan. Bake at 350 degrees for 30 to 35 minutes. Do not overbake. The top may look bubbly. Dust very well with powdered sugar. Best if made a day in advance and allowed to stand overnight. Can be frozen.

Once you eat these brownies, no other brownie will be chocolatey or delicious enough. Don't try to eat them right away; they are too gooey.

Chocolate Almond Cheesecake

Serves 12

1¼ cups graham cracker crumbs

¼ cup packed brown sugar

¼ cup slivered almonds

⅓ cup butter, melted

1 6-ounce package semisweet chocolate chips

16 ounces cream cheese, softened

½ cup packed brown sugar

¼ teaspoon salt

1 teaspoon vanilla

2 eggs, separated
  few drops of almond extract

¼ cup packed brown sugar

1 cup whipping cream
  almond slices
  whipped cream

Combine first 4 ingredients. Press in bottom of a greased 9-inch springform pan. Bake at 300 degrees for 10 minutes. Cool.

Melt chocolate. Mix thoroughly with softened cream cheese, ½ cup brown sugar, salt, vanilla, egg yolks and almond extract. In a separate bowl, beat egg whites until smooth. Slowly add ¼ cup brown sugar and beat until very stiff. Beat 1 cup whipping cream until stiff. Carefully fold egg whites and cream into chocolate mixture. Pour into baked crust and chill for several hours. Remove sides of pan. Garnish with almond slices and whipped cream.

The mousse-like texture is enhanced by chocolate and almonds.

239

Black Sin Gâteau

Serves 20

1 **cup unsalted butter, cut into ½-inch cubes**

8 **ounces bittersweet chocolate, broken**

4 **ounces semisweet chocolate, broken (do not use chocolate chips)**

5 **large eggs at room temperature**

1 **cup sugar, divided**

2 **teaspoons vanilla pinch of salt**

⅓ **cup light corn syrup**

The name says it all.

In a double boiler over warm water, melt butter and chocolates, stirring constantly until melted. Remove from heat. Cool 5 to 10 minutes. In the large bowl of an electric mixer beat eggs, ½ cup sugar, vanilla and salt on medium high 8 to 10 minutes, until volume is tripled. In a saucepan, combine remaining ½ cup sugar and corn syrup. Stir constantly over medium heat, bringing mixture to a full boil. Resume beating the egg mixture on medium high. Very slowly add the syrup mixture in a slow, steady stream. On a lower speed, blend in the chocolate mixture.

Lightly butter the bottom and sides of a 9 or 10-inch springform pan. Line the bottom with waxed paper. Securely wrap the outside with heavy duty aluminum foil. Pour batter into pan and smooth the top. Place springform pan in a shallow roasting pan and fill with 1 inch of hot water. Bake in center of oven at 350 degrees for 40 to 45 minutes; do not overbake. Remove springform pan from water and cool 30 minutes. Invert cake onto a serving plate; remove waxed paper. Chill.

This sinful dessert warrants a worthy garnish. The possibilities are endless — Chambord whipped cream arranged to interact with garden fresh, ruby red raspberries; individual servings on a delicate dessert plate sauced with stark white chocolate sauce and piped with Bittersweet Sauce; an edible violet fantasy interspersed with strawberries and mounds of Grand Marnier whipped cream.

Gingerbread Cake

Serves 12

A sweet aroma fills the air with holiday spirit.

Cake:

- ½ cup butter
- 1 cup sugar
- 1 cup dark molasses
- 2 egg yolks, beaten
- 3 cups cake flour
- 1 teaspoon salt
- 1 teaspoon baking soda
- 2 teaspoons ground ginger
- 2 teaspoons ground cinnamon
- 1 cup buttermilk
- 2 egg whites, stiffly beaten
  Hard Sauce

Hard Sauce:

- ½ cup butter, softened
- 1½ cups sifted confectioners' sugar
- 1 egg yolk
- 2 teaspoons grated lemon peel
- 1 egg white, stiffly beaten

Cake:
In a bowl, cream butter; add sugar and cream and beat until light and smooth. Add molasses and egg yolks and mix thoroughly. Sift flour; measure. Sift flour again with salt, soda and spices. Add flour mixture alternately with buttermilk to molasses mixture. Fold in egg whites. Turn batter into a greased and floured 9-inch tube pan. Bake at 350 degrees for 30 to 40 minutes. Serve hot with Hard Sauce.

Hard Sauce:
In a bowl, cream butter and sugar. Add egg yolk, beating constantly. Blend in lemon peel. Fold in egg white; chill.

Pumpkin Cupcakes

24 cupcakes

Cupcakes:

2 **cups sugar**

1 **cup vegetable oil**

4 **eggs**

2 **cups flour**

1 **tablespoon pumpkin pie spice**

2 **teaspoons baking soda**

1½ **cups canned pumpkin**

Frosting:

8 **ounces cream cheese, softened**

3 **tablespoons margarine, softened**

2 **teaspoons vanilla**

2½ **cups sifted confectioners' sugar**

Cupcakes:
In the large bowl of an electric mixer, combine sugar and oil; add eggs and continue beating. Add the next 4 ingredients and mix well. Pour batter into a cupcake pan that has been greased or lined with cupcake papers. Bake at 350 degrees for 25 to 30 minutes. Let cool completely. Freezes very well.

Frosting:
In a bowl, blend cream cheese and margarine. Add vanilla and sugar and mix well. Frost cooled cupcakes.

Use Halloween or Thanksgiving cupcake liners. Top with a cluster of roasted pumpkin seeds.

In 1873, Susan Elizabeth Blow founded the first public kindergarten in the United States, at the Des Peres School in Saint Louis, with sixty-eight students. Based on the German model, kindergarten was designed to help ease the transition from home to school. Although punctuality, obedience and silence were among the lessons emphasized, the children were also encouraged to learn through "directed play" . . . a radical concept at the time . . . using blocks, modeling clay and drawing to develop specific skills.

Amaretto Butter Squares

40 squares

  1 cup butter, softened
  1 cup sugar
  1 egg, separated
  1½ tablespoons amaretto or
      ½ teaspoon almond extract
  2 teaspoons grated orange peel
  ¼ teaspoon salt
  2 cups flour
  ¾ cup sliced almonds

Melts in your mouth.

In a large mixing bowl, beat butter with sugar 3 minutes until light and creamy. Add egg yolk, amaretto, orange peel and salt; beat until well blended. Stir in flour and blend again. Spread and pat dough evenly into a 12 x 15-inch jelly roll pan. In a small bowl, beat egg white until foamy; brush evenly over dough. Sprinkle with almonds. Bake at 300 degrees for 40 to 45 minutes, or until light golden. Cut into 2-inch squares while still warm. Transfer to a rack to cool. Can be frozen.

Keep these in your freezer to have on hand when you need a sweet for ice cream or coffee.

Kirsch Butter Cream

4 cups butter cream

  ¾ cup butter, softened
  ½ cup vegetable shortening
  ¼ teaspoon vanilla
  5-6 cups sifted confectioners'
      sugar
  1 egg white
  2 ounces kirschwasser
      (cherry brandy)
      heavy cream

Cream butter and shortening. Add vanilla. Slowly add confectioners' sugar. When sugar is combined, add the egg white, then kirschwasser. Adjust consistency by adding additional sugar or heavy cream.

A delightful frosting for a special cake or an ordinary cake that you want to make special. It can also be used as a base for a fruit tart.

Fresh Apple Cake with Hot Rum Sauce

Serves 12

Apple Cake:

  2 **cups sugar**
  ½ **cup vegetable shortening**
  2 **eggs**
  1 **teaspoon vanilla**
  2 **cups flour**
1½ **teaspoons baking soda**
  ½ **teaspoon baking powder**
  ½ **teaspoon salt**
  1 **teaspoon cinnamon**
  ½ **teaspoon nutmeg**
  4 **cups peeled, chopped apples**
  1 **cup chopped walnuts (optional)**

Rum Sauce:

  ½ **cup sugar**
  ½ **cup brown sugar**
  4 **tablespoons butter**
  ½ **cup cream**
    pinch of salt
  1 **teaspoon rum flavoring**

Butterscotch Bars

16 bars

  6 **tablespoons butter**
  1 **cup packed brown sugar**
  1 **egg**
  1 **teaspoon vanilla**
  1 **teaspoon baking powder**
  ¾ **cup flour**
  1 **cup walnuts, chopped**

A divine rum sauce sets this cake apart.

Apple Cake:
Cream together sugar and shortening; beat in eggs and vanilla. Sift together flour, baking soda, baking powder, salt, cinnamon and nutmeg. Add dry ingredients to creamed mixture. Add apples and nuts and stir well. Pour into a greased 9 x 13-inch baking pan. Bake at 350 degrees for 45 minutes.

Rum Sauce:
In a saucepan, cook sugars, butter and cream until thickened. Add salt and rum flavoring. Spoon sauce over warm cake.

In a heavy saucepan, melt butter and brown sugar over low heat. Stir and cool slightly. Add the egg, vanilla, baking powder and flour; stir until thoroughly mixed. Add nuts. Pour into a 9 x 9-inch baking pan. Bake at 350 degrees for 35 to 40 minutes. Cool and cut into bars.

White Chocolate Mousse with Raspberry Sauce

Serves 4

Mousse:

> 4 ounces white chocolate
>
> 2 tablespoons plus ½ teaspoon warm milk
>
> 1 egg white
> few drops of lemon juice
> pinch of salt
>
> ½ cup whipping cream, beaten until stiff
> dark chocolate shavings

Raspberry Sauce:

> 1 10-ounce package frozen raspberries, thawed
>
> ¾ teaspoon cornstarch
>
> 2 tablespoons sugar
>
> 1 teaspoon fresh lemon juice
>
> 2 teaspoons light rum or brandy, or liqueur of choice

Mousse:
Melt chocolate in top of a double boiler. Add milk and stir until smooth. Cool to room temperature. Beat egg white with lemon juice and salt until it forms stiff peaks. Fold egg white into chocolate. Fold in whipped cream. Spoon into individual molds or small dishes suitable for unmolding. *Refrigerate overnight.* Unmold onto chilled plates. Garnish with shaved chocolate. Surround with Raspberry Sauce.

Raspberry Sauce:
Place raspberries and liquid in a saucepan. Add cornstarch; bring to a slow boil over medium heat while stirring. Let the sauce thicken, stirring frequently. Add sugar. Simmer 5 minutes, stirring frequently. Press mixture through a strainer into a bowl. Pour into a blender and add lemon juice and liqueur. Blend until smooth. Yields 1 cup.

Equally delicious served with Bittersweet Sauce.

Bittersweet Sauce

1 cup sauce

> 8 ounces bittersweet chocolate
>
> ½ cup whipping cream or light cream

In a heavy saucepan, melt chocolate over low heat. Cool slightly; stir in cream. Serve the sauce warm or cover and chill. Warm chilled sauce to serve.

Rum Raisin Apple Pie

Serves 8

- ⅓ **cup raisins**
- 2 **tablespoons dark rum pastry dough for double crust 9-inch pie**
- ½ **cup packed light brown sugar**
- 3 **tablespoons flour**
- ¾ **teaspoon ground cinnamon**
- ¼ **teaspoon freshly grated nutmeg**
- ¼ **teaspoon grated lemon peel**
- ¼ **teaspoon salt**
- 2½ **pounds Golden Delicious apples, peeled and cored**
- 2 **teaspoons fresh lemon juice**
- ¾ **cup chopped pecans**
- 2 **tablespoons cold unsalted butter, cut into pieces**
- 1 **tablespoon milk**
- 1½ **teaspoons sugar vanilla ice cream**

In a small saucepan, combine raisins and rum. Bring to a simmer over moderate heat. Quickly remove from heat. Let stand 15 minutes or until rum is absorbed.

On a lightly floured surface, roll out one half of the dough and place in a 9-inch pie plate, leaving a ½-inch overhang. Chill while preparing filling.

In a large bowl, combine brown sugar, flour, cinnamon, nutmeg, lemon peel and salt. Thinly slice apples and add to brown sugar mixture. Add raisins and lemon juice. Stir well. Roll out remaining dough. Mound apple mixture in chilled pie shell and sprinkle with pecans. Dot with butter. Cover with dough. Fold top crust over bottom crust overhang and crimp edges. Cut several decorative steam vents. Brush with milk and sprinkle with sugar. Bake at 425 degrees for 30 minutes. Reduce to 375 degrees and bake an additional 20 to 25 minutes or until apples are tender. Let cool on a rack. Serve warm or at room temperature with ice cream.

Bread Pudding with Whiskey Sauce

Serves 8 to 10

1 **loaf French bread**

4 **cups milk**

3 **eggs, slightly beaten**

2 **cups sugar**

2 **tablespoons vanilla**

1 **cup raisins**

3 **tablespoons butter, melted**

½ **cup butter or margarine**

1 **cup sugar**

1 **egg, well beaten**

2 **tablespoons cream or milk**
  whiskey to taste

In a large bowl, soak bread in milk. When bread is saturated, mash with hands until well mixed. Add eggs, sugar, vanilla and raisins; stir well. Coat an 8 x 10-inch baking pan with melted butter. Pour batter into pan. Bake at 350 degrees for 45 to 60 minutes until very firm. Let cool.

To prepare Whiskey Sauce, melt butter in a double boiler and stir in sugar. Heat until very hot and sugar is dissolved. Quickly whisk beaten egg into sugar and butter mixture. Add cream and whiskey to taste.

To serve, cut pudding into squares and place on individual serving plates. Top with sauce and heat under broiler until bubbly. Pudding can be made in advance. Before serving, top with Whiskey Sauce and heat in microwave.

Known as the Old Cathedral, "The Basilica of Saint Louis, King of France," was completed in 1834 and is the oldest cathedral west of the Mississippi. Its clean Greek Revival lines and plain construction stand in marked contrast to the ornate splendor of the New Cathedral located in the Central West End. The New Cathedral's splendid interior domes are covered with mosaics that are considered some of the finest in the world. Covering over an acre of square footage, the installation of these mosaics spanned a period of more than 56 years.

GATEWAYS
TO EATING
FOR HEALTH
&
FITNESS

Eating for Health and Fitness

Welcome to the 1990's. Americans are looking more closely at the relationship of good nutrition to health and fitness.

We are aware of the effects of exercise on our cardiovascular system as well as our muscle tone. We are watching our fat and cholesterol intake, eating more vegetables and whole grains and limiting our salt intake. Moderation is the name of the game.

We are paying attention to information, of which there is much, on the relationship of healthy diets and exercise to the prevention and cure of disease.

Our goal with this section is to present ideas, suggestions and recipes that make enjoyable the benefits of eating well. We do not intend to discuss good versus bad cholesterol or the technical aspects of nutrition. That information is readily accessible and, it seems, subject to change.

We believe that light cooking is a state of mind. We are convinced it is possible to enjoy good cuisine while lowering caloric and fat contents. By blending a few low calorie, low fat commercial products with creative imagination, you can offer glamorous, gourmet menus.

To aid the quest for healthy eating, your inventory should include the following items:

Low salt chicken broth. Lower salt versions can be purchased, but we suggest making your own, omitting the salt. Freeze broth in ice cube trays and store in an airtight container. Just pop a cube out of the freezer to sauté or cook vegetables or to flavor your favorite rice.

Nonfat yogurt. There are only 55 calories in $\frac{1}{2}$ cup nonfat yogurt. Use it as a base for sauces, creams and dips. With a touch of flavored mustard, it makes an excellent sandwich spread. Add chives or herbs for a light topping on baked potatoes. For Yogurt Cheese, a thicker creamier yogurt, line a strainer with cheesecloth and fill with yogurt. Cover with plastic wrap and chill 12 hours. Store and use as you would commercial yogurt.

Mustards. Select a variety to keep on hand, including sweet, hot and champagne. A small amount of mustard will add a large amount of flavor to many recipes.

Vinegars. Keep an assortment of vinegars on the pantry shelf. Raspberry, tarragon, rice, wine, fine herbs, basil and garlic are some of our favorites. Sprinkle on salad greens, vegetables or use on meats and fish to avoid oil rich marinades.

Herbs. Both fresh or dried can add real flavor to meats and vegetables and significantly reduce the salt in your diet.

Lemon juice. Frozen lemon juice is a timesaving product. It adds zest to poultry, fish and fresh vegetables. For a quick, refreshing Summertime Cooler, combine ¼ cup lemon juice, 4 packets Equal® and ¾ cup water. Serve over ice garnished with a lemon slice.

Artificially sweetened gelatins, pudding mixes and Equal® sweetener. These are invaluable to those watching their sugar intake. They give a sweetness that otherwise might be forsaken. Equal® can be added to recipes after cooking. We suggest these ways to sweeten cooked or baked foods:

Substitute Equal® for sugar when preparing no bake graham cracker crusts or no bake cookies.

Sprinkle warm muffins, breads, and oven baked fruits with Equal® or a combination of Equal® and cinnamon.

Dissolve 24 packets of Equal® in ¼ cup boiling water. Drizzle glaze over unsweetened pies, tarts or baked fruits. Another idea is to pour the glaze over plain cakes that have been pricked with a fork at 1-inch intervals.

Egg substitutes. Can be used in most recipes quite successfully in place of whole eggs. There are several on the market or make your own by combining 1 egg white, 2¼ teaspoons nonfat dry milk, 2 teaspoons safflower oil and a few drops of yellow food coloring. Two tablespoons of this mixture equal 1 egg. In recipes, 2 egg whites can also be substituted for 1 egg, eliminating the cholesterol-laden yolk.

Reduced calorie salad dressing. Add to Yogurt Cheese for a delicious low fat sandwich spread. Can also be used as a marinade for meats and seafood.

Natural flavored seltzer waters. These no calorie, no salt, naturally flavored beverages are a pleasant substitute to an evening cocktail and a refreshing replacement for higher sodium diet drinks.

Reduced fat dairy products. Sour half and half, light cream cheese, light mayonnaise, reduced calorie margarine and evaporated skim milk are products that lower fat content without sacrificing flavor.

The following recipes have been created specifically by cooks who are eating lighter. The nutritional analyses and exchanges give approximate values. We offer this gateway as an entrée to your good health and fitness.

Equal® Sweetener and NutraSweet® Brand Sweetener are registered trademarks of the NutraSweet Company.

Berry Best Breakfast

Serves 6

¾ **cup bulgur wheat**
¾ **teaspoon ground cinnamon**
   dash of ground nutmeg
1 **cup fresh orange juice**
¼ **teaspoon grated orange peel**
2 **cups fresh blueberries**
2 **small peaches, peeled and sliced**
⅓ **cup broken walnuts**
1 **cup low fat yogurt**
2 **tablespoons honey**
1 **teaspoon vanilla**

What a way to start the day!

In a large bowl, stir together bulgur wheat, cinnamon and nutmeg. In a small saucepan, combine orange juice and peel. Bring to a boil and pour over wheat mixture. Stir, cover and let stand 30 minutes until juice is absorbed and mixture is completely cooled. Fold in fruits and nuts. In a small bowl, combine yogurt, honey and vanilla. Serve over wheat and fruit mixture.

Bulgur wheat is cracked wheat that has been hulled, steamed and dried. Increasingly popular, it is known for its lightness and nutty flavor.

Per serving:
224 calories
6.3 gm protein
41 gm carbohydrates
5 gm fat
1.4 gm fiber
2.3 mg cholesterol
30 mg sodium
Exchanges: milk .5, fruit 2, bread 1, fat 1

A year before the United States was to go to war in 1812, the Saint Louis area experienced devastation of a different sort. In the early morning hours of December 16, 1811, the residents of nearby New Madrid found themselves being shaken by a violent earthquake. The quake was the strongest ever experienced in this country, even surpassing the famous San Francisco jolts. The Mississippi River rose and fell pulling down groves of trees and wiping out small islands. The waters even reversed direction flowing north instead of south and the course of the river was permanently altered.

252

Apple Waldorf Salad

Serves 4

- 1 **Granny Smith apple**
- 1 **Red Delicious apple**
- 1 **tablespoon fresh lemon juice**
- ½ **cup chopped celery**
- 1 **tablespoon pecan halves**
- ¼ **cup nonfat yogurt**
  dash of ground cinnamon
  dash of freshly grated nutmeg
- 4 **purple cabbage leaves**

Be Good to Your Heart Salad

Serves 6

- 1 **pound fresh spinach**
- 1 **cup sliced and quartered fresh strawberries**
- ¼ **pound fresh bean sprouts**
- 1 **cup seedless grapes, halved**
- 1 **cup vegetable oil**
- ¾ **cup sugar**
- ⅓ **cup white vinegar**
- 1 **small onion, minced**
- 1 **teaspoon salt**
- 1 **teaspoon Worcestershire sauce**

A luscious low calorie salad.

Chop unpeeled apples and sprinkle with lemon juice. Add celery, pecans, yogurt and spices. Serve on purple cabbage leaf.

Per serving:
62 calories
1 gm protein
13 gm carbohydrates
1.4 gm fat
.6 gm fiber
.25 mg cholesterol
169 mg sodium
Exchanges: milk .1, fruit 1, fat .3

Wash spinach thoroughly; drain and pat dry. Remove tough stems. Break into bite size pieces and place in a large salad bowl. Add strawberries, bean sprouts and grapes. Toss gently. Combine remaining ingredients in a small bowl. Whisk to blend well. Toss with salad and serve immediately.

Salad per serving:
51 calories
3.1 gm protein
11.6 gm carbohydrates
.5 gm fat
1.2 gm fiber
0 mg cholesterol
62.5 mg sodium
Exchanges: 1 fruit, .5 vegetable

Dressing per tablespoon:
105 calories
0 gm protein
6.5 gm carbohydrates
9 gm fat
0 gm fiber
0 mg cholesterol
84 mg sodium
Exchanges: .5 fruit, 2 fat

Champagne Chicken Salad

Serves 4

1 pound boneless, skinless chicken breasts, cooked and cubed

2 green onions, tops and bottoms, sliced

2 tablespoons coarsely chopped pecans

2 cups hulled and quartered strawberries

½ cup nonfat yogurt

2 tablespoons champagne mustard

Combine all ingredients and chill for at least half an hour. Serve on a bed of greens.

Per serving:
341 calories
56 gm protein
6 gm carbohydrates
9 gm fat
.3 gm fiber
146 mg cholesterol
250 mg sodium
Exchanges: milk 0.2, vegetable 0.2, fruit 0.2, meat 4.0, fat 0.5

Lemon Sauce

Serves 6

⅔ cup light mayonnaise

1 tablespoon minced chives

1 tablespoon prepared horseradish

1 tablespoon Dijon mustard

2 tablespoons fresh lemon juice

A versatile light sauce.

Combine all ingredients and mix thoroughly. Serve with vegetables or seafood.

For a special salad, serve with Belgian endive and asparagus.

Per serving:
75 calories
2 gm protein
2.5 gm carbohydrates
7.2 gm fat
0.0 fiber
9 mg cholesterol
61 mg sodium
Exchanges: fruit 3, fat 1.4

Toasted Cauliflower

Serves 8

1 **head cauliflower**
3 **tablespoons margarine, melted**
½ **teaspoon garlic powder**
   freshly ground pepper
½ **teaspoon salt**

A light crunchy appetizer.

Break cauliflower into bite size pieces. Place on a baking sheet and brush each piece with margarine. Dust with garlic powder and pepper. Broil 10 minutes until cauliflower appears toasted. Sprinkle with salt. Serve with toothpicks.

Per serving:
 72 calories
  3 gm protein
  7 gm carbohydrates
 4.5 gm fat
 1.2 gm fiber
   0 mg cholesterol
 193 mg sodium
Exchanges: vegetable 1.4, fat .9

Grilled Tuna

Serves 6

8 **ounces low calorie Italian salad dressing**
2 **pounds tuna steaks**
4 **tablespoons teriyaki sauce**
1 **teaspoon garlic powder**
1 **teaspoon salt free seasoning**
6 **green onions, diced**
¼ **cup dry sherry**
   freshly ground pepper to taste

Pour salad dressing in a 9 x 13-inch glass baking dish. Place tuna in baking dish. Cover tuna with remaining ingredients. Marinate at least 3 hours, turning tuna after 2 hours. Grill tuna 15 minutes or until tender. Watch closely as tuna cooks quickly.

A wire fish basket is a worthwhile tool when grilling seafood. It eliminates the problems of fish sticking to the grill or falling apart.

Per serving:
220 calories
  38 gm protein
   5 gm carbohydrates
11.2 gm fat
  .1 gm fiber
  61 mg cholesterol
696 mg sodium
 Exchanges: vegetable .5, meat 5, fat 4

Swordfish Tandoori

Serves 4

2 tablespoons plain low fat yogurt
1 scallion, minced
1 small clove garlic, minced
1 tablespoon minced cilantro leaves
¼ teaspoon grated lime peel
¼ teaspoon minced fresh ginger
⅛ teaspoon salt
⅛ teaspoon freshly ground pepper
   pinch of ground cumin
   pinch of dried red pepper flakes
1 pound swordfish steaks, 1-inch thick
   lime slices or wedges

In a small bowl, mix all ingredients except swordfish steaks and lime slices. Place swordfish in a microwave safe dish. Spread sauce over fish. Cover dish with plastic wrap, leaving 1 side open for venting. Microwave on high 3 to 4 minutes, rotating plate halfway through cooking time. Transfer to serving plates and garnish with lime. Serve immediately.

This recipe also works well with halibut or salmon steaks.

Per serving:
208 calories
* 32 gm protein*
* .5 gm carbohydrates*
6.5 gm fat
* .5 gm fiber*
* 4 mg cholesterol*
12 mg sodium
Exchanges: meat 4.5

Honey Crunch Chicken

Serves 4

2 chicken breasts, halved, boned and skinned
2 tablespoons light mayonnaise
2 tablespoons nonfat yogurt
1½ ounces grape-nut cereal, crushed
1 tablespoon honey
   salt to taste (optional)

Wash chicken and pat dry. Place in a shallow baking dish. Combine mayonnaise and yogurt. Cover both sides of chicken with mayonnaise mixture. Process cereal in a blender or food processor to crush. Sprinkle crushed cereal evenly over chicken. Salt to taste. Drizzle evenly with honey. Bake, uncovered, at 350 degrees for 40 to 45 minutes.

Per serving:
220 calories
* 28 gm protein*
* 14 gm carbohydrate*
5.1 gm fat
* .2 gm fiber*
* 75 mg cholesterol*
142 mg sodium
Exchanges: bread .6, meat 3.8, fat .04

Low Calorie Chicken Dijon

Serves 2

2 **chicken breast halves, skinned**

¼ **teaspoon freshly ground pepper**

4 **teaspoons reduced calorie margarine, melted**

1 **tablespoon Dijon mustard**

1 **teaspoon dried parsley flakes**

¼ **teaspoon dried rosemary, crushed**

¼ **teaspoon paprika**

¼ **teaspoon dried thyme**

Place chicken in a shallow baking dish that has been sprayed with nonstick vegetable spray. In a small bowl, combine remaining ingredients. Mix well and spread over chicken. Cover and bake at 350 degrees for 30 minutes. Remove cover, baste chicken and bake 15 additional minutes.

Per serving:
184 calories
25.8 gm protein
1.8 gm carbohydrates
9.2 gm fat
.1 gm fiber
73 mg cholesterol
185 mg sodium
Exchanges: meat 3.8, fat 0.8

Slim Chicken Yogurt

Serves 6

3 **pounds chicken breasts, skinned**

2 **tablespoons fresh lemon juice**
salt and freshly ground pepper (optional)

½ **cup nonfat yogurt**

¼ **cup light mayonnaise**

1 **tablespoon Dijon mustard**

1 **tablespoon Worcestershire sauce**

½ **teaspoon dried thyme**

¼ **teaspoon cayenne pepper**

½ **cup grated onion**

½ **cup freshly grated Parmesan cheese**

Place chicken in a baking dish. Drizzle with lemon juice. Sprinkle with salt and pepper. In a bowl, blend yogurt, mayonnaise, mustard, Worcestershire sauce, thyme, cayenne pepper and onion. Spread over chicken. Bake, uncovered, at 350 degrees for 50 minutes. Sprinkle with cheese and broil until melted.

Per serving:
272 calories
40 gm protein
3.6 gm carbohydrates
10 gm fat
0.03 gm fiber
107 mg cholesterol
345 mg sodium
Exchanges: meat 5.6, fat 1.0

Poulet au Citron

Serves 8

4 **tablespoons margarine, divided**

4 **chicken breasts, halved, boned and skinned**

  grated peel of 2 lemons

  juice of 2 lemons

1 **teaspoon salt**

  freshly ground pepper to taste

2 **tablespoons chopped fresh parsley**

2 **tablespoons chopped fresh chives**

1 **teaspoon dried marjoram**

2 **tablespoons paprika**

1 **cup chicken broth**

¼ **cup white vermouth**

2 **tablespoons cornstarch**

3 **tablespoons cold water**

  watercress sprigs

  lemon peel spirals

In a large skillet, melt 2 tablespoons margarine and brown chicken until golden. Transfer to a baking dish. Sprinkle with lemon peel, lemon juice, salt and pepper. Bake, covered, at 350 degrees for 45 minutes. Uncover and add parsley, chives, marjoram and paprika. Dot with 2 tablespoons margarine. Broil 5 minutes until crisp. Remove chicken to a serving platter and keep warm.

Pour baking dish liquids into a saucepan. Add chicken broth and vermouth. Bring to a boil. Dissolve cornstarch in cold water and add to saucepan. Simmer 2 minutes. Pour over chicken and serve immediately. Garnish with watercress and lemon peel spirals.

Per serving:
254 calories
71 gm protein
4 gm carbohydrates
16 gm fat
0 gm fiber
193 mg cholesterol
331 mg sodium
Exchanges: fruit .3, meat 6, fat 1.5

Low Cholesterol Turkey Breast

Serves 8

1   **3-pound turkey breast, skinned**
    light olive oil
    salt free seasoning
    garlic powder
4   **carrots, peeled and sliced into thirds**
1   **large green pepper, sliced**
2   **ribs celery, sliced into thirds**
1   **red onion, quartered**
2   **potatoes, quartered**
3   **zucchini, sliced**
¼   **pound green beans**

Place turkey in a roasting pan. Rub generously with olive oil. Sprinkle with salt free seasoning and garlic powder to taste. Bake, uncovered, at 400 degrees for 1 hour or until crispy brown. Place vegetables around the turkey and sprinkle them with a small amount of olive oil and seasonings. Cover well with aluminum foil. Bake an additional 1½ hours.

Per serving:
342 calories
54 gm protein
23 gm carbohydrates
21 gm fat
1.5 gm fiber
111 mg cholesterol
118 mg sodium
Exchanges: meat 7, fat .5

Vegetarian Spaghetti

Serves 4

6   **green onions, sliced, including tops**
1½   **cups sliced mushrooms**
1   **green pepper, cut into strips**
1   **head of cauliflower, broken into florets**
2-3   **tablespoons low cholesterol margarine**
3-4   **medium zucchini, sliced into 2-inch diagonal strips**
3   **medium tomatoes, cut into wedges**
2   **8-ounce cans no salt added tomato sauce**
    freshly ground pepper to taste
1   **8-ounce package thin spaghetti, cooked until al dente**
2   **tablespoons freshly grated Parmesan cheese**

In a large saucepan, sauté onions, mushrooms, green pepper and cauliflower in margarine 4 to 5 minutes. Add zucchini and tomatoes; sauté an additional 2 minutes. Add tomato sauce and pepper. Cook 2 to 3 minutes. Pour over pasta and sprinkle with Parmesan cheese.

Per serving:
373 calories
15 gm protein
58 gm carbohydrates
11 gm fat
3 gm fiber
2.5 mg cholesterol
221 mg sodium
Exchanges: vegetable 2.9, bread 2.9, fat 2.0

Fettuccine in Light Alfredo Sauce

Serves 6

1 pound fettuccine

2 packages powdered butter flavor mix dissolved in 1 cup hot water, divided

1½ cups freshly grated Parmesan cheese, divided

1 cup evaporated skim milk, divided

1 cup hot liquid reserved from cooking pasta

salt and freshly ground pepper to taste

Cook fettuccine in boiling water until al dente. Drain fettuccine, reserving 1 cup of the liquid. Return pasta to pan over low heat. Immediately add one half of the butter flavor mixture, cheese and milk and a few tablespoons of the cooking liquid. Add salt and pepper. Toss gently to mix well. Repeat the process, adding remaining half of butter flavor mixture, cheese and milk. Toss again. If mixture is too thick, thin it with some of the cooking liquid. Preheat the serving dish; this must be served hot.

Per serving:
310 calories
20 gm protein
46 gm carbohydrates
8.5 gm fat
.13 gm fiber
21 mg cholesterol
586 mg sodium
Exchanges: milk .4, bread 2.6, meat 1.7, fat .7

Vegetables with Linguini

Serves 6

- 1 medium yellow squash
- 1 medium zucchini
- 1 medium red pepper
- 2 tablespoons olive oil
- 1½ cups sliced fresh mushrooms
- 3 cloves garlic, minced
- ¼ cup dry white wine
- ¼ teaspoon salt
- ¼ teaspoon dried basil, crushed
- ¼ teaspoon dried tarragon, crushed
- ¼ teaspoon crushed red pepper
- 6 ounces linguini
- ¼ cup freshly grated Parmesan cheese

Colorful and healthy side dish.

Slice yellow squash and zucchini lengthwise into ¼-inch slices, then slice into very thin horizontal strips. Slice red pepper into thin strips. Heat olive oil in a large skillet over high heat. Add squash, zucchini, red pepper, mushrooms and garlic. Stir-fry 2 to 3 minutes until vegetables are crisp tender. Combine white wine, salt, basil, tarragon and crushed red pepper. (If the vegetable mixture has created juice, add a mixture of a little cornstarch and water to vegetable mixture to thicken.) Drizzle wine and herb mixture over vegetables. Toss to coat and heat thoroughly. Cook linguini according to package directions. Drain, return to pan and add cooked vegetable mixture. Serve on a large platter. Sprinkle with Parmesan cheese.

Per serving:
130 calories
4.8 gm protein
13.5 gm carbohydrates
6 gm fat
.75 gm fiber
3.2 mg cholesterol
163 mg sodium
Exchanges: vegetable 1, bread 1, fat 1

No Egg Lower Cholesterol Cheesecake

Serves 12

1¼ **cups graham cracker crumbs**
 3 **tablespoons sugar**
⅓ **cup margarine, softened**
24 **ounces light cream cheese**
1½ **cups sugar**
 4 **teaspoons vanilla**
 2 **teaspoons fresh lemon juice**
 2 **cups sour half and half**
 7 **tablespoons sugar**
 2 **teaspoons vanilla**

Wickedly delicious.

Combine graham cracker crumbs, 3 tablespoons sugar and margarine. Pat into bottom of a springform pan. Combine cream cheese, 1½ cups sugar, vanilla and lemon juice and beat 5 minutes or until frothy and light. Spread over crust. Cake will settle during baking. Bake at 350 degrees for 15 to 20 minutes or until firmly set. Cool. Blend remaining ingredients and pour over cooled cheesecake. Bake at 350 degrees for 10 minutes. Chill 5 hours or until thoroughly cooled. Keep chilled until ready to serve.

Can also be made in individual servings. Line muffin cups with foil and prepare as directed. Individual servings can be frozen and served without thawing.

Per serving:
222 calories
*   7 gm protein*
* 13 gm carbohydrates*
15.5 gm fat
*   1 gm fiber*
* 51 mg cholesterol*
288 mg sodium
Exchanges: fruit .5, bread .4, fat 3.3

Cappuccino Cream

Serves 7

1 **envelope unflavored gelatin**

6 **tablespoons sugar**

2 **cups skim milk**

2 **eggs, separated**

1 **teaspoon instant expresso coffee**

2 **teaspoons coffee flavored liqueur**

2 **tablespoons semisweet chocolate chips, crushed in a food processor**

3 **tablespoons finely chopped walnuts**

7 **thin cinnamon sticks grated unsweetened chocolate**

Combine gelatin and sugar in a 2½-quart saucepan. Set aside. Beat together milk, egg yolks and coffee in a 1-quart bowl until frothy. Stir into gelatin. Cook mixture over low heat 7 minutes, stirring constantly until slightly thickened. Remove from heat and transfer into the 1-quart bowl. Stir in liqueur and chill 1½ to 2 hours until mixture mounds when dropped from a spoon. (If coffee mixture jells, beat until smooth). Stir in chocolate chips. Beat egg whites until stiff, then fold into the coffee mixture. Divide among 7 champagne glasses, sprinkle with nuts and chill 2 to 3 hours or overnight. Garnish with a cinnamon stick and a dusting of grated chocolate.

Per serving:
130 calories
* 5 gm protein*
18 gm carbohydrates
* 5 gm fat*
* 1 gm fiber*
80 mg cholesterol
60 mg sodium
Exchanges: milk 3, fat 1

No Clo Brownies

24 brownies

²⁄₃ **cup safflower oil**
2 **cups sugar**
1½ **teaspoons vanilla**
3 **egg whites**
1 **cup flour**
²⁄₃ **cup cocoa**
½ **teaspoon baking powder**
¼ **teaspoon salt**
1 **cup chopped walnuts**
   several drops peppermint
   extract (optional)

Combine all ingredients and blend well. Pour into a 9 x 13-inch baking pan. Bake at 350 degrees for 20 to 25 minutes. Cool 10 minutes. Cut into squares. Frost if desired.

Per Serving:
172 calories
  28 gm protein
  21 gm carbohydrates
   9 gm fat
   3 gm fiber
   0 mg cholesterol
  27 mg sodium
Exchanges: bread 1.5, fat 1.5

Faux Crème and Berries

Serves 1

½ **cup nonfat yogurt or**
   Yogurt Cheese
¼ **cup sliced strawberries**
½ **teaspoon almond or**
   vanilla flavoring
1½ **teaspoons sugar or 1**
   packet sugar substitute
   sprig of mint

Combine all ingredients. Stir gently. Serve chilled in a stemmed glass. Garnish with a strawberry and a sprig of mint.

Per serving:
  97 calories
   7 gm protein
  17 gm carbohydrates
  .3 gm fat
  .2 gm fiber
   2 mg cholesterol
87.5 mg sodium
  Exchanges: milk .7, fruit .7

High Fiber Apple Crisp

Serves 6

¼ cup packed brown sugar
4 tablespoons whole wheat flour, divided
¼ teaspoon ground cinnamon
4 tablespoons margarine, softened
½ cup rolled oats
3 tablespoons wheat germ
3 tablespoons chopped walnuts
6 medium apples, sliced
¾ teaspoon ground nutmeg
¾ cup apple juice
ice milk or flavored yogurt

Combine brown sugar, 3 tablespoons whole wheat flour, cinnamon, margarine, oats, wheat germ and walnuts in a food processor or blender. Set aside. In a medium bowl, combine apples, 1 tablespoon whole wheat flour and nutmeg. Place in an 8 x 8-inch baking dish. Pour apple juice over apples and sprinkle with brown sugar mixture. Bake at 375 degrees for 30 minutes. Serve with ice milk or flavored yogurt.

Per serving:
268 calories
4 gm protein
42 gm carbohydrates
11 gm fat
1.2 gm fiber
0 mg cholesterol
94 mg sodium
Exchanges: fruit 3.5, bread 1, fat 2

Light Fruit Bavarian

Serves 4

1 3-ounce package strawberry sugar free gelatin
2 cups frozen strawberry yogurt
1 tablespoon light rum, brandy or liqueur

Dissolve gelatin in 1 cup boiling water. Add frozen yogurt in large spoonfuls and stir until melted. Add rum. Pour into 4 individual serving dishes and chill until set.

Per serving:
110 calories
3 gm protein
20 gm carbohydrates
1.2 gm fat
0 gm fiber
6.4 mg cholesterol
103 mg sodium
Exchanges: fruit .2, bread 1, fat .5

Honorary Chairman
Lucille Osterkamp

Chairman
Nancy Spewak

Co-Chairman
Peggy Burris

Production
Michelle Werley

Finance
Peggy Luth

Marketing
Candace Martz

Recipe Collection
Ellen Umlauf

Recipe Testing
Carol Hatfield

Typing
Carol Holmdahl

Index
Lois Miller

Public Relations
Carolyn Kolman

Patrons
Jean Wood
Kathy Atwood

Advisors
Leslie Dimit
Jackie Baker

Committee Members

Barbara Archer
Sandy Bouchein
Anne Bowen
Suzanne Boyle
Judy Bryant
Pattie Canter
Cindy Carney
Ginger Cornelius
Ann Cortinovis
Susan Edison
Christy Ehrenreich
Patricia Hanna
June Hardy
Mary Henderson
Barbara Hibbard
Nancy Hillhouse
Barbara Kenney
Becca Klingler
Katie Klingler
Patti Korn
Harva Leigh Lambert
Connie Lohr
Renee McCaffrey
Fay McKenna
Chris Parks
Ann Russell
Sharon Sienaski
Debbie Stahlhuth
Bonnie Stansen
Ellie Svenson
Sandy Terrill
Jane Tucker
Sharon Venables
Kay Wren

Recipe Testers

Carol Hatfield
Maggie Albers
Anne Albrecht
Carolyn Allen
Marilynn Anderson
Laura Barnett
Cheryl Behan
Cindy Belmont
Susan Block
Joanne Bodine
Sandy Bouchein
Anne Bowen
Debbie Brass
Peggy Burris
Susan Cauttrell
Judy Cohen
Karma Crowell
Alisia Dargan
Barbara Deater
Sue Derrington
Leslie Dimit
Jeannie Dolson
Debby Edwards
Helen Edwards
Christy Ehrenreich
Barbara English
Vida Fabric
Carol Fisher
Marianne Fournie
Karen Frates
Susie Goode
Patricia Hanna
Mary Kay Hays
Mary Henderson
Sheila Hoffmeister
Carol Holmdahl
Jeanne Hunter
Sally Irwin

Jo Ann Kindle
Becca Klingler
Katie Klingler
Mary Kniep
Carolyn Kolman
Patti Korn
Harva Leigh Lambert
Jane Landsbaum
Nancy Lane
Patricia Leigh
Connie Lohr
Peggy Luth
Dee Mace
Jean Marglous
Candace Martz
Fay McKenna
Pixie Messey
Merle Millar
Debra Moore
Jane Moseley
Kathie Mundschenk
Anita O'Connell
Kristi Peterson
Sue Rapp
Debbie Reimer
Randee Roberts
Ann Russell
Jackie Sanderson
Kim Scherrer
Marsha Schwesig
Sharon Sienaski
Skip Smith
Nancy Spewak
Sibi Striebeck
Carla Sweetwood
Ellen Umlauf
Sharon Venables
Mary Ann Virant
Michelle Werley

Recipe Contributors

The Auxiliary-Twigs is grateful to our many members and friends who have shared their favorite recipes. We greatly appreciate your generosity and hope we have not inadvertently omitted anyone's name. We regret that space did not permit us to include all the recipes submitted.

Anne Albrecht

Kathy Atwood

Sarah Babington

Mary Barker

Cheryl Behan

Marcia Bell

Jeanne Belle

Joanne Bodine

Tony Bommarito

Sandy Bouchein

Anne Bowen

Carolyn Bower

Heather Breindel

Martha Bromley

Judy Bryant

Martha Buck

Peggy Burris

Sarah Butler

Joyce Cammon

Pattie Canter

Bill Cardwell

Nancy Caverly

Judy Cohen

Isabell Corge

Sandra Corry

Karma Crowell

Alicia Dargan

Penny Davis

Mimi Denes

Sue Derrington

Marcel Desaulniers

Carolyn Dickens

Leslie Dimit

Mary Ann Dowling

Peggy Dunbar

Trish Ebsworth

Debby Edwards

Joan Edwards

Anita Eftimoff

Christy Ehrenreich

Hanna Evens

Vida Fabric

Carol Fisher

Bonnie Freeland

Art French

Susan French

Giovanni Gabriele

Ginger Gaebe

Andrea Gardner

Ivy Garnholz

Alice Gerdine

Alice Ghazarian

Liz Glazer

Mary Goellner

Annette Gohagan

Mary Gosney

André Gotti

Chris Green

Bonnie Grenney

Joann Guth

Ann Haack

Bonnie Hana

Carol Hatfield

Susan Haverstick

Mary Kay Hays

Mary Henderson

Lynn Hickel

Sally Higgins

Carol Holmdahl

Marion Horton

Winnie Hounsom

Jeanne Hunter

Susan Husted

Christy James

Dorothy Johnson

Vicki Johnson

JoAnn Kindle

Becca Klingler

Katie Kiingler

Carolyn Kolman

Patti Korn

Harva Leigh Lambert

Carol Lasher

Mary Ann Lee

Connie Lohr

Jane Luedde

Dee Mace

Carole Marcum

Candace Martz

Sue Mattern

Muffy Matthews

Barbara McCarthy

Robin McClanahan

Fay McKenna

Timothy McQueen

Polly Mellinger

Jerry Meyers

Merle Millar

Lois Miller

Janine Moden

Jill Morris

Jenny Nixon

Anita O'Connell

Anne O'Connell

Gretchen O'Neal

Jenny O'Neil

Lucille Osterkamp

Kristi Peterson

Karen Pic

Carolyn Pokorny

Rochelle Popkin

Mary Purvis

Muzzi Qualy

Christine Randall

Jean Ray

Leah Richert

Jean Roessler

Jane Rohrbaugh

Jane Rouse

Martha Rowe

Beverly Rumage

Ann Russell

Jackie Sanderson

Colette Sasina

Kim Scherrer

Joellen Schonwald

David Schwartz

Nancy Schwartzman

Peggy Shepley

Nancy Spewak

Ellie Svenson

Carla Sweetwood

Barbara Taylor

Sharon Thiemann

Grace Ann Titone

Vicki Todd-Smith

Jeanne Toma

Pam Tvedt

Ellen Umlauf

Bob Vickers

Ny Vongsaly

Mary Ann Wafer

Jim Wallace

Mary Weinstock

Michelle Werley

Carole Ziemann

Judy Zimmerman

John Zwolinski

Patrons

Dr. and Mrs. Robert Spewak

Dr. and Mrs. Fred Fabric
Mr. and Mrs. Ron Lohr
Mr. and Mrs. Maurice Wood

Mrs. Charles M. Babington, Jr.

Evadne A. Baker
Mr. and Mrs. W. Randolph Baker
Mrs. H. Nulsen Baur
Ellie Beckers
Mrs. Robert J. Bodine
Mrs. Holly Bry
Dr. and Mrs. Garrett C. Burris
Susan J. Colten
The Coovert Foundation
Mr. and Mrs. William E. Cornelius
Mr. and Mrs. Theodore P. Desloge, Jr.
Mrs. Burl Dillard
David and Leslie Dimit
Mr. and Mrs. Charles S. Drew, Jr.
Mrs. Neal J. Farrell
Ira and Judy Gall
Suzanne S. Harbison
Mrs. Lewis T. Hardy
Mrs. Paul Hatfield
Mrs. Jack K. Higgins
Margaret Jackes
Mrs. Donald Klingler
Mr. and Mrs. Charles Knight
Mrs. Robert Kresko
Mrs. John F. Krey, II
Mary Ann Krey
Mrs. Oliver M. Langenberg
Dr. and Mrs. Félix E. F. Larocca
Mr. and Mrs. Ned Lemkemeier
Mrs. Stanley Lopata
Mrs. John N. MacDonough
Jane Hunter MacMillan
Mrs. Francis A. Mesker
Mr. and Mrs. Lee A. Miller
Mr. and Mrs. John W. Moore
Mrs. Vaughan Morrill, Jr.
Mrs. William J. Oetting
Jane O'Neill
Mrs. Roy W. Osterkamp
Ben and Dorothy Peck
Mrs. Frank E. Pipe
Southwest Pediatrics
Mrs. Andrew C. Taylor
Mrs. Jack C. Taylor
Mr. and Mrs. Joseph G. Werner
Mrs. Donald D. Wren
Mrs. Milton L. Zorensky

Mrs. Nan Stout

Mrs. George W. Achuff
Mr. and Mrs. Douglas Albrecht
Mrs. Charles B. Anderson
Mrs. Charles M. Babington, III
Virginia Baird
Crystal Beuerlein
Mrs. Van-Lear Black, III
Mr. and Mrs. Jack A. Blake
Mrs. V. Patton Braxton, Jr.
Barbara R. Cole, M.D.
Mrs. Herbert D. Condie, Jr.
Dr. and Mrs. M. B. Conrad
Mr. and Mrs. Harold J. Corbett
Mr. and Mrs. Howard Elliott, Jr.
Mrs. Ronald Evens
Frieda and Milton Ferman
Mr. and Mrs. John H. Ferring, IV
Suzanne Fischer
Mrs. Lee T. Ford
Billie Frey
Dr. and Mrs. Robert H. Friedman
Mr. and Mrs. William Friedman
Emily Gladders Gebhard
Mr. and Mrs. David Gifford
Mrs. Vernon Goedecke
Mr. and Mrs. Robert D. Goellner, Jr.
Mrs. Ed Gomes, Jr.
Raymond and Karen Griesedieck
Bonnie Hana
John and Mary Henderson and Family
Mrs. Bruce S. Higginbotham
Mrs. Robert E. Kindle
Mr. and Mrs. Richard W. Kniep
Mrs. Michael Kolman
Mrs. Ernest Kretschmar
Mrs Fred M. Lanz
Dr. and Mrs. Sherman J. Le Master
Daniel B. Lichtenstein
Mrs. William L. Luth
Dr. and Mrs. Jeffrey L. Marsh
William and Victoria McAlister
Mr. and Mrs. Tom McRaven
Mrs. Raymond W. Meckfessel
Nikki Mercer
Keithley and Dwight Miller
Maude E. Mueller
John and Anita O'Connell
Dr. and Mrs. William H. Peterson
Mrs. Vernon W. Piper
Mrs. A. Charles Roland, III
Mrs. Donald O. Schnuck
Dr. and Mrs. Thomas Shaner
Mr. and Mrs. Jack Spewak
Mrs. William D. Stamper
Alexis Sternhell
Doris B. Stinnett
Mrs. Robert Trulaske, Sr.
Mrs. Robert Tschudy
Mr. and Mrs. Lewis Tubbesing
Mrs. Larry D. Umlauf

Mr. and Mrs. Steven Vagnino
John Virant Family
Mrs. Mahlon B. Wallace, Jr.
Barbara Wells
Mr. and Mrs. Ralph Werley
Trey and Peter Wiegand
Jo Lynn Winer
Susan Young

Maggie Albers
Mrs. LeGrand Atwood
J. Ellen Bangert
Mrs. George Barnes, Jr.
Leo C. Belknap
Mrs. Brooks Bernhardt
Mr. and Mrs. Scott Berry
Dr. and Mrs. Gordon R. Bloomberg
James Boedeker, M.D.
Carol and Charles Boudreaux
Deborah Brass
Holland Vose Brigham
Mrs. Saul Brodsky
Mrs. Douglas Brown
Judy Bryant
Mrs. Anthony A. Buford
Dr. and Mrs. Max Burgdorf
Dr. and Mrs. Dean Burgess
Mrs. Robert R. Burke
Barbara Bush
Mr. and Mrs. Joseph C. Campbell
Mrs. W. L. Canfield
Mrs. John Capps
Mrs. John R. Cassin
Mrs. James T. Chamness, Jr.
Mrs. James H. Cohen
Shirley W. Cohen
Juanita Polito-Colvin, M.D., and
Grant Colvin
Mrs. James L. Cox
Dave Sinclair Ford, Inc.
Jim and Penny Davis
Dr. and Mrs. Ray S. Davis
Mr. and Mrs. Henry P. Day
Mrs. John Dillon
Mrs. Steven Dix
Philip R. Dodge, M.D.
Catherine M. Dunn, M.D.
Mrs. Kathy Edwards
Rose F. Elliott
Jean M. Ewing
Mr. and Mrs. William C. Fikes
Dr. and Mrs. Edward Fliesher
Margery C. Fort
Mrs. Terry Franc
Mrs. R. C. Garrett
Elliot and Jody Gellman
Dr. and Mrs. James A. Gerst
A. C. and Jan M. Giessman
Mrs. Louis S. Goltermann, Jr.
Mr. and Mrs. T. E. Halstead
Ann Hamsher
Mrs. E. Douglas Harbison

Mrs. Roy W. Harper
C. D. Hoffman
Mr. and Mrs. Mark Hofstein
Mrs. David M. Hollo
Mrs. Arthur K. Howell, Jr.
Mrs. Wm. Richard Huey
Dr. and Mrs. Carl S. Ingber
Mrs. W. Boardman Jones, Jr.
Dr. and Mrs. Harold Joseph
Dr. and Mrs. Henry J. Kaplan
Lynne Drohlich Kaufman
KDNL Fox 30
Mrs. Meyer Kopolow
Bruce and Patti Korn
Betty and Bob Kortkamp
Katherine L. Kreusser, M.D.
Mrs. Stephen Lambright
Julia M. Lamy
Paul and Jan Latta
Dr. and Mrs. Richard Lazaroff
Patricia Leigh
Mrs. Sidney Levinson
Mr. and Mrs. Lee M. Liberman
Mr. and Mrs. Ronnie Light
Mrs. D. Michael Linihan
Clarice Lodder
Caroline K. Loughlin
Dr. and Mrs. Robert H. Lund
Nancy Lurie
Mrs. Paul S. Mace
Mr. and Mrs. John Martz, Jr.
Mr. and Mrs. M. J. May
Mrs. Charles N. McAlpin
J. Richard McEachern
Mrs. J. Dale Meier
Mr. and Mrs. Robert J. Messey
Mrs. Roswell Messing, Jr.
Mrs. Stuart F. Meyer
Mrs. Ronald Moore
Mr. and Mrs. H. Leighton Morrill
Mrs. David B. Mueller
Helen E. Nash, M.D.
Chris L. Palcheff, M.D.
Dr. and Mrs. Carlos A. Perez
Donna D. Perkins
Julie and Steve Plax
Mrs. B. F. Rassieur, III
Jan and Craig Rathjen
Mrs. Linda Reed
Eugene J. Reiter
Fran Reither
Riley, Barnard and O'Connell
    Business Products, Inc.
Mr. and Mrs. Donald Ross
Mrs. Ernest T. Rouse, III
Dr. and Mrs. Michael Rumelt
Mrs. Steven Schankman
Mrs. Frederick W. Scherrer
Mrs. Arthur E. S. Schmid
Mr. and Mrs. David Schwartz
Edith R. Schwartz
Dr. and Mrs. William G. Sedgwick

Rick and Sheri Shapiro
Mrs. Richard Shelton
Gary and Janice Sherman
Mr. and Mrs. C. Samuel Sinnett
Southwestern Bell Telephone Company
Dale and Janet Steinback
Ellie Svenson
Kathi Tacony
Dr. and Mrs. Marc Wallach
Dr. and Mrs. Todd Wasserman
Mrs. John D. Weiss
Anonymous

Helen M. Erickson

AAA Remodeling Company, Inc.
Steve and Nancy Abram
Adele Baur Adam
Helen M. Aff-Drum, M.D.
Patricia Amato, M.D.
Laurence and Carol Avins
Mrs. Marge Aylward
Laurie Badler
Mr. and Mrs. James G. Baker, Jr.
Mary Barenkamp
Mildred Barhan
Mrs. Vincent H. Barreca, Jr.
Mrs. Andrew H. Baur
Mary S. Behnke
Dr. and Mrs. Joe Belew
Mrs. Douglas H. Bell
Mr. and Mrs. Paul Belmont
Elliot and Linda Benoist
Mr. and Mrs. Peter F. Benoist
Mrs. Irvin Bettman, Jr.
Camille Bishop
Anne Bowen
Mr. and Mrs. Tim Boyle
Diane Breckenridge
Mrs. John F. Brewer
Carole Ann Brown
Mrs. David Brown
Mr. and Mrs. Harvey M. Brown
Joan Brown
Mr. and Mrs. Frederic C. Brussee
Mr. and Mrs. James A. Buck
Loraine P. Budke
Mr. and Mrs. Ralph W. Canter
Mrs. Emmett A. Capstick
Jennifer Carrick
Mrs. William A. Claypool
Lisa and Paul Cobbledick
Dr. and Mrs. Darryl Cohen
Mrs. Sheldon Cohen
Lucie Convy
Mrs. C. William Cook
Mrs. Alvin M. Corry
Mrs. G. Newton Cox
Mrs. Robert Cranston
Mrs. John Crick
Mrs. Timothy Crowley

Mrs. Robert K. Crutsinger
Mrs. Edward H. Cunliff
Mrs. John E. Curby
Mrs. H. Douglas Day
Mrs. Richard Dickherber
Thomas J. Donovan, M.D.
Mrs. John J. Dowling, III
Mrs. Derick Driemeyer
Ellen Dubinsky
Mrs. William Claiborne Dunagan
Mr. and Mrs. Terry Dunaway
Dorcas H. Dunlop
Mrs. Peter A. Edison
Mrs. Benjamin F. Edwards, III
Anita K. Eftimoff
Christy Ehrenreich
Iris S. Elliot
Mrs. Robert P. Elsperman
McRee Leschen Engler Fund
Mrs. Bruce English
Barbara Ernst
Mrs. Dennis D. Fales
Mr. and Mrs. John R. Feldmeier
Mrs. James G. Forsyth, III
Karen Frates
Delia Garcia
Mrs. David L. Gardner
Mrs. Charles Garrison
Margene Gerfen
Edith Gevers
Henry J. Gherardi
Mrs. Harold M. Gilbert
Dr. and Mrs. Louis Gilula
Peggy P. Gissendanner
Mrs. Liz Glazer
Mr. and Mrs. Paul Goessling, Jr.
Mr. and Mrs. Edward Goldberg
Joseph and Zeena Goldenberg
Mrs. Gregory L. Goltermann
Mr. and Mrs. Denny Goode
Mrs. James W. Graham
Randy and Susie Graham
Mr. and Mrs. Paul V. Grenney
Harriet and Wendall Griffin
Dr. and Mrs. Robert L. Grubb
Mrs. Julie Hagnauer
Dorothy M. Hanpeter
Dr. and Mrs. Tom Harrison
Mrs. David Hatfield
Mr. and Mrs. William P. Haviluk, Jr.
Mrs. George Hays
Diane G. Hennessey
Ina and Edward Hensley
Miss Dorothy E. Hermann
Mrs. Frederick Hermann
Mr. and Mrs. George L. Hibbard
Dolores K. Hill
Mrs. John D. Hirsch
Mr. and Mrs. Thomas Hizar
Mr. and Mrs. Jim Hoffmeister
Mr. and Mrs. David Holley
Mr. and Mrs. Jerry Holmdahl

Nancy E. Holmes, M.D.
Tennie Hoppin
Mrs. Douglass D. Horner
Mrs. Richard W. Horner
Mr. and Mrs. Fred P. Hubert
Ruth E. Jacobs
Christy Franchot James
Mrs. James Lee Johnson, Jr.
Dr. and Mrs. Robert L. Kaufman
Michele E. Kemp, M.D.
Barbara Kenney
Mrs. Edward F. Kercher, III
Mr. and Mrs. Frank L. Key
Barbara A. Kirtley
Don and Becca Klingler
Kathryn E. Kniep
Mr. and Mrs. Cornelius W. Krentz
Mr. and Mrs. F. Mark Kuhlmann
Mrs. A. Joseph LaCovey
Mrs. William D. Lambert, III
Mrs. Walter R. Lamkin
Anita Buie Lamont
Mrs. Doris E. Lanam
Mrs. Raymond E. Lange
Dolores K. Lansche
Mary Ann Lee
Richard and Faye Levey
Mrs. Marvin E. Levin
Jane and Mike Lewis
Lida National Yellow Pages Service
Mrs. Charles Limberg
Mrs. Carl E. Lischer
Mrs. Robert W. Lloyd
Mrs. Ralph S. Lobdell
M. Kevin Lueders
Jane S. Mackey
MagneTek Century Electric
Mrs. Kevin A. Maher
Mrs. Sawyer Marglous
Mr. and Mrs. K. Ray Mashburn
Sally McCarthy
Diane and Mike McGovern
Clancey McKay
Fay S. McKenna
Mrs. William McLaurine
Barbara Meldrum
Mrs. Michael J. Mellinger
Diane Merritt, M.D.
Renée Michelson
Mrs. Linda Misanko
Janine and Noel Moden
Mr. and Mrs. Robert S. Morris
Mrs. Lucius B. Morse, III
Ann R. Moskowitz
Mrs. Stephen C. Murphy
Cissy and Steven Nissenbaum
Margaret Grigg Oberheide
Mrs. Robert F. O'Connell
Sharon C. Olson
Mrs. William Owens
Sallie Painter
William E. Peacock

Dr. and Mrs. William Peck
Mrs. David E. Perkins
Mrs. L. W. Peterson
Gordon and Susie Philpott
Mrs. Darrell Plocher
Nancy Potter
Mrs. Sally P. Powell
Mrs. J. Wilson Rainer, Jr.
Mrs. P. J. Rapp
Mrs. Rudyard K. Rapp
Mrs. Timothy K. Reeves
Mrs. Henry C. Reiner
Carol Ann Reininger
Sarah Remington
Randee Roberts
Mr. and Mrs. Richard Roessler
Dr. and Mrs. James Rohrbaugh
Mrs. Thomas Rosen
Mr. and Mrs. Allan John Ross
Mrs. William M. Rowe, Jr.
Lucinn Sams
Mr. and Mrs. James R. Samuel, Jr.
JoAnn Sanditz
Jeff Santilli
Barbara Sapot
Colette J. Sasina
Richard Scherrer Family
Margaret C. Schmidt
Robert Schmidt Family
Mayor and Mrs. Vincent Schoemehl
Susie Littmann Schulte
Sharon Sienaski
Mrs. Sherman Silber
Caryl Green Simon
Mrs. Jerry L. Smith
Mrs. Robert B. Smith
Michael L. and Rosemary W. Somich
Mr. and Mrs. Carl J. Spector
Mrs. Melford Spiegelglass
Mrs. Carl C. Stifel
DeeDee Stivers
Mrs. James M. Stolze
Joanne Strathearn
Sibi Striebeck
Roy and Karen Stueber
Mrs. Carla Sweetwood
Ellinere Tabbert
Hannah Tenenbaum
Mrs. Nat Tettlebaum
Dr. and Mrs. Brad Thach
Mrs. Robert Thiemann
Mrs. George S. Thomas
Jean H. Thurston, M.D.
Jeanne B. Toma
Mr. and Mrs. James J. Venables, Jr.
Mrs. Jerry Vouga
Lee and Barbara Wagman
Mary Waltke
Mrs. David G. Watkins
Roger J. Waxelman, M.D.
Stephen and Diane Weinstock
James and Suzanne Werley

Marguerite Wetterau
Mrs. Clarence T. Wilson
Mrs. Steven R. Wilson
Patricia B. Wolff, M.D.
Mrs. Robert Wunsch
Mrs. Ron L. Yates

Judy Zafft
Judy Zimmerman

Connie Finger

Index